AF806353

Philosophy of International Law

Second Edition

Anthony Carty

EDINBURGH
University Press

Edinburgh University Press is one of the leading university presses in the UK. We publish academic books and journals in our selected subject areas across the humanities and social sciences, combining cutting-edge scholarship with high editorial and production values to produce academic works of lasting importance. For more information visit our website: edinburghuniversitypress.com

© Anthony Carty, 2007, 2017

Edinburgh University Press Ltd
The Tun – Holyrood Road
12 (2f) Jackson's Entry
Edinburgh EH8 8PJ

First edition published in 2007

Typeset in 11/13 Adobe Sabon by
IDSUK (DataConnection) Ltd, and
printed and bound in Great Britain by
CPI Group (UK) Ltd, Croydon CR0 4YY

A CIP record for this book is available from the British Library

ISBN 978 0 7486 7550 0 (hardback)
ISBN 978 0 7486 7551 7 (paperback)
ISBN 978 0 7486 7552 4 (webready PDF)
ISBN 978 0 7486 7553 1 (epub)

The right of Anthony Carty to be identified as author of this work has been asserted in accordance with the Copyright, Designs and Patents Act 1988 and the Copyright and Related Rights Regulations 2003 (SI No. 2498).

Contents

Acknowledgements

The present volume is a second edition of a book which appeared ten years ago. The questions which I set for the first edition have continued to preoccupy me since, and indeed continue to preoccupy me. I have adapted and integrated into the second edition parts, sometimes considerable, of some especially relevant articles and book chapters which I wrote in the intervening time. There are two key articles written before 2007 which are, in part, adapted to chapter 2 of the second edition. In addition, the first edition has been considerably restructured to allow realigning and reformulating of the questions which preoccupy me.

Carty, 'The Continuing Influence of Kelsen on the General Perception of the Discipline of International Law', *European Journal of International Law* (1998) 344–54.

Carty, 'Scandinavian Realism and Phenomenological Approaches to Statehood and General Custom in International Law', *European Journal of International Law* 14 (2003) 817–41.

Carty, 'The Moral Theologian, Oliver O'Donovan and International Law', *Political Theology* 9.3 (2008) 339–62.

Carty, 'From a Unipolar to a Multipolar World. A Post-Bush Presidency for a Post-Western World', in *Power and Justice in International Relations: Interdisciplinary Approaches to Global Challenges*, Marie-Luisa Frick and Andreas Oberprantacher (eds) (Routledge, 2009) 13–28.

Carty, 'Vattel's *Natural Liberty of Conscience of Nations in a New Age of Belief and Faith*', in *Vattel's International Law in a XXIst Century Perspective / Le droit international de Vattel vu du XXIe siècle,* Vincent Chetail and Peter Haggenmacher (eds) (Brill, 2011) 189–210.

Carty, 'Doctrine versus State Practice in International Law', in *Oxford Handbook of the History of International Law* ed. A. Peters and B. Fassbender (Oxford University Press, 2012) 972–96.

Carty and Zhang, 'From Freedom and Equality to Domination and Subordination, Feminist and Anti-Colonial Critiques of the Vattelian Heritage', *Netherlands Yearbook of International Law* 43 (Springer, 2012) 53–82.

Carty, 'From Classical Natural Law to "New Natural Law": Where Natural Law Becomes Ideology', in Russell Wilcox and Anthony Carty, *Natural Law and Comparative Law* (Simmonds and Hill, 2015) 375–96.

Introduction: What Place for Doctrine in a Time of Fragmentation?

A DEFINITION OF DOCTRINE AND ITS PRESENT PROBLEMATIC IN PUBLIC INTERNATIONAL LAW

I intend to begin simply by referring to two recent French works, the *Dictionnaire encyclopédique de théorie et de sociologie du droit* and a colloquium organised by the legal history department of the University of Picardie (Amiens), *La Doctrine juridique*. The first provides us with an authoritative and vital distinction between legal doctrine and legal dogmatics, while the second explains the problematic of keeping the former alive.

The French dictionary distinguishes doctrine from 'dogmatique juridique' (legal dogmatics). The former is defined as 'opinion, theory or thesis', while the latter means the domain of the science of law concerned with the interpretation and systematisation of juridical norms.[1] An essential element of doctrine is that it is supposed to have authority. The theory, opinion, and so forth must be capable of exercising influence. Coming from the tradition of Roman law and canon law, particularly in French and German legal communities, doctrine has authority not as a source of law as such, but as freely and spontaneously held opinion, which is likely to become accepted. Since the seventeenth century the nature of this authority has become contested. It is seen as rooted in theories of *natural right* that were increasingly regarded as the ideological apparatus of a dominant bourgeois class.

Legal dogmatics works within the assumptions of legal positivism, particularly with respect to the sources of law. It is concerned with the interpretation of statutes and jurisprudence. There may be,

1. *Dictionnaire*, 2nd edition, gen. ed. A. J. Arnaud (1993), entries by Sylvie Cimamonti and Aulis Aarnio, respectively.

within this framework, theories of interpretation and methods for the systematisation of written and customary law. However, this supplementary role for the legal writer, whether an academic or practitioner, is not challenged one way or the other by the controversies surrounding doctrine. Theories of interpretation and systematisation do not have to operate only with logic, but any explicit reference to values will be confined to those that it can be argued are immanent to the system of legal norms actually accepted as legally binding in a society. This type of legal activity is an inevitable and integral part of any positive legal order, however narrowly understood.

The crisis facing doctrine, on the contrary, appears to be fatal. It is attributable above all to the collapse of the natural law or law of nature background to both continental civil law and international law that can be taken to have been completed in the West, especially in Europe, by the 1950s, notwithstanding a brief renaissance of natural law after the Second World War. This tradition had allowed the jurist, since the glossators and canonists of the medieval period, to resort freely to notions of natural justice, equity, personal responsibility, public order, harmony, and so forth to develop freely otherwise fragmentary pieces of local custom, regional law, judicial precedents, and even general legislation.

In a sense the tradition was pre-democratic and pre-liberal, in that it is always assumed that somehow there will be present a group of erudite and morally serious people who are able to wrap up legally significant human actions in the texture or framework of reasonableness. It is also assumed that standards are universal and everywhere the same, not only in space but also in time. This favours an old-fashioned form of inter-disciplinarity, which now appears as mere eclecticism. The doctrinal writer will look to history, philosophy, and even literature to support what appears to him just and reasonable in the circumstances.

It is, in the view of the Picardy study on *La Doctrine*, above all Kelsen with his Pure Theory of Law, who is easily recognisable as taking away the foundation for the working method of *doctrine*.[2] According to the Pure Theory of Law, theories of natural law or equity merely conceal the personal preferences of the authors and are subjective. Insofar as the structure of a legal order contains gaps and ambiguities, these can only be filled through political decision, in

2. See, in the Picardy Colloquium, Annick Perrot, *La Doctrine et l'hypothèse du declin du droit* (1993) 180, the entire article, but esp. 198 f.

which the individual jurist has no special part to play. Liberal, voluntarist democracy means that, to find law, one has to return to the primary means that the legal order has agreed for the creation of new norms. In the Pure Theory of Law these primary means do not have to be democratic, although Kelsen himself was a democrat. Given an increasingly regulatory function for law, in Kelsen's view, the details of social life to be so regulated would have to be dealt with by the appropriate public legal authority, whose success would be more or less a matter of effectiveness. Deficiencies could be best remedied by giving authority to the judiciary, an extension of the State, or, as Kelsen preferred, the legal order, to take the necessary additional decisions. Allied to the Pure Theory of Law, as an enemy of the natural law schools, comes Scandinavian realism, which also serves to bury the traditional role of doctrine. Not only does this school attack natural law and so on on epistemological grounds, but it uses the same weapons to attack the basic concepts of positive law that it sees as a legacy of the natural law tradition. These include the concepts of subjective or individual right, the will of the State or of the legislator. The Scandinavian realists would replace such activity with a form of legal sociology that entailed identifying law as a psychological datum, evidence of a sense of obligation in a society, that people felt themselves to be bound by rules that they regarded as law. Instead of the concept of validity, the lawyer should work with a theory of verification that allowed him to identify that there was a social belief that rules existed that were binding upon the people who held the belief.[3]

Given the present structure of international law, which is still primarily customary, this gives a full place to writers, but only within a framework of legal dogmatics.

THE CLASSICAL PLACE OF DOCTRINE IN INTERNATIONAL LAW

The aim of this introduction of the figure of Paulus Vladimiri will be to illustrate how, during the classical medieval period, the distinction between doctrine and dogmatics was clearly understood precisely in the sense outlined in the *Dictionnaire* discussed in the first section. It is only with the coming of the modern period that the former comes to be swallowed up by the latter.

---

3. *Dictionnaire*, entry on Realism, Scandinavian, by Enrico Pattaro. A. Ross produced a *Textbook of International Law* in 1945.

Vladimiri and the 'Higher' Medieval Period

Vladimiri was anxious to carve out a proper space for judicial practice against the hegemonic claims of doctrine in medieval legal disputations. At the same time his doctrinal method, that is the types of material upon which he relied to develop his argument, shows clearly how this method rested upon certain epistemological assumptions that have not been regarded as valid since the classical period. It mattered enormously to Vladimiri, involved in a dispute with the German (Teutonic) Order on behalf of the Polish king, to argue that the proper resolution of the conflict had to be through a judicial process and not merely a reliance upon doctrine. To demonstrate this, he made a clear distinction between the two, which remains valid in a legal culture where it is the claims of judicial practice that are hegemonic. To leave disputations about heresy or the rights of infidels against Christians in the hands of doctrinalists is very dangerous because the nature of doctrine or of science is that it excludes all doubt, and therefore does not accept proof to the contrary, since it is from propositions, which are known by themselves.[4] Whether a war against a heretic or infidel is just and can therefore be undertaken involves questions of evidence as well as of doctrine. Whether in a particular case there is a legitimate cause of attacking, and hence an illegitimacy in resisting, are questions that cannot be answered 'except by way of justice, namely by proof brought in law or by sentence and in consequence by a legitimate declaration'.[5]

Vladimiri's method receives a very lucid analysis from Stanislaus Belch. Here I wish to highlight the place that is nonetheless left to doctrine as against judicial practice. For instance, confusion about what may be done by Christians to infidels arises from a factually incorrect assumption that all infidels commit blasphemy, persecute Christians, and seize their territories. Factually inaccurate assumptions lead to pseudo-doctrinal justifications of what can be done to infidels. Where none of this has been proved, the question arises, which doctrine can appropriately answer: what can be done to infidels as such? The answer comes from natural law: they are entitled to be left in peace. It is the nature of the Christian faith that it is grounded in love. Therefore, nothing coercive can be done in its

4. Ludwig Ehrlich (ed.), *Works of Paulus Vladimiri (A Selection)* (1968) Vol. II, from 1st Tractatus (1417) 203.
5. Ibid., Vol. I, Controversy with Frebach, Quoniam Bror (1417) 308.
6. Stanislaus F. Belch, *Paulus Vladimiri and his Doctrine Concerning International Law and Politics* (1965) Vol. 1, 213–14.

name.[6] The correct question for doctrinal debate was whether 'the infidel nations have the same human rights as the Christians'. To answer this question meant the establishment of the truth of certain principles that alone could serve in any argument as a major premise.[7] This involved Vladimiri in sifting through the opinions of the great doctors of the Church, some of whom did not share this doctrine on the rights of infidel nations. He applied a quite simple style of reasoning to reach his goal. For instance, there was scriptural support (c.3, D 45) concerning directly the prohibition of force in the conversion of the Jews. There, the essence of this canon is that it applies equally to the conversion of all infidels. Again, to take another example, Vladimiri's opponent Vrebach takes Paul's admonition that Christians should not fight infidels to mean not those who recognise the dominion of the Church and the empire. Vladimiri objects that in law we do not usually make distinctions, and so we should not here.[8]

The Renaissance Universality of Resemblances

The justification for this rather extensive treatment of a medieval figure is that it is now widely accepted in the scholarship that modern figures who may compete for the 'fatherhood' of international law, above all Vitoria and Grotius, belong firmly within this medieval world. Haggenmacher emphasises the pre-modernity of Grotius. That is, Grotius's work, which is mainly about the doctrine of just war, is the culmination of a medieval scholastic tradition, which depended upon a medieval and classical Greek concept of natural law. The main feature of this doctrine is that *Man* is embedded in a universal society and in the *Cosmos*.[9] Equally, Vitoria, who was concerned with the same question as Vladimiri, approached it against the backdrop of a presumed universal order. As Bartelson puts it,

> The question was not how to solve a conflict between competing sovereigns over the foundation of a legal order, but how to relate concentric circles of *resemblant* laws, ranging from divine law down to natural and positive law. In his effort to work out a coherent relationship between them, Vitoria relies on a lexicon of legal exempla, in which a wide variety of textual authorities are invoked.[10]

---

7. Ibid., 233.
8. Ibid., 233–6.
9. P. Haggenmacher, *Grotius et la doctrine de la guerre juste* (1983).
10. Jens Bartelson, *A Genealogy of Sovereignty* (1995) 128; emphasis in the original.

The transition from the medieval to what Bartelson calls the classical period, from the seventeenth century at the latest, already disturbed the place of doctrine, if not among international lawyers, then certainly among serious students of international society. Bartelson provides a very illuminating account of the epistemological foundations of the transformation. The essence of this perspective is, of course, a retrospective reflexivity (thanks to a neo-platonic revival). Renaissance knowledge became a knowledge of resemblances between entities whose unity had been shattered. Bartelson sums up what is, in effect, the method of Grotius in the following phrases: 'Through the resemblance of events and episodes it becomes possible to describe and discuss present affairs by drawing on the almost infinite corpus of political learning recovered from antiquity, without distinguishing between legend and document';[11] it becomes possible to describe the deeds of a Moses or a King Utopus in the same terms as one describes 'the recent behaviour of Cesare Borgia or Henry VIII, because it is assumed that they share the same reality, and occupy the same space of possible political experience'.[12] It is inevitable that such a conception of legal order will be, in the modern sense, monist. Neither Vitoria nor Grotius will countenance any opposition between the kind of law that applies between States and within States, since this would imply an absence of law.[13]

THE SOVEREIGN: OR THE OBJECTIVITY OF SUBJECTIVE INTEREST

The epistemological break with the medieval–Renaissance picture supposes a combination of political and philosophical events. The so-called modern State arising out of the wars of religion of the sixteenth and seventeenth centuries is taken as traumatised by its bloody foundation and hence silent about its origins. It becomes the subject of Descartes' distinction between the immaterial subject and the material reality that it observes, classifies, and analyses. Knowledge presupposes a subject, and this subject, for international relations, is the Hobbesean sovereign who is not named, but names, not observed, but observes, a mystery for whom everything must be transparent. The problem of knowledge is that of security, which is attained through rational control and analysis. Self-understanding is

11. Ibid., 108.
12. Ibid., 110.
13. Ibid., 130–1. Bartelson applies these remarks to Vitoria.

limited to an analysis of the extent of power of the sovereign, measured geopolitically. Other sovereigns are not unknown 'others' in the modern anthropological sense, but simply 'enemies', opponents, with conflicting interests, whose behaviour can and should be calculated.

The purpose of knowledge, once again, is not to re-establish resemblances in a fragmenting medieval Christian world, but to furnish dependable information with which to buttress the sovereign State, whose security rests precisely upon the success with which it has banished disorder from within its boundaries on to the international plane. Mutual recognition by sovereigns does not imply acceptance of a common international order, but merely a limited measure of mutual construction of identity resting upon an awareness of sameness, an analytical recognition of factual, territorial separation, combined with a mutual accord of reputation, which, so long as it lasts, serves to guarantee some measure of security.

However, the primary definition of State interest is not a search for resemblances, affinities of religion, or dynastic family. Instead, it is a matter of knowing how to conduct one's own affairs, while hindering those of others. Interest is a concept resting upon detachment and separation. Society is composed of a collection of primary, unknowable, self-defining subjects, whose powers of detached, analytical, empirical observation take absolute precedence over any place for knowledge based on passion or empathy, whether oriented towards sameness or difference.[14]

THE ROLE FOR DOCTRINE IN THE CLASSICAL THEORY OF SOVEREIGNTY

This structure of sovereign relations remains the basic problematic that international lawyers face today. The origin of the State is a question of fact rather than one of law. One may not enquire into its composition or nature. Law is whatever the sovereigns choose to define as such through their will, in treaties or customs as implied treaties. The instability of this supposed legal order is patent. The status of mutual recognition as a means of assuring security is unstable. There is no agreement about the legal significance of recognition. International law is binding but not enforceable. Adjudication exists, but its impact is sporadic. Fundamentally, the problem can be encapsulated in a

14. Ibid., summary of the whole of chapter 5, 'How Policy Became Foreign', 137–85.

sentence. There is what all the parties are willing to identify as law, but there is auto-interpretation of the extent of obligation.

Given the preponderance of the State, the role for doctrine has become marginalised and confined to the question of whether international law is law at all. Perhaps the majority view among the profession is that the question is unnecessary. Emer de Vattel made the point that international law is a law precisely suited to the nature of the State, as a form of independent corporation. Institutional defects in the character of international law, viz. the absence of legislature, judicature, and so on, do not affect the basic need for and suitability of inter-State law for law among States. So Jouannet sees no difficulty in the Vattelian sovereign being integrated into an international legal order. The lack of difficulty is hardly surprising because this new legal order is made by States specifically for their relations with one another. The crucial feature of her argument is that the character of the sovereign is corporate. Because sovereign nations deal only directly with one another, they can only see one another as societies of men of whom all the interests are held in common. It is not a law of nations derived from human nature that rules them, but a law derived from the particular character of the State.[15]

The difficulty remains, accepted by Bartelson and Jouannet, that there is no superior juridical order immediately binding upon States. They agree that sovereignty includes the right to decide the extent of an obligation. Again, both may quote Vattel that 'each has the right to decide in its conscience what it must do to fulfil its duties; the effect of this is to produce before the world at least, a perfect equality of rights among Nations'.[16]

Jouannet describes Vattel as introducing the logic of Hobbesean and Lockean individualism into international law, liberty, and sovereignty that are not unlimited but not subject to any higher order. Bartelson would rather describe this order as the objectivity of subjective interest.

This dilemma is what is meant by the question of whether international law is binding. It troubled doctrine in international law as long as a natural law or Law of Nature tradition continued to have any life in it, thereby posing the question of whether norms or values could have objective character. It was a main preoccupation of international law

15. E. Jouannet, 'L'Emergence doctrinale du droit international classique. Emer de Vattel et l'école du droit de la nature et des gens', PhD thesis, Paris (1993) 447–8, 458–9.
16. Ibid., 472–5; Bartelson, 'How Policy Became Foreign', 194–5.

doctrine in the nineteenth century and early twentieth, encapsulated in debates about whether (1) international law was binding, (2) whether treaties were legal instruments that had to be kept, and (3) whether the sovereignty of States could be legally limited or restricted.

When the traditions of natural law, even of a Vattelian character, evaporated after 1945, there seemed to be nothing left but a legal pragmatism, until the so-called critical legal debate resurrected the issues. The critical legal debate, particularly associated with Kennedy and Koskenniemi, appears to resurrect the role for doctrine at least in the narrow and marginal sense described here. They agonise about the paradox of the need for an international order if equally sovereign States are to have any peace with one another. At the same time they recognise that an objective international order, one that is binding upon its subjects albeit not created by them, is incompatible with the structure of State sovereignty, taken from Vattel, that they do not dispute.[17] This debate now takes upon itself a post-epistemological turn insofar as the parties debate through rhetorical devices that are neo-positivist and neo-naturalist, in that they do not willingly espouse the foundations of either school, even if they continue to contrast the language of the two schools.

In my view, the critical legal approach is useful as a heuristic device for exposing the failure of practitioners to ground appeals to rules of law in *actual*, rather than supposed, evidence of State consent, or in *actual*, rather than concealed or disguised, reference to objective values. However, its 'postmodernism' (its opposition to the idea of any fundamental or absolute values) does not allow it to resurrect any creative role for doctrine, even less so Vladimiri's. Their own sharing of liberal value scepticism leaves critical legal studies with no more than repetitive demonstrations that international law decisions (whether of courts or of States) are precisely that – decisions – so that international lawyers must accept responsibility for the political character of their decisions, in the sense that they are free, undetermined by prior legal rules. Indeed, debate with critical

17. The literature on this subject is now legion. I offer a survey of the main characters in Anthony Carty, 'Critical International Law: Recent Trends in the Theory of International Law', *The European Journal of International Law* 2 (1991) 66–95. The continued dynamic of this debate is illustrated by the opening and closing paragraphs of John Tasioulas, 'In Defence of Relative Normativity: Communitarian Values and the Nicaragua Case', *Ox. JLS* 16 (1996) 85–128. He draws a distinction between the positivist statist concept of international society and a natural law orientation that gives a communitarian concept of the society.

theorists has revealed that there is a partiality for the authority of the State that precludes any return to naturalism or any possible contemporary equivalent. For instance, this may be seen in a discussion between Allott and Koskenniemi on this point.[18] I will juxtapose their positions from quotations of their work. According to Allott, international law does not recognise the total social process by which reality is formed, but only that of the interacting of the governments of State societies, as if they constituted a self-contained and self-caused social process. This is precisely the sense of epistemological positivism that Bartelson has focused on in Descartes and Hobbes. Koskenniemi objects that statehood functions precisely as that decision-making process that, by its very formality, operates as a safeguard that different (theological) ideals are not transformed into a globally enforced tyranny.[19] It is obvious that Koskenniemi imposes upon existing State structures the liberal idea of a political order as arbitrator. However, he nowhere demonstrates that States function internationally in this way, even those that suppose themselves to be liberal. Indeed, Tasioulas points out how Koskenniemi's further response to this encounter leads to the odd conclusion that there is a 'tendency of some of these recent trends to yield conclusions surprisingly congruent with Weil's positivist stance'.[20] So, the problem posed by the classical doctrine of sovereignty remains, only now it seems that international lawyers, in a 'postmodern' epoch, are bereft of any tools with which to complement or, alternatively, deconstruct the State. This is the sense in which I pose the question of whether there is any future for doctrine in a world beyond positivism, namely beyond the exclusive role of States as law-definers?

AND MEANWHILE, IN ENGLAND?

I have argued:

> the theory of international law was deliberately 'killed off' by the 'greats' of the discipline in the 1920s and 1930s, in particular by Oppenheim, McNair, Brierly, and even Lauterpacht. It was they who laid the

---

18. See 'Conclusion', British Institute of International Law (ed.) *Theory and International Law, An Introduction* (1991) 119–21.
19. Referring to M. Koskenniemi, 'The Future of Statehood', *Harvard ILJ* 32 (1991) 397 at 407.
20. Tasioulas, 'In Defence of Relative Normativity', 128.

> intellectual foundations for the so-called practitioners' approach to the discipline, and then sent their successors off into the courtrooms.[21]

This statement risks a number of ambiguities, the first of which has to do with the word 'theory'. This has come to mean the rather abstruse application of French poststructuralism to legal formalism, leaving much of the profession baffled, even intimidated, but hardly convinced that a connection had been made with their concerns.[22] Obviously the argument that theory has died out in England, as everywhere else, needs to be restated in several essential elements.

First, theory should be understood to mean the symbolic, or cultural, ethical significance of the body or system of international law in ordering the relations among States. This disappeared in Britain with the shock of the First World War and the rush to institutions to defend humanity against the sovereignty of States. No more eloquent statement of this view has been made than by Thomas Baty:

> The difference between the 19th century and the present becomes vividly apparent if one peruses such a book as Sir R. Phillimore's *Commentaries on International Law*, written in the 1850s. Grandiloquent, discursive, illbalanced, inconclusive as it often is, one feels as one reads its pages the pervasive presence of a conclusive standard of right and wrong. No such moral standard permeates the works of today.[23]

Whether one esteems such figures as Phillimore as thinkers or intellectuals (and clearly Baty did not), they considered themselves as international lawyers as having a responsibility to address statesmen about how the rule of law should prevail in international society. This had nothing to do with being university teachers, because their primary audience was not the university student. Nor does it help to describe them as 'practitioners' without defining what they practiced.

21. A. Carty, 'Why Theory? – The Implications for International Law Teaching', in *Theory and International Law, An Introduction*, 75, 77.
22. J. Crawford, 'Public International Law in Twentieth-century England', in J. Beatson and R. Zimmermann (eds), *Jurists Uprooted, Germanspeaking Émigré Lawyers in Twentieth-century Britain* (2004) 681 at 699. 'Self-conscious exercises in "grand theory" in international law are a more recent phenomenon', referring to the work of David (not Duncan) Kennedy, M. Koskenniemi, P. Allott, and S. Marks. These are the theorists mentioned in the last section.
23. T. Baty, *International Law in Twilight* (1954) 10.

The word is as slippery as 'theory'. For instance, Crawford describes Phillimore as an English-educated civilian. His three-volume international law text 'was written by a civilian practitioner and later judge of the Admiralty Court'.[24]

Phillimore's concept of law rested upon an appeal to the spirit of a God-given moral law governing the universe.[25] So, 'Obedience to the law is as necessary for the liberty of States as it is for the liberty of individuals.' Moral truth demonstrates that independent communities are free moral agents, and historical fact demonstrates that they are mutually recognised in the universal community of which they are members. Law is not to be equated with the notion of physical sanction. Instead, one has to judge critically the impact of historical events upon States as free moral persons. So Phillimore's view, writing in 1879, was that European history since the Danish War of 1864 had been very critical. In 1864 there was a violent change of territory and States did not come to assist as they ought to have done. There followed further injuries that States did not assist others to prevent. So in the 1870s we find that Europe is subject to the prevailing notion that 'a state must seek territorial aggrandisement as a condition of her welfare and security'. There may have been little 'theory' underlying these remarks, but clearly he was addressing them to his political leaders, at least one of whom, his friend William Gladstone, may have been expected to have some sympathy. While it is mentioned that he was a judge of Admiralty, he was also a member of the House of Commons in the 1850s when he wrote the first edition of his textbook. An essay by Gladstone may illustrate how a leading Victorian politician understood law and morality in relations among States. 'England's Mission' gave a central place to the equality of independent States. To Gladstone, an immoral policy is a 'vigorous' policy, which excites the public mind, apathetic with the humdrum detail of legislation, thereby covering up domestic shortcomings; it disguises partisan interests as national and enlists jingoist support. The self-love and pride, which all condemn in individuals, damage States as well, destroying their sobriety in the estimation of human affairs, as they vacillate from arrogance to womanish fears:

24. Crawford, 'Public International Law in Twentieth-century England', 686 and 689.
25. What follows comes from Carty, 'Why Theory?', 88, with citations omitted.

> The doctrines of national self-restraint, of the equal obligations of States to public law, and of their equal rights to fair construction as to words and deeds, have (however) been left to unofficial persons . . . [T]o overlook the proportion between our resources and our obligations, and above all to claim anything more than equality of rights in the moral and political intercourse of the world, is not the way to make England great, but to make it both morally and materially little.[26]

Phillimore's association with Gladstone was hardly exceptional. In his survey of the English tradition of international law Johnson quotes F. E. Smith (later the Earl of Birkenhead) referring to it as an English tradition that 'Professors of International Law shall also be men of affairs'.[27]

There is no mistaking McNair's unease with this intellectual atmosphere. He remarks how the nineteenth-century textbook was a descriptive rather than an analytical work, a history of international relations.[28] Now the output of judicial decisions makes international law 'comparable in technique and educational value to the common law or equity'. The topics one can now consider in teaching international law are much more often dealt with in the national courts, the conclusion being permitted that such law is part of a barrister's training. These topics are: recognition of belligerency, effects of insurgency and civil war, immunities of foreign States and public ships, diplomatic and sovereign immunities, territorial waters and jurisdiction on the high seas, nationality, treatment of aliens, effects of war, and so forth. Jennings began his tenure of the Whewell Chair in Cambridge with a ringing endorsement of McNair's sentiments. He emphasises the importance of judicial, primarily municipal, decisions that are found in the *International Law Reports:* 'It is impossible to exaggerate the importance of this publication which has transformed

26. In *The Liberal Tradition, From Fox to Keynes*, eds Bullock and Shock (1967) 165–7.
27. D. H. N. Johnson, 'The English Tradition in International Law', *International and Comparative Law Quarterly* 11 (1962) 416 at 425, with a quotation from the first edition of his *International Law* (1900). Smith held numerous offices of State, but, for Johnson, the most significant example of the practice was Sir William Harcourt, who was both Whewell Professor of International Law in Cambridge and a leading Liberal statesman through the Gladstone ascendancy.
28. What follows is taken from 'Why Theory – Implications for International Law Teaching', 78.

international law into a case law subject, thus making it not only a better teaching material, but also a very much stronger and more useful law.'[29]

When McNair and Lauterpacht were presenting the first volume of what was then called the *Annual Digest of International Law Cases* in 1929 their expectation was:

> The feature of the twentieth century, particularly after the year 1919, is likely to be an abundant growth of judicial activity in international relations, and there is little reason to doubt that, before half that century has elapsed, international law will be developed almost out of recognition.[30]

Concerning the authority of such material, the authors clearly have reference to the fruitfulness of the judicial style of reasoning, that is the concern with the resolution of a specific problem. So the authors continue,

> in any field of human activity it is impossible for one mind faced with the task of solving a problem not to give weight to the solution of a similar problem which has commended itself to another mind elsewhere. That is not a principle of law but of common human experience.[31]

This is not necessarily 'ignoring state practice in favor of judicial decisions, or the analysis of ideas in favor of textual exegesis',[32] but it is to create the expectation that the best synthesis of this practice, and indeed the most authoritative interpretation of this practice, will be provided by the judiciary, whether national or international.

Elsewhere, I have recently argued that it is a focus on the prospect of adjudication that heightens the concern of the positivist international lawyer, with the bilateral or reciprocal aspects of legal relationships at the expense of the wider aspects for international order that concerned Phillimore or Birkenhead. The problems of State power and sovereignty, and the exigencies attaching to the nature of

29. R. Y. Jennings, 'The State of International Law Today,' *Journal of the Society of the Public Teachers of Law* (1957–58) 95 at 96.
30. Preface to the *Annual Digest of International Law Cases, Years 1925 and 1926* (1929) x.
31. Ibid.
32. Crawford, 'Public International Law in Twentieth-century England', 700.

an international legal system and its legal structure, are unlikely to be central to the concerns of a consensus-based judiciary, which still resembles permanent arbitration. The tendency will be to rely upon areas of State practice that are fairly well settled and have implications for the individual, for example, for the purposes of extradition law, which State may be taken to have effective jurisdiction. A casuistry of the equity of the particular case is combined with the necessity of having regard to the seesaw of recognition and acquiescence with respect to the two most engaged parties, for example with respect to title to territory, in what will usually become a concrete context of arbitration.[33]

What is lost thereby is the confidence to address directly the behaviour of States in terms of some independent international standard. This had disappeared with the Victorian and Edwardian confidence in the capacity of international lawyers as opinion-makers to sway the conscience of nations. When exactly this happened is disputed and may vary from country to country,[34] but the gradual process of technical transformation of the discipline of international law has taken place everywhere, and in Britain that form has accentuated the place of the judiciary. In the nineteenth century, the confidence of English international lawyers to influence State behaviour rested on a utilitarian sense of the power of international opinion to sway State behaviour to a social sense of what was in the interest of the majority. It supposedly reproduced the role of opinion in shaping legislation in England itself. Here key figures were the professors of international law in universities such as Oxford (T. E. Holland) and Cambridge (John Westlake).[35]

---

33. See further A. Carty, 'Visions of the Past of International Society, Law, History or Politics', *Modern Law Review* 69(4) (Spring 2006) 644–60.
34. Martti Koskenniemi places the change in continental Europe in the 1950s, in *The Gentle Civiliser of Nations* (2002) 3, while David Kennedy is closer to the view expressed here that the shock of the Great War led international lawyers to hope, in his view somewhat magically or mysteriously, for peace through institutions, or even the language of institutions, see David Kennedy, 'The Move to Institutions', *Cardozo Law Review* 8 (1987) 841, esp. to 849.
35. See Casper Sylvest, 'International Law in 19th Century Britain', *British Yearbook of International Law* LXXV (2004) 9–70; and John Anthony Carty '19th Century Textbooks on International Law', unpublished thesis, Cambridge University (1973) esp. Part VII, 'International Law in England, The Textbooks', 277–379.

The alternative, post-1918 view in England was instead institutional, one in which the international lawyer had no distinctive role as an opinion-shaper. Brierly represented it well in his study of the foundations of international law. As with Oppenheim,[36] Brierly saw the State as a complex institutional labyrinth. He took a view that effectively excluded any place for an evolving international public opinion, or even an evolving customary practice of States. He had the following perspective on the relation of opinion to law creation:

> '[T]he public' which is supposed to direct political events in a democratic state is a 'phantom'; there is no overmastering social purpose in it, but a vast complex of individual purposes . . . Somehow or other we know that out of these chaotic materials there are precipitated the public policies . . . which the organs of government proceed to carry into effect in legislation or administration, but the process by which this takes place is far too intricate either to be traced in detail or to be summarized in a single formula.[37]

The sequel to this development appears to be very unfortunate in the case of England. Commenting on the English scene in the early 1960s in his inaugural lecture at the London School of Economics (LSE), Johnson provides a remarkable panorama of the richness of the classical English international law tradition. It cannot be reduced to the role of nineteenth-century utilitarianism and the manipulation or legitimate shaping of public opinion. It goes back to a rich medieval and Renaissance civilian, Roman law, and natural law tradition, alongside the important prize law field, protected by the ancient universities and having so prominent a place even into the nineteenth century.[38] However, at the time of writing Johnson noticed the serious gulf in England, wider than elsewhere, between the study of international law and the study of ethics. Johnson blames this not on John Austin, who did not oppose international law as a form of international morality, but on the international lawyers themselves,

36. Carty, 'Why Theory? – The Implications for International Law Teaching', 79–82 describing the State as an institution, a perspective most amenable to the superimposition of international institution, although obviously not causing them, merely catching the mood of the times, as a representative thinker.
37. J. Brierly, *The Basis of Obligation in International Law, and Other Papers*, ed. H. Lauterpacht (1958) 41–2.
38. Johnson, 'The English Tradition in International Law', 432 ff.

who wished to make their subject appeal to their fellow law school colleagues. This led English international lawyers, wishing to impress their colleagues with the positive character of international law,

> to go too far in severing the links which connected international law with the principles of morality and natural law. International law may by this presentation have been made respectable to practicing lawyers, although, as we have seen, even that result was only very partially achieved. The price paid was that international law came to have, and still has, very little meaning to that substantial portion of English public opinion which tends to view world events in moral terms. What relevance has international law today to those people, and especially young people, who feel passionately about such questions as the hydrogen bomb and race relations? Unfortunately very little.[39]

FOUNDATIONS FOR A NEW ROLE FOR DOCTRINE

As Mark Twain said of himself, rumours of the death of natural law are somewhat exaggerated. Instead, it is better to see its eclipse of popularity in intellectual circles – international law is only a system of ideas – as a reflection of the triumph of ideas associated with liberal democracy and the rule of law. What are these ideas?

Richard Ned Lebow's *A Cultural History of International Relations* offers a typology of cultural representations of world society in historical perspective, which offers an ideological or structural explanation of the phenomenon of liberal democracy as the political theory for, and systematic representation of, appetite.[40] At the same time, there are two other human motives or drives that help to understand conduct, the drive for honour and away from fear.[41] Liberalism views the human drive of appetite positively and imagines peaceful, productive worlds in which material well-being is a dominant value. Liberals imagine their theories are descriptions of societies that already exist or are coming into being, with proponents of globalisation predicting a worldwide triumph of liberal democratic trading States. Its starting point is a fundamentally welfare-oriented,

39. Ibid., quote on 432, esp. 432.
40. Richard Ned Lebow, *A Cultural Theory of International Relations* (2008) 72–6.
41. Ibid., 61–72, 88–93.

consumerist, and therefore politically post-modern, privately interested, even apolitical *individual*, described by Cooper in *The Breaking of Nations*.[42]

Persons may nominally be the best judges of their own interest, but the invisible hand of collective egotism is what ensures public survival. Beyond that there is no formally acknowledged interest in power politics, not to mention aggressive wars of conquest. There is no further need for a critique of human conduct by reference to a transcendent standard of 'right reason'. This function for doctrine will be lost in the face of the tasks of the management of human welfare, above all economic administration, so as to satisfy human appetites. International society needs to be managed skilfully, which may explain the appropriateness of the emergence of international administrative law as a governing concept to describe the phenomena of contemporary world, not simply State, practice.[43]

Indeed Koskenniemi appears to be arguing that the development of a natural law foundation to international law became lost in the intricacies of economic management at the point when Adam Smith abandoned natural jurisprudence for political economy.[44] His complaint that international law, as a dream of the Gentle Civilisers, comes to an end about 1960, with the triumph of European Law and the assignment of the Frenchman, international lawyer Paul Reuters, to Brussels, is another way of saying that international law is about a functionalist management of socio-economic frictions among States, rather than a search for the meaning of their narrative in the onward march of their historical destinies.[45]

An extended introduction to Vattel's place in both the European Enlightenment and in the development of international law thinking, is provided by Martti Koskenniemi.[46] He appreciates the slippery nature of the concept of 'voluntary law' within which Vattel embeds his

42. R. Cooper, *The Breaking of Nations: Order and Chaos in the Twenty-First Century* (2003) 62.
43. The Global Administrative Law Project at New York University Law School <http://iilj.org/GAL/>, accessed 14 August 2016.
44. M. Koskenniemi, 'The Advantages of Treaties: International Law in the Enlightenment', *Edinburgh Law Review* 13 (2009) 27–67.
45. M. Koskenniemi, *The Gentle Civilizer of Nations* (2002).
46. Martti Koskenniemi, 'From Dante to Vattel', in *Vattel's International Law in a XXIst Century Perspective, Le droit international de Vattel vu du XXIe siècle,* Vincent Chetail and Peter Haggenmacher (eds) (2011) 73–5. All of the subsequent quotations from Koskenniemi on this page are from the same source.

formulation of equality. It is that part of the law that takes account of the specific nature of the international system. It reflects the 'presumed consent' of States to what they would consent if they possessed full knowledge of their interests and their relative position at each moment vis-à-vis their rivals'. This is not an equation of 'voluntary law' with actual rules attributable to treaty or tacit custom. Says Koskenniemi, 'something is not in accordance with a nation's interest merely because a nation happens to do it'. Instead, says Koskenniemi, 'voluntary law is what progressive expertise tells us is needed for a nation's "Bonheur et perfection"'. The voluntary law is firmly grounded, he says, in the eighteenth-century reality, where progressive elements can be chosen that 'look for a more harmonious existence in the future. Like Mandeville's *Fable of the Bees,* voluntary law's dual realist/idealist structure consecrates the liberal world-view under which private vices become producers of the greatest public good.' Koskenniemi ends his chapter equivocally by saying that Vattel 'buys freedom from Empire and the public law of the State at the cost of capitalism and expert rule'.

This book will explore more fully the negative implications of Vattel's theory of voluntary law and equality being embedded so fully in the eighteenth-century Enlightenment optimism that 'private vices become producers of the greatest public good'. As Dany-Robert Dufour explains, the equilibrium of desire about which Mandeville was so optimistic quickly developed into the 'delights' of domination and subordination. This received the fullest philosophical exposition by the Marquis de Sade at the end of the eighteenth century, before becoming 'codified' in Hegel's dialectic of 'Master and Slave' in his *Phenomenology of the Spirit.* While it is possible for 'desires' to be exchanged there is nothing in the logic of the pursuit of interest, whether by individual men or by nations, which says that where 'desires' clash, each should not insist on the triumph of their own 'desires', indeed that the most exquisite 'desire' is precisely where one's own 'desire' absorbs, quashes or eliminates the 'desires' of the other, while still leaving a certain place for the exchange of 'desires'.[47]

It would be possible to reintroduce a classical natural law role for doctrine if it was possible to show that there was some place in the contemporary practice of States, for individual choice and responsibility, a capacity to shape events constructively according to some measure or standard of reasonableness. In fact, Lebow contrasts appetite societies, such as the liberal, democratic West primarily with 'spirit societies'

47. Dany-Robert Dufour, *La Cité perverse: Libéralisme et pornographie* (2009).

where the primary motivation is esteem, both self-esteem and esteem that one has won from others, society and so on, according to agreed rules. This drive for self-worth is at least as strong as appetite and often takes over when the former is in some measure satisfied.[48]

Lebow recognises that what appears strange is that the liberal paradigm of State interest for individual welfare appears to offer no ballast to resist the tendency to fear that the precariousness of an international society without any overriding authority repeatedly engenders through the competition that is the main form of contact among States. This is because liberalism does not acknowledge that appetite, like spirit-based societies have their roots in human motivation, ultimately individual even if inherently socially contagious. Of human motivation Lebow says:

> Spirit and appetite based worlds are inherently unstable. They are intensely competitive, which encourages actors to violate the rules by which honor or wealth is attained. When enough actors do this, those who continue to obey the rules are likely to be seriously handicapped[49] . . . The difficulty of appeasing the spirit or appetite, or of effectively discriminating among competing appetites, sooner or later propels both kinds of people and regimes down the road to tyranny. Tyranny is initially attractive because the tyrant is unconstrained by laws. In reality, the tyrant is a true slave because he is ruled by his passions and is not in any way his own master.[50]

Of course fear is the other face of tyranny. Fear is a negative emotion essentially derivative, marking an anticipated loss of other goods, self-esteem and the esteem of others and, of course, wealth.[51] As the fear grows the counter-measures for protection become self-defeating and intensify the sense of danger. The search for security in this more usual sense of the word – not Foucault's – knows no bounds and spreads fear in the community, whether national or international. This is because the final root of this derivative emotion is always the *unrestrained* drive for either appetite or the spirit of honour, or both together. This lack of restraint will be a failure of leadership by elites, although it may be accompanied by a revolt by the less advantaged who consider that the rules for acquisition of wealth and honour are not being met.[52]

48. Lebow, *A Cultural Theory of International Relations* esp. at 61 et seq.
49. Ibid., at 82.
50. Ibid., at 83.
51. Ibid., 88 et seq.
52. Ibid., also at 83–6.

It is the place of reason to exercise restraint on the pursuit of honour and appetite, by which Lebow means *phronēsis,* not an instrumental reason – David Hume's slave of the passions – but a capacity to reformulate behaviour on the basis of reflection. This goes beyond simple feedback to make conduct more effective, to a learning about one's environment and how it works, to an appreciation that the ability to satisfy appetite and spirit rests on a robust society. That, in turn, rests upon affection and the role of close relationships in self-actualising, where meaningful co-operation becomes possible. This is all drawn from Aristotle, Socrates, and Plato. The fundamental difficulty leading to the breakdown of orders, for Aristotle, is the parochial pursuit of factional goals, leading others to fear exclusion from the ability to satisfy their goals. For Socrates dialogue is the surest means of making us recognise the parochial and limited range of our goals. For Plato *eros* can be educated by reason and directed towards the good and the beautiful and even the kind wisdom concerned with ordering of States and societies.[53]

After setting out this normative framework, Lebow illustrates it with the whole sweep of Western history, including some of East Asia in the last hundred years. While international diplomacy virtually always has appetite trumped by the spirit in pursuit of honour, the high point of this tendency was the period 1660 to 1789. Of course the significance of this period is that it is precisely when legal historians are agreed that whatever influence the Grotius tradition of international law doctrine had, it was then. While the State was all the time increasingly consolidated as an institution it was still visibly directed by sovereign individuals, above all Louis XIV, Peter I of Russia and Frederick II, all of whom sought and obtained the title of Great. Lebow's argument is not at all that these rulers studiously read and followed Grotius's maxims. Rather it is that the primary problem they all represented was a lack of restraint in the pursuit of glory, after a period – the Wars of Religion – where public consciousness was especially aware of the absence of all constraints. The function of a classical ethic of reason – right reason – was then not to ensure a balance of power – an unstable concept in an atmosphere of fear – but to restore and maintain balance, an equilibrium in the mentality of the elites of Europe. While wars would frequently have dynastic pretexts, historians are agreed that dynasties usually restrained an ultimate destructiveness in conflict.[54]

53. Ibid., 76–82
54. Ibid., 262–304, chapter 6: 'From Sun King to Revolution'.

The 'Advantages of Treaties' and the Move from Natural Law to Economics and from Economics to Materialism

In another important article Koskenniemi remarks, commenting on David Hume's views about treaties, 'It is only with arguments about the "advantages of treaties" that a stable and realistic sphere of the international seems to emerge. This is not a sphere of law, however, but of economics.'[55] Koskenniemi explains the context of the new natural law approach that sought to make 'self-interest appear consistent with life in society'. Koskenniemi quotes the same famous remark from Adam Smith as does Dufour, that our dinner comes not from the kindness of the butcher and brewer or the baker, but from their own interest (64). So says Smith, we should address not their humanity but their self-love (64). The question was still whether an impartial spectator could encourage a secondary sociability in a society of self-centred individuals (64). What appeared to be useful for long-term happiness had to be an argument that reflected the possibilities of long-term interest. As Smith could see, the weakness of international law was that there was no legislature or judicial system to resolve disputes (65). However, as the Physiocrats and others such as Frederick II realised increasingly in the eighteenth century, 'the proper language for modern *salus populi* would have to be that of political economy' (65).

The first resort of *raison d'etat* appeared to be mercantilism, a zero-sum game of States in their struggles with one another. However, liberalism has to come up with an invisible law of economics that will reconcile conflicting interests. The abolition of import restrictions and free trade encourages the individual, as the nation, to pursue his own advantage, which, at the same time, works to the advantage of society and the world (66). The study of one's own advantage automatically works to that of the society. Here Smith makes an important move. The political is concerned with irrational, negative passions, while the economic realm turns our passions into beneficial and calculable interests. These can be subjected to a universal system of rational exchanges (67).

Where people are concerned only to fulfil their needs, with free economic activity given full reign, welfare and happiness will be produced (67). Koskenniemi points to a widespread consensus among international lawyers. What is said 'by a very large part of professional international

55. Koskenniemi, 'The Advantage of Treaties: International Law in the Enlightenment', *Edinburgh Law Review* 12 (2008) 27. Subsequent page references are in the text.

lawyers in the past half century emerges from viewing the international world in terms not of politics but of economics'. This is international law as a universal commercial society. As heads of State proliferate at the United Nations (UN) representing increasingly insignificant political communities in the General Assembly, 'the crowd retreats to drinks in the adjoining lounge' (67).

The single most radical element of Dufour's apparently outrageous intellectual history is to trace the link, as a matter of intellectual history, from Mandeville to Smith and then to Sade. Indeed, the starting point is a fateful remark by Pascal in his *Thoughts* fragment 106, 'The grandeur of man is to have drawn from concupiscence such a beautiful order.'[56] Classical Greek and especially Christian thought was built on the pillar of reining in the passions and ensuring their permanent subordination to reason. Love of the other, ultimately of God, had to be the exclusive alternative to love of the self. For the classical La Rochefoucauld, self-love makes men idolaters of themselves and tyrants of others if fortune gives them the means (112). Mandeville's *Fable of the Bees,* in contrast, is about the liberation of passions as the way to opulence, their control leading to misery (30). Mandeville preaches in the *Fable* 'Be as greedy, egoist, as wasteful for your pleasure as you can be, for, this way you will do the most for the prosperity of your nation and the happiness of your fellow citizens' (133). It is this idea that is white-washed without acknowledgement by Adam Smith (esp. 150), the word 'vice' replaced by 'self-love' (133).

Dufour quotes Dumont's work, that *Homo aequalis,* the victor over *homo hierarchicus*, is the product of the economic ideology from the eighteenth century. We leave a wholistic world, transcendent, dominated in Europe by a totality represented by a divine thought (139) to which one must submit, to enter instead to a world dominated, in Smith's cosmic structure, by a play of forces resting upon a principle of attraction. The human world is organised, although humans do not know it, by a play of forces resting upon personal interest, which plays the role of attraction, comparable to Newton's law of gravity for physical beings, an organising principle as an invisible hand, a modernised divine design (143). There is a place for discipline, but it is, in Smith's world, a discipline for the poor, the sick and the victims of whatever calamity, who should realise what the order and the perfection of the universe requires that they accept (158). The ravages in

---

56. Dufour, *La Cité perverse* 94. All of the subsequent references to Dufour in this section are in the text.

the 'third world', especially in the Americas, still served the purpose, in Smith's eyes, of bringing the survivors the fruits of European progress, industry and the arts, without which these empires could never have become civilised or cultivated (152).

It was Augustine who realised that love of the self subordinates the common good, through an arrogant domination and that the self-love is a rival of God, requiring everything for itself and wishing to make the other submit to its interest (60, 165). This is precisely what de Sade follows in chapter 12 of *The New Justine*. Egoism is the first law of nature and of reason. 'We ought only to hold sacred what delights us' (169). In *The Philosophy of the Boudoir* de Sade repeats a principle taken from Mandeville that regarding their own happiness makes honest men through egotism and this is the surest of laws among men (170). For de Sade relationship with the other is simply not necessary. The other is nothing but the object of my enjoyment (172). Of course the desire of the other may resist one's own desires. So, for myself to enjoy, it is necessary that the other does not. Hence, it comes to the fact that the exaltation of my ego requires me to be a tyrant. Writes de Sade 'il n'est point d'homme qui ne veuille être despote quand il bande' (173) and 'l'idée de voir un autre jouir comme lui le ramène à une sorte d'égalité quit nuit aux attraits indicibles que fait éprouver le despotisme alors' (174). Dufour concludes from this analysis that 'laissez faire' is to allow the construction of a demonic enterprise, essentially pornographic (174).

Contrasting two texts of Smith and de Sade, Dufour italicises the phrases of Smith – give me that of which I have need and you will have of me what you need, and de Sade – loan to me for a moment the part of your body that can satisfy me and enjoy yourself that part of me that is agreeable to you, if you please (178). But how free will the exchange really be? Dufour notes how de Sade helps us to question the ambivalence of the dimension of consent in exchange. May there not be a secret clause in the maxim of exchange? The true world of self-love, in perversion, takes what it wants. In de Sade's words, ' Je ne te demande rien. . .je prends et je ne vois pas que de ce que j'use d'un droit sur toi, il doive résulter qu'il me faille abstenir d'en exiger un second' (179). Dufour concludes by explaining that the essence of this coercion is that one aims to undo the other, to twist her body into parts, by dissecting and singling out her particular sexually potent organs, to disorganise her (185). The depersonalising focus on particular aspects of the sexual anatomy of the other is the surest way to enjoy the other while at the same time unravelling and so completely obliterating her personality (185).

A Renaissance of Ethically Grounded Legal Reasoning in Natural Law

The person who provides the most lucid concretisation of the dissipation of the natural law tradition of legal thinking is Janne Haaland Matláry, who shows the way to a Natural Law Grounded Legal Reasoning. After reviewing the onward march of empiricism through Locke, Hume, and Kant, Haaland remarks on the latter, whose ideas are so close to the new classical natural law school, that Kant tried to rescue objective human nature by postulating it a priori, a postulate of a rational being endowed with dignity.[57] Yet it remains a postulate because nothing about human nature in itself can be known. This is the final conclusion of Hume's empiricism. The idea that the world community and all within it can have a telos or purpose, an overall sense of meaning, is negated by our consciousness that knows only ourselves as a series of sense experiences. Since we cannot observe ourselves, but only notice our own behaviour, we have no substance or identity.

Haaland opposes to this the telos of man as *eudaimonia*, happiness. This is found not just through reason, but also the classical virtues of justice, prudence, and temperance. The word for rational ability in ethical matters comes from the Latin word 'VIR', which means in Latin manly or strong. This classical concept of the person, with intelligence married to virtue, leads inevitably to an unclouded or uncorrupted vision with respect to the 'free-running' of natural inclinations in 'the furniture of the world' – personal, social, national, and international. The objective capacity for moral judgement leads to objective assessments of the quality of these natural inclinations, whether, to borrow Robert Gahl's expression – itself an interpretation of Aquinas – they are being ruled and measured, as they should be, by right reason. There is no doubt that 'the furniture of the universe' is present as the deep structures against which the 'free run of inclinations' is to be judged. As Gahl explains, the right reason of man merely participates in the eternal reason of God. Again, as Gahl has said, one has to keep in place three factors: that natural law is promulgated by God, that it is human nature, and that it is the work of reason.[58]

---

57. <http://thomasmoreinstitute.org.uk/papers/democracy-and-human-rights-in-europe-the-problem-of-relativism/>. What follows from Haaland in this and the next paragraph is taken from this lecture given to the Thomas More Institute in London on 9 May 2007, revisited 1 October 2014.
58. R. Gahl, 'Natural Law Approaches to Comparative Law:Methodological Perspectives, Legal Tradition and Natural Law', *Journal of Comparative Law* 2 (2014) 189.

Robert Gahl himself stresses seven dimensions of natural law: the neo-platonic metaphysic; the Aristotelean four causes in the definition of law of Aquinas; the anthropic, epistemic, and theonomic; the natural inclinations towards the good and the ends of human flourishing; practical reasoning; moral virtues; and cognitive discovery and narrative temporality.[59] Gahl points out how this vast panorama is narrowed down by the 'so-called new classical natural law theory' that puts an emphasis on the epistemic focus of natural law at the expense of the anthropic and theonomic.[60] Gahl sees in this new school an under-appreciation of the divine and natural law character of natural law. He singles out the view of John Finnis. Gahl quotes Finnis, that '[m]oral standards. . .make legal rules binding rationally, and shape concept formation in even descriptive social theory'.[61] However, Gahl retorts that it is sounder to 'consider morality 'natural' precisely because reasonable (in an understanding neither consequentialist nor Kantian)'. Following Hittinger, Gahl stresses that Natural Law is founded principally in God and only secondarily in the human being.[62] Therefore, one has to keep in place three factors: that natural law is promulgated by God, that it is human nature, and that it is the work of reason.[63]

This apparently abstract and abstruse knowledge lays the foundation for Gahl's discussion of the relationship of reason to 'natural inclination' in classical Christian Natural Law theory. The new classical natural law sets up, probably following Kant, a profound dichotomy between rational moral judgement and desire. Hence it is important to understand how natural inclination was viewed previously. The question for Aquinas, according to Gahl, is whether natural law is 'only in reason or is it also somehow in the other powers or faculties of nature? Is it correct to speak of inclinations as being at once natural and as somehow constituting the law?'[64] Concretely, this concerns such matters as the natural inclination 'to conserve one's own life, to procreate, to make friends, to make intellectual progress through new discoveries of understanding and so on'.[65] It appears 'even the concupiscent and irascible appetites can be law'.[66]

59. Ibid., 179 at 179–80.
60. Ibid., at 188.
61. Ibid.
62. Ibid.
63. Ibid., at 189.
64. Ibid.
65. Ibid., at 189–90.
66. Ibid., 190.

This is because natural inclinations, natural powers, and faculties are law insofar as they are ruled and measured by right reason. In this way they also participate in the divine reason of the eternal law.[67] Natural inclinations are rational inclinations, consequent upon the cognitive understanding of the goods as ends of human perfection.[68]

Haaland's book, *When Might becomes Human Right*, can very well be read as her judgement of right reason, married to virtue, about the 'free run of natural inclinations' at present. While there is a common human nature discovered through reason – the 'furniture of the universe'[69] – Haaland diagnoses that the problem at present is that individual preference dominates in politics, a complete subjectivism. Reasoning from the self-referential man rather than a principled analysis of human nature is what dominates.[70] Yet people refuse to talk about what is a human being; indeed today there is no overt, systematic ideological debate.[71] Instead narcissism reigns – nothing exists objectively, independently of me (what George, Finnis et al., would deride as 'furniture of the universe').[72] A family is whatever we say it is – pure nominalism.[73] You, the subject, can choose infinitely and there need be nothing permanent in your choice – all options are open all the time.[74] We forget telos, the purpose or intention of any thing or person, any meaning, an order connecting the parts to the whole, a sense of the metaphysical, of the order of things existing prior to our knowledge, all assumed away as essentialism. Haaland's corresponds to Gahl's critique of the new classical natural law theory. So Gahl says that George dispenses with metaphysics by mocking 'Platonic forms' as somehow detached from the real world of human persons.[75]

Haaland identifies how the practice of social movements such as feminism or gay-lesbianism rests upon constructivism. This is the view that social roles are constructed by society and that 'meaning' is there merely a function of social practices. Meanings can therefore change and individual stipulation is a part of the process.[76] This applies to

---

67. Ibid.
68. Ibid.
69. Janne Haaland Matlary, *When Might becomes Human Right: Essays on democracy and the crisis of rationality* (2007) 4.
70. Ibid., at 7 and at 15.
71. Ibid., at 19 and 21.
72. Ibid., at 32.
73. Ibid., at 34.
74. Ibid., at 39.
75. Ibid., and see Robert George, *In Defence of Natural Law* (1999) 232–3.
76. Ibid., at 69 et seq.

the whole parameter of debates about family and especially adoption. Haaland argues that international conventions such as that on the Rights of the Child 1989 give the child a right to parentage by biological parents, also implicitly excluding one parent raising a child alone or in a homosexual relationship.[77] However, she treats this particular field of social activity as merely one among many. Haaland relates it also to a changing identity of the nation state, globalisation, and the failure of any convincing international order.

Furthermore, political research in Norway shows that Norwegians generally use human rights language to support their political claims, not by referring to any particular human rights convention or declaration, but in the sense of their political claim having a generalised legal character, somehow a good thing in itself. So, she paraphrases the contemporary Norwegian political discourse that it is my right and my dignity demands, for example, a larger pension, good working conditions, parental leave and high-quality health care, regardless of income and social status.[78] Haaland may appear to oppose this discourse because she is conservative politically. However, Haaland is not politically sectarian. She recognises that today 'market liberalism and its corollary, consumerism, are the key problems. . .(as) more and more power is vested in market actors to the detriment of political actors'.[79] As the labour force has largely lost the capacity to protect itself, 'there seems to be no ethos whatsoever left on the part of the employer – short term profit and not development that benefits employers and community. . .(which) in turn makes it almost impossible for an employee to settle down and plan a family'.[80]

Haaland diagnoses the actual institutional response to these developments at a national and global level, before recommending an essential role for classical natural law in future progressive legal development. As the nation state declines as a source of social cohesion – with the fading of notions of national identity – the only ethical anchor remaining is international human rights law. Yet ethical insecurity is related to the same weakening of the nation state and the absence of any as yet formed norms of international governance. Neo-liberalism and consumerism face each other across the divide of corporate power and the individual.[81] Judges in supranational tribunals adjudicate human rights questions based on criteria of

77. Ibid., at 116.
78. Ibid., at 101 et seq.
79. Ibid., at 142–3.
80. Ibid., at 143.
81. Ibid., at 84–6.

more or less trying to follow political trends, nominally presented as law. The European Court of Human Rights (ECHR) relies upon a so-called evolutionary interpretation to deal with, for example, discrimination in employment, the place of religious symbols in schools or whatever. It reaches supposedly sociological assessments of changing societal developments, but without documentation on precise changes in the climate of opinion or analysis of the significance of the changes.[82] In fact, human rights paragraphs are really policy statements, meaning that there are few indications of how a lawyer should interpret them. While States do frequently expose themselves to international adjudication, of international human rights bodies at the instigation of newly empowered global citizenry,[83] the fundamental problem is, throughout, a radically subjectivised individualism, with no objective judicial ground for constraint.

It is, hence, in the final analysis, a problem that only a classical, natural law grounded legal philosophy can answer. She follows the metaphor of Hans Petter Graver, that legal rules have become 'liquid law', where legal rules are unable to hold their shape for long, responding to the pressure not merely from political bodies but, above all, articulated social interest groups, hence the title her book, *When Might becomes Human Right*.[84] The metaphor of 'liquid law' is taken by Graver from Zygmunt Baumann's 'concept of "liquid modernity" where everything is "individualized, privatized, without given or self-evident rules, codes and patterns to conform to"'.[85] So Haaland treats as most urgent to re-establish sound reasoning in the nature of law and politics. Evoking Aristotle's notion of man as being a zoon politikon and the ontological realism that truth exists independently of my subjective personal view of things, 'the concern of the Christian must therefore be to show, through reason and logic, that the very concept of law implies universal, i.e. moral, reasoning'.[86] So she concludes:

> The first step is one of reintroducing logical reasoning: the language of universals, the moral language, is one about the truth of things: is this right or wrong? Here natural law is the only viable road. Normative questions cannot be determined by majority voting, and posing the question of right and wrong in and of itself implies that there is a truth to be discovered.[87]

82. Ibid., at 100–3.
83. Ibid., at 103, 106–7.
84. Ibid., at 103–6.
85. Ibid., 108.
86. Ibid., 138, also at 139.
87. Ibid., at 140.

FURTHER READING

Bartelson, Jens, *A Genealogy of Sovereignty* (1992).
Brierly, James, *The Basis of Obligation in International Law*, Hersch Lauterpacht (ed.) (1958).
Carty, Anthony, 'International Law as a Science, The Place of Doctrine in the History of its Sources', in *The Indian Yearbook of World Affairs Part II* (1980) 128–60.
de Vattel, Emer, *The Law of Nations* (2008).
Dupuy, Pierre Marie and Vincent Chetail (eds), *The Roots of International Law, Liber Americorum Peter Haggenmacher* (2014).
Johnson, D. H. N., 'The English Tradition in International Law', *International and Comparative Law Quarterly* 11 (1962) 416–45.
Koskenniemi, Martti, *From Apology to Utopia* (2006).
Lebow, Richard N., *A Cultural Theory of International Relations* (2008).
Nuzzo, Luigi and Milos Vec (eds), *Constructing International Law, The Birth of a Discipline* (2012).
Pagden, Anthony and Jeremy Lawrence (eds), *Vitoria's Political Writings* (1992).
Sylvest, Casper, 'International Law in 19th Century Britain', *British Yearbook of International Law* LXXV (2004) esp. 9–70.
Wilcox, Russell and Anthony Carty (eds), *Natural Law and Comparative Law* (2015).

1

Continuing Uncertainty in the Mainstream

INTRODUCTION: CAN INTERNATIONAL CUSTOMARY LAW BE A FORMAL SOURCE OF LAW AMONG SOVEREIGN STATES?

There is no consensus among international lawyers on a workable or operable concept of general customary law, supposed to be the fundamental source of an international law binding upon States. It is thought to represent an analytical framework within which one can assess whether States recognise a rule, principle, or practice as binding upon them as law. Jurists are to examine the same 'raw material' of international relations as diplomats, statesmen, historians, and political scientists. Yet according to the most orthodox view, expressed in the jurisprudence of the International Court of Justice (ICJ), the jurists are to find that States have, in some sense, a legal conscience or sense of conviction. In the *North Sea Continental Shelf* cases the ICJ said that the 'practice of states' relevant to the assertion that a rule of customary international law exists must:

> be such, or be carried out in such a way, as to be evidence of a belief that this practice is rendered obligatory by the existence of a rule of law requiring it (*opinio juris sive necessitatis*) . . . The states concerned must therefore feel that they are conforming to what amounts to a legal obligation.[1]

The basic problems with this formulation have been put squarely by Sorensen and D'Amato. Sorensen points out how the very nature of relations among States makes ascertainment of an evolving customary law virtually impossible. Diplomatic negotiations remain so closed and secret that not even the representatives of one State will know what are the underlying motives of their opposite numbers. Yet

1. *ICJ Reports* (1969) 3 at 77.

such motivation is essential to the psychological element of custom.[2] D'Amato has been equally direct in questioning any possible legal method of observing customary law evolving out of the consciousness of a modern bureaucratic State.[3]

It appears impossible to speak of States having an identity that allows one to suppose that, as centres of subjectivity, they have acquired a sense of obligation with respect to a particular matter. If the State is viewed as a corporate entity, the legal order that supports it should define the organs of the State competent for the purpose of creating general custom, and, furthermore, specify when in fact the organs are acting to this end. Yet the international legal order does not do this. Jurists are left fumbling with the idea that the State is itself, as a totality, in some undefined way, capable of having a 'legal sense' that it is bound by a general custom, which may even be supposed to be already existing. The reaction of some jurists has been to try to dispense with the psychological element of general custom altogether, yet without abandoning the concept of general custom itself.[4]

Pierre-Marie Dupuy provides an exhaustive and authoritative account of the formal problems for the international legal profession. In his *Hague Academy Lectures* he draws attention to the fact that the profession must face a deficiency: 'that, precisely, of the existence of *procedures*, duly formalised by the law itself, for the creation of customary norms'.[5] Dupuy remarks how there are very detailed rules for the conclusion of treaties,

> but, there are not, to the contrary, to borrow the terminology of Hart, secondary rules governing the conditions of formation of custom . . . One contents oneself to affirm unilaterally that the rules of custom exist or one awaits a judge to say so himself, in place of the states.[6]

Until there is some form of revelatory proof of its existence, generally judicial, a rule of custom remains a virtual rule. The paradox is that, trapped in its theoretical premises, the most classical positivist

---

2. M. Sorensen, *Les sources du droit international* (1946) esp. 109.
3. A. D'Amato, *The Concept of Custom in International Law* (1971) 82–4.
4. Ibid., 52; Sorensen, *Les Sources du droit international* 52.
5. *L'Unité de l'ordre juridique international, Cours général de droit international public* (2003) 160; the author's translation; emphasis in the original.
6. Ibid., 160–1.

doctrine, says Dupuy, nonetheless persists in seeing in custom, despite this absence of forms, a formal source of law with respect to the conditions of its creation, and not merely with respect to its content.[7]

There is a clear residual confidence among international lawyers that the international judiciary can 'reveal', to use Dupuy's language, the presence of custom, and turn it from virtual to real law. Yet, it is almost a commonplace of legal doctrine that the ICJ has reached decisions in such cases as the *Fisheries Jurisdiction* (1974) or the *Advisory Opinion on Namibia* (1971), in the face of so much conflicting State interest and interplay of power, as to leave one at a loss as to how general custom is supposed to arise out of State practice.[8]

What is needed is a framework of analysis of State activity that allows a court to engage in effective analysis of the conduct of States as actors in international society. This entails actually lifting the corporate veil of the State in order to understand both facts and intentions. For some purposes this may not be strictly necessary, for example if the matter under observation is purely one of legal/State responsibility. Positions taken by governments would, then, be of more importance than understanding actions in contexts. However, investigation of customary practice is a matter of deciphering the normative significance of the behaviour of collective entities and of evaluating, comparatively, clashing collective actions. As has been seen in the first part, doctrine has virtually talked its way into the position that somehow the very idea that States have intentions, minds, and so on is regarded as absurd. Instead, the notion of legal obligation of States is to be inferred from the results of their behaviour, externally observed as a sort of material fact. As Akehurst put it some time ago: 'We cannot know what states believe. First of all, states being abstractions or institutions do not have minds of their own; and in any case since much of the decision-making within governments takes place in secret, we cannot know what states (or those who speak for them) really think, but only what they say they think.'[9]

7. Ibid., and the literature cited therein: a comprehensive survey of doctrine, especially 'continental'.
8. For instance, N. K. Hevener on the 1971 *South West Africa* opinion, 'A New International Legal Philosophy', *ICLQ* 24 (1975) 790, at 793–4; and R. Churchill on the *Fisheries Jurisdiction Cases,* 'The Contribution of the ICJ to the Debate on Coastal Fisheries Rights', *ICLQ* 24 (1975) 82.
9. M. Akehurst, 'The Concept of Custom in International Law', *BYIL* 47 (1974–5) 195.

It is possible to imagine what a purely materialist approach to conduct can mean.[10] Philosophical sociology has grappled with the problem. Wittgenstein has called 'mentalism' the belief that subjective mental states cause actions. In other words, it is no less problematic to ask what are the intentions, the internal subjective state of an individual person, than it is to explore the activities of a collective entity. Instead, we merely ascribe motives in terms of public criteria that make behaviour intelligible. Therefore, it is better for social scientists to eschew intentions as causes of actions and focus on the structures of shared knowledge that give them content.[11] Wittgensteinians say that, in the hypothetical court case, the jury can only judge the guilt of the defendant – having no direct access to his or her mind – by means of social rules of thumb to infer his or her motives from the situation (a history of conflict with the victim, something linking them to the crime scene, and so forth). They go further and argue that the defendant's motives cannot be known apart from these rules of thumb and so there is no reason to treat the former as springs of action in the first place.[12]

However, it is possible to argue – and will be done so here – that no matter how much the meaning of an individual's thought is socially constructed, all that matters for explaining his behaviour is how things seem to him. In any case, what is the mechanism by which culture moves a person's body, if not through the mind or the self: 'A purely constitutive analysis of intentionality is inherently static, giving us no sense of how agents and structures interact through time.'[13] Individuals have minds by virtue of independent brains and exist partially by virtue of their own thoughts. These give the self an 'auto-genetic' quality, and are the basis for what Mead calls the 'I', an agent's sense of itself as a distinct locus of thought, choice, and activity: 'Without this self-constituting substrate, culture would have no raw material to exert its constitutive effects upon, nor could agents resist those effects.'[14]

It is the corporativist character of the State that dominates in international law and that leads to the conclusion of Akehurst that 'we cannot know what states believe but only what they say they

10. The following reflections of Alexander Wendt on Wittgenstein also appear in chapter four.
11. A. Wendt, *Social Theory of International Politics* (1999) 179.
12. Ibid.
13. Ibid., 181–2.
14. Ibid.

believe'. It is this framework, taken from the international law of Personality or Subject-hood, which comes to paralyse the law of the sources, especially customary law – since the latter calls for an examination of the legal conviction of States, their *opinion juris,* which is normally called the subjective element. It will be the argument of this work that the origin of the modern idea of the State, from, at the latest the seventeenth century, is inimical to any idea of a binding international legal order, because it is grounded in an absolutist claim to legitimacy as a way of securing internal order and security. States face one another as 'bundles of anxiety' that compulsively determine the nature and extent of their obligations to one another across morally vacant boundaries of distrust. This is why it is impossible to know what they are 'really thinking' and also makes it sound incongruous that they should have legal conviction.

If one is to reconstruct a natural law doctrine of individual responsibility as the ground-stone for international legal order, this has to be done in a subsequent chapter concerned with international legal personality, paying attention especially to the destruction of the medieval natural law order by the modern absolutist State. However, international customary law as a conceptual frame, has, as Dupuy has shown, become embedded ineradicably in the minds of international lawyers, and so it is necessary to offer an explanation of how it has evolved as an intellectual framework within the discipline. In other words, this source of law is entirely a construction of international legal doctrine – the imaginations of international lawyers – and carries with it all of their ideological ambitions and in particular the desire to bury any doctrine of natural law. It has nothing to do with what international historians or diplomats may call the practice of States. This doctrinal activity is itself intimately bound up with the rejection of a natural law foundation to international law, but this is very much a historical accretion rather than a logical necessity. The heart of the exercise of reinstituting a natural law approach to international law is not customary law as such but the construction of the modern State in international law. Its deconstruction is necessary if one is to emerge from the sterility of the doctrine of international customary law, but that will have to come after a historical excursus into the doctrinal construction of this 'source of law'.

Legal Doctrine and the Creation of State Practice

The distinction is easy enough to make between proposals of writers, for instance, for State conduct, their attempts to describe State practice and the State practice itself. If it is a matter of contrasting the second two, one can say that, for example, writers describe State practice on the use of force and, alternatively, one may simply describe that practice directly, without reference to the opinion of doctrine, although, of course, one becomes oneself, thereby, an addition to doctrine. Writers may expound a just war theory, while states resort to a practice of unlimited discretion to wage war, or, alternatively, states may adhere in practice to a just war theory while authors adopt a strict positivism, interpreting State sovereignty as unrestrained.

Nonetheless, a surprising difficulty can arise when one sets oneself precisely the task of describing what is the State practice itself. This is when it emerges that there is a real problem with the way the conceptual framework of State practice works out. Consider, for instance, the way that diplomatic history is used to describe the practice of states. Parry says that one cannot construct what is identifiably international law from treaties or diplomatic practice.[15] The great European treaties are part of political history not legal history, never mind law.[16] The series of entries in the *Max Planck Encyclopaedia of Public International Law* (MPEPIL) from ancient times to 1918 do precisely that.[17] They appear to fail to recognise what Hueck regards as the importance of the history of the science of international law in itself shaping the agenda of relevant material.[18] While it is perfectly legitimate to decide to treat international law as an appendage of diplomacy, at the very least there is needed some kind of theory of what role international law plays. That would mean understanding how and when it is allowed to come into play.[19]

---

15. C. Parry, *The Sources and Evidences of International Law* (1965) 34–5, 37–8
16. Ibid., 37–8
17. In particular the entries by W. Preiser: History of International Law: Basic Questions and Principles, S. Verosta: History of International Law 1648 to 1815 and H-U Scupin: History of International Law 1815 to World War I on <www.mpepil.com> . These entries were completed in the 1980s.
18. I. J. Hueck, 'The Discipline of the History of International Law: New Trends and Methods on the History of International Law' *Journal of the History of International Law* 3 (2001) 194.
19. Grewe has such a theory, that both writers and practice are an expression of the same Zietgeist of their epoch. W. Grewe, *The Epochs of International Law* (2000), at 25. The author broadly agrees with this approach and will come back to it later, when discussing connections between the relationship of the historical school of law and new archival diplomatic history in the nineteenth century.

Otherwise there is a crude equation of any treaty with a legal instrument in the sense of the Vienna Convention and so forth.

As Parry says, the importance of say Vienna 1815, or Paris 1856 'lies primarily not in their character as examples of the operation of a law-making process . . . but in their status as politico-military affirmations of a law made largely by other means'.[20] As this great author of the *Consolidated Treaty Series*[21] writes, commenting in particular on Vienna 1815, 'If a new age had to be sought, it would be more correct to seek its beginnings in Vattel rather than Vienna.'[22] Concentrating on epochs reflecting the influence of Great Powers appears an alternative to the apparently tired old conflict between natural law and positivism. It must surely be the case that at least in repositories of State chancelleries and court jurisdictions there are other sources of law that can be contrasted with doctrine. However, the reality is strangely different. International law chancelleries were only set up in the late nineteenth century, and many after World War I.[23] Court cases in turn cover a narrow field of prize, maritime jurisdiction and diplomatic immunity cases.[24]

In fact, the reason that international legal history is almost impossible to write is that there is no consensus on what international law is. Even the notion of positive law is not agreed. From Suarez to Bynkershoek to Vattel there was no concept of general customary law. Hence there was no concept of State practice at all, as we now understand it.[25] There was only the notion of consent, formal or tacit, in which case one could only have a history of international law based on treaties, to which Parry objects.

---

20. Parry's complaint, supra, note 15, at 40.
21. Edited and annotated by C. Parry (1969–81).
22. Supra, note 15, at 39.
23. G. Marston, 'The Evidences of British State Practice in the Field of International Law', in *Perestroika and International Law*, A. Carty and G. Danilenko (eds) (1990) 27–47.
24. A. Carty, *The Decay of International Law* (1986) 12, and literature cited therein, particularly the work of A. M. Stuyt and, again, C. Parry, at 23.
25. Paul Guggenheim, 'Contribution à l'histoire des sources du droit des gens', *Hague Recueil* 94 (1958) provides, in chapter III, 'La Coutume', the most erudite and exhaustive account of the development of the concept of custom in international law writing from the late fifteenth century until the beginning of the twentieth. It is the starting point of research in this area.

In the final analysis, what present international lawyers recognise as international law rests in a combination of the Parry–Hueck picture that the construction of the discipline comes first in providing the means to recognise what constitutes legally significant State practice. This need not be absolutely the case. Indeed, the author would like to stress that the more the power of the discipline is appreciated the easier it is to contest the narrowing of the field of historical enquiry that the discipline represents. It is probably this that drives the predominantly German historical tendency[26] to go searching for international legal history among the Assyrians and the rather narrowed Francophone resistance to this on recognisably legal ideological grounds.[27] Indeed, within the history of the discipline itself it may always be possible to recover new parameters for exploring the history of State practice precisely by reverting to a different theory of doctrine. For instance, the natural law school of Grotius, so long as it continues to adhere to the 'just war theory', has a much broader remit to be critical of the conduct of international relations than a strict positivism, which regards 'high politics' as indifferent legally. Conversely, the historical school of legal positivism, itself fairly closely allied to the German school of diplomatic history, is capable of awakening or giving credibility to a much broader range of historical investigations of State practice than classical positivism. The reason is that the historical school approach to customary law treats practice as a narrative of the whole conduct of States and does not just limit itself to registering the treaties that they sign. The field is wide open to a variety of directions of enquiry.

So this chapter endeavours to set up a number of oppositions as heuristic devices to illustrate how doctrine and State practice may play off against one another in the writing of the history of international law, both positively and negatively. The following may be taken as examples that serve to support the Parry–Hueck thesis about the decisive influence of the discipline (effectively the doctrine) in constructing the practice. The concept of the sovereign State as being above all moral standards and free to do as it pleases unless it chooses to

---

26. Represented in the <www.mpepil.com> entries on the History of International Law.
27. See, for example, R. Kolb's dismissal of ancient India and Chinese contributions to international law as quite simply not conforming to modern Western ideas of law and international law since modern times. *Ésquisse d'un droit international public des anciennes cultures, extra-européennes* (2010).

restrict itself, comes from the reconstruction of the Renaissance State from Hobbes onwards. Cassese explains this clearly in his textbook.[28] At the same time it is possible to insist, as do the German school, that the Treaty of Westphalia incorporated an anti-hierarchical idea of equality in the sense of absence of subordination to either Pope or Emperor, that is, viewing international legal history as diplomatic history.[29] Nonetheless, the understanding of formal equality of States, as similar to individuals, comes with Vattel, as a form of natural law theory that then became accepted by doctrine as international law in the course of the nineteenth century, through constant doctrinal repetition, through, for instance, Wheaton to Oppenheim.[30] Doctrine develops the idea of equality from the time of Vattel, as including the principle of non-intervention and the voluntary character of judicial or arbitral settlement of disputes. That is, the developments within doctrine also shaped the way that States were regarded and shaped and also the perhaps mistaken belief of international legal doctrine that its own views, for example, of the principle of non-intervention, represented customary international law.

Yet again, the German school of international legal history, while appearing to be determined to get away from doctrine and write history from State practice, is really objecting to a view of the history of international law as a gradual development of limits on State sovereignty, in favour of the view that true historical narrative, of which international legal history is also a part, must take whatever normative attitudes the rulers or managers of independent entities, like nations, peoples or whatever, actually had in their relations with one another.[31] On this view 1648 and indeed Europe itself need not be central.[32]

---

28. A. Cassese, *International Law* (2001) paragraph 16.
29. That is, in the entry on 1648–1815 by Verosta in <www.mpepil.com>.
30. Carty, *The Decay of International Law* esp. 89–93.
31. See especially for this theoretical reflection on the German school, H. Steiger, 'Universality and Continuity in International Public Law?' in *Universality and Continuity in International Law*, T. Marauhn and H. Steiger (eds) (2011) 13 at 14.
32. Steiger still criticizes Eurocentrism within the German school, particularly Grewe, ibid., at 40. Such criticism is being given no weight in this chapter since European perspectives on the discipline are still absolutely dominant worldwide; see: A. Carty and F. Lone, 'Some New Haven International Law Reflections on China, India and Their Various Territorial Disputes', *Asia Pacific Law Review* 19 (2011) 93–111.

At the same time, the nature of the Vattelian doctrine contrasts effectively with international legal history as diplomacy in another respect, actually making diplomatic legal history more difficult. Hinsley and others (Hedley Bull) say that just as Europe was consolidating into a Christian historical community, he prepared the way for a uni-disciplinary legal formalism, gradually driving international law away from any contact with diplomacy.[33] Indeed, for the legal formalism coming out of Vattel it is difficult to see what interest history can have. Vattelian formalism, as a product of the Enlightenment, is anti-historical. In fact, it represents a confidence of an epoch, so that a belief in a mature anarchy among nations prevailed for the whole of the nineteenth century, the Vattelian period, finally formalised in the clarity of Oppenheim's International Law, the pure statement of positivism.[34] International legal history, in the sense of State practice, if it is to exist at all, can then consist of a Whig-style history of gradually increasing acceptance of regulation, especially in the nineteenth century.[35] Here, the historical drive need not be very strong, as such histories are of outdated law.

However, there is a fundamental aspect of the story of the history of doctrine and practice that gives the advantage to doctrine. The doctrine of State practice as the ground of general custom is a product of the historical school of law, in other words a construction of the discipline or science of international law. There is no comprehensive history of the concept of customary international law. Part of the reason is probably that natural law thinking dominated the discipline until the nineteenth century. Paul Guggenheim, a Swiss French scholar, provides the most complete overview of custom between the late fifteenth century and the beginning of the twentieth century in 1958.[36] The concept of custom first came out of the Roman Law and Canon Law traditions, says Guggenheim, where custom was a tacit legislation of the people. Francisco Suarez, a sixteenth-century Spanish Jesuit theologian and

33. F. H. Hinsley, *Power and the Pursuit of Peace: Theory and Practice in the History of Relations between States* (1967) and also Sir Herbert Butterfield and Martin Wight (eds) *Diplomatic Investigations: Essays in the Theory of International Politics* (1968).
34. See above all B. Kingsbury, 'Legal Positivism as Normative Politics: International Society, Balance of Power and Lassa Oppenheim's Legal Positivism', *EJIL* 13 (2002) 401–37.
35. See especially the contribution of H.-U. Scupin 1815 to World War I on <www.mpepil.com>.
36. See note 25 supra.

specialist in Roman and Canon Law, presented custom as a positive *ius gentium* (law of peoples), an expression of the tacit will of the peoples of the world. Although it was subordinate to natural law, it still had a valid and independent place. In *De Legibus* (Of Laws), especially in Books II and VII, Suarez carves out a space for *ius gentium*, including a general customary law of peoples – regarded as radical at the time because Suarez was arguing that not all law came directly by God or from a God-given reason.[37] Tierney also explains that Suarez was assimilating custom to legislation, as the will of the community.[38]

Indeed, as Guggenheim argues, even an early eighteenth-century international lawyer, such as Cornelius van Byjnkershoek, who was known as a positivist – that is, he thought positive law more important than natural law – still persisted in the view that custom was a form of tacit convention. He wrote his views down in *De foro legatorum*, or *The Jurisdiction over Ambassadors*. Van Bynkershoek asserts, especially clearly in chapter XIX, that the law of nations is nothing but tacit agreement, a presumption that can always be barred by an express wish, because there is no international law other than what is based on the tacit agreement of voluntary participants.[39]

Guggenheim does explain how in the course of the nineteenth century international lawyers came to believe that all law rested ultimately on custom in the different sense that the practices and usages of communities, including the international community, preceded the gradual growth of the conviction that these practices were binding as law. However, Ago explains more explicitly the break that this represents from the older Roman and Canonist traditions. The latter always saw custom as a product of conscious will. Yet, says Ago, it is the essence of the modern idea of customary international law that it distinguishes a conscious will to create law from a growing consciousness that laws have simply grown up spontaneously out of State practice, so that States gradually become aware of them through reflection on the outcomes of their practice. Ago argues that the distinguishing feature of custom is precisely that, as spontaneous law, it is found by inductive inference from the types of claims that

37. Francisco Suarez, 'Selections from Three Works', in *The Classics of International Law*, James Brown Scott (ed.) (1995).
38. B. Tierney 'Vitoria and Suarez on *ius gentium*, Natural Law, and Custom', in *The Nature of Customary Law: Legal, Historical, and Philosophical Perspectives*, Amanda Perreau-Saussine and James B Murphy (eds) (2007).
39. Cornelius van Bynkershoek, *De foro legatorum*, or *The Jurisdiction over Ambassadors*, text of 1744 (Clarendon Press, 1946).

States make against one another, rather than by evidence of States adhering to a tacit law-making form.[40]

It is remarkable that the doctrine is first most clearly expressed by von Kaltenborn in 1847, but then, in Guggenheim's view, becomes incorporated into international legal science with Alfonse Rivier towards the end of the nineteenth century. This view was incorporated into mainstream international law doctrine through Oppenheim's acceptance of it, he taking it from Rivier's German colleague von Holtzendorff.[41] Even more remarkably, Koskenniemi says that such a way of thinking of custom was only authoritatively accepted in mainstream international law jurisprudence in the *North Sea Continental Shelf Case* of 1969.[42]

It is suggested that there is an additional aspect of the historical school of law that has not been sufficiently appreciated. It has considerable implications both for the rewriting of the history of international law and for the continuing political significance of customary international law. Kaltenborn's work must be seen in the context of the rise of nationalism, in the first case, German nationalism, after 1815. This was the context in which historical and legal studies were tied together. History was revalued after the Enlightenment. This is attributable to one simple cause: the belief that only from the 'internal' or personal experience of a subject could any indication be gathered as to what that subject could or should do or be expected to do. The increased 'scientific' study of history was tied to this belief.[43] In the early nineteenth century the place of philosophy in providing a rational account of man was replaced by history. The new emphasis on historical change *and the insistence upon a new precision of documentation were the expression of a desire to see the past from the inside, to relive experience through the eyes of those whom one is studying.*[44] The most outstanding historian of the time, Leopold Ranke, could apply this perspective to international relations since the

40. Roberto Ago 'Science Juridique et Droit International', *Hague Recueil* 90 (1956). In chapter 5, Ago distinguishes the canonist, legislative tradition of custom from contemporary customary law
41. See further Carty, *The Decay of International Law* esp. 34–6.
42. M. Koskenniemi, History of International Law since World War II, para. 31 <www.mpepil.com>.
43. A. Carty, 'International Law as a Science (The Place of Doctrine in the History of its Sources)', in *XVIII, Part II Special Issue, Indian Yearbook of International Affairs* (1980) 128 at 140 and for what follows in the text subsequently, at 140–1.
44. In particular, see A. Marwick, *The Nature of History* (1970) 35; see also H. Butterfield, *Man on His Past* (1969) 103.

'documents' that were becoming available were the archives of 'princes and prelates'.[45] At the same time it was not merely the importance of empathy in the researcher – whether jurist or historian – that transformed his role.

Compared to Ranke's counterpart of the Enlightenment, in the search for the normative, it was precisely the nation state that was becoming the source of 'Enlightenment'. The political State was central to human development. Ranke would have it that States were unique individuals, that they were thoughts of God, who had chosen to express the idea of humankind in various peoples. If there had been only one possibility for the State, then only universal monarchy would be reasonable.[46] So, for Savigny also, the essential role of the jurist/historian was not to legislate but to gather together the elements of custom. It is only by reflection upon historical experience that we can come to a knowledge of our time.[47]

So the Historical School of Law and the Rankean theory of history writing are tied together. They combined two elements that have shaped the consciousness of international lawyers. First, they revalued the actual behaviour of State nations or nation states as powers themselves of moral significance in history. It is not the simple doings of princes but the life spirit of nations that makes history meaningful and that has to be grasped as accurately as possible. At the same time, this task has to be undertaken as scientifically as possible. Through archival research one can come to understand and empathise with the intentions and ambitions of the people responsible for the running of the nation states. This can then be a starting point for debate about the ethical and legal implications of their conduct. This is language that is by no accident very similar to that of Steiger, who wishes to justify the open-minded study of all the history of 'peoples-states' from the perspectives that they had of the normative, regardless of time or place.[48]

The Doctrinal Creation of a State Practice, which Doctrine Cannot Decipher

It is this historical drive, just described, which explains the continued paramount authority of general customary law as evidenced in the

45. Marwick, *The Nature of History*, 37–8.
46. H. Kohn, *The Mind of Germany* (1960) 59–60.
47. J. Droz, *Le Romantisme Allemand et l'Etat* (1966) 217–19, also quoting Savigny.
48. See note 31 above.

practice of States. Indeed, the movement of the German school to rewrite the histories of international law, too burdened with a history of doctrine and legal ideas, has the same motivation. Nonetheless, it produces a paradoxical situation, at the present time, in any attempt to understand the history of international law as a history of the practice of States. That practice is bound to be significant because it is bound up with the history of human beings in their life among the communities of nations. However, these communities are secretive towards one another.

Back in 1949 the Secretariat of the United Nations submitted a more than 100-page memorandum to the International Law Commission, in the context of an obligation by that body to report to the UN General Assembly on ways and means to make the evidence of customary law more available. The Secretariat 1949 memorandum, in its conclusions, recognised very well that providing official declarations as documents without what it recognises as contextualising 'background materials' renders the documents of imperfect value. The Secretariat outlined four possible categories for organising the digests: topically; chronologically; by country; and by categories of evidence, for example, national law or judicial decisions.[49] However, the final report of the International Law Commission 1950 simply did not take the matter further, merely recommending to States and the Secretariat to make collections of categories of evidence, as defined above. It excused itself by saying there was little that could be done to persuade governments to stimulate the production of more of their practice, that is, the essential 'background documents'. This would be too arduous.[50] Therefore, the International Law Commission in 1950 declared that there was no reasonable prospect of States making available to one another the archival material necessary to construct a picture of customary law.

This has led to a division in how to assemble what is taken to be customary law. Following Council of Europe Guidelines many national Yearbooks of International Law produce copious statements

---

49. Memorandum submitted by the Secretary General of the United Nations to the International Law Commission, 1949: *Ways and Means of Making the Evidence of Customary International law more Readily Available: preparatory work within the purview of article 24 of the Statute of the International Law Commission*, UN DOC. A/CN. 46 and Corr.1 New York, United Nations 1949.
50. Report of the International Law Commission 1950: Ways and means for making the evidence of customary international law more readily available , from the *Yearbook of the International Law Commission*, Vol. II, 367–74.

by their politicians as to what their country regards as international law.[51] Together with national court decisions, legislation, participation in international organisations – replete with numerous more statements by politicians – doctrine has plenty to tidy up and systematise in digests. There is a voluntarism in this approach. International law is what States say it is, in their public statements, not only because one cannot know what States are really thinking, but also because such statements are closest to expressions of *will*.

However, there is a minority academic opinion that is more challenging in calling for what is really a Rankean view of the practice of States. In the 1960s Parry argues that full historical background is necessary to understand evidence of *opinio juris* in the practice of States. Rejecting the conclusions of the Council of Europe, he said that leaving out 'background materials' rendered official documents difficult to evaluate as to meaning and impact. There is no sound reason to accept declared intentions or attitudes of State officials as a reliable indicator of the real intentions that explain the meaning of actions. States are essentially communities and the processes whereby they form intentions and execute them are evidenced by many different materials that show the different stages of development of actions.[52] Parry in the 1960s and 1970s undertook the publication of a *British Digest of International Law,* managing a total of six volumes before he died in 1982, each about eight hundred pages, probably remaining the definitive method of compiling complete historical pictures of legal incidents in a chronological narrative over long periods. One such example concerned issues of aliens, that is, asylum seekers and extradition.[53] These surveys of official and

51. Council of Europe Resolution 68(17): Model Plan for the classification of documents concerning State practice in the field of public international law <www.coe.int/t/e/legal_affairs/legal_co-operation/public_international_law/Texts_&_Documents/Resolution%20(68)%2017%20E.pdf>* (adopted by the Ministers' Deputies on 28 June 1968).
52. Parry, *Sources and Evidences of International Law,* at 67–8. The problems of gathering evidence of practice in the sense of when and with what effect legal advice is called upon, directed to other states and produces a response, is described exhaustively through the chapter 'Custom or the Practice of States'. These problems are indistinguishable from historiographical problems: how to construct what Steiger has called the narrative that reveals the normative perspectives of the actors.
53. Clive Parry, *British Digest of International Law*, Vol. 6, Phase One, Part Six, *The Individual in International Law, Aliens and Extradition 1860–1914* (1965) xxxvii, 852.

unofficial British documents explain practice in the half a century before 1914, for example, the treatment of foreign political dissidents. The representational skills of the jurist working on such materials, in Parry's case, put international law writing about practice on par with credible history writing. In his case, the assumption is not challenged that States, as communities, have intentions, some of which are legally relevant, which can be understood in narrative form, provided that sufficient rigour in skills of representation exists. However, as can be seen in Parry's case, the representation will not be contemporary. So the work will really be history of international law, *while at the same time explaining the evolution of customary international law in a particular State's practice.*

History and law have come together in Guggenheim's and Ago's historical explanation of the development of the modern international law concept of general custom through the nineteenth-century German historical school. Their assumption is that a pattern of consciousness or awareness of States has to be traced continuously from the past to the present, making historical narrative an integral part of legal evolution. Yet it is precisely the closure of contemporary archives of States, already noted by the International Law Commission, which makes the exercise of searching for general custom through State practice problematic, thereby problematising the whole idea of general customary international law, as now understood to be the practice of States, evidencing a conviction as to what is law.

In other words, the representational function of doctrine comes up against the 'sécret de l'état', in particular of the modern, liberal, democratic State, supposedly governed by the rule of law. It is Allott who has highlighted the difficulty repeatedly since the publication of *Eunomia.* The attempt to represent what Aron has called the 'Cold Monsters' of the state is bound to bring a historically guided hermeneutic, archival approach to State practice into bitter conflict with the State in attempting to penetrate its practice. In Allott's words, the modern State evacuates the active presence of reason, faith, conscience and personal responsibility in a legal system whose subjects are not subjective subjects of the system but law-making and law-recognising, law-applying and law-enforcing robots. Allott attributes this disaster to what he calls a post-Vattelian era whereby predominantly Western, supposedly liberal democratic, politicians justify their participation in the international system on the ground of some theory of the representation of the people, whereas international affairs remain largely beyond the purview of national electorates, even of intellectual elites.

The explosion of international organisations and courts still takes place in the context of the absence of an international public.[54]

Nonetheless, the history of State practice, which actually grasps the true legal significance of events, while not comprehensively feasible, is certainly doable on occasions and these occasions can set the standard for what is really the goal to attain. For instance, in the second edition of the first volume of *International Law* in 1911, Oppenheim, the arch or classical, positivist, described the absorption of Korea into Japan as having occurred voluntarily as a result of a Treaty. In the same sentence, Oppenheim described this form of territory transfer or State recreation as voluntary subjugation. The subsequently released historical record shows that Britain agreed with Japan under a secret clause of a renewed Anglo Japanese Treaty in 1905, that Japan could use – and did use – whatever coercion was necessary to compel Korea's becoming part of Japan. The record shows that the Japanese Korean treaties were induced with physical coercion against Korean officials. At the same time, Oppenheim represents in the second volume of his work, in 1912, that Japan's occupation of Korea during the Russian Japanese war was necessitated by the inability of Korea to defend itself against Russian encroachment. Japan's action was an intervention in Japan's own vital interests, to liberate Korea from Russian occupation. If this representation by a doctrinal writer is legally *and* historically incorrect, it is only in the sense that he does not have access to the decision-making process through access to diplomatic archives.[55] Indeed the UK's fifty- and thirty-year rules, with respect to document release, while probably the most liberal in the world, condemn doctrine to a truncated historical role in representing State practice.

This revaluation of State practice, paradoxically, does not mean that the practice of States begins only where doctrine has constructed the concept in the course of the nineteenth century. It means that the whole history of nations can be explored to see what it reveals of

54. P. Allott, *Eunomia: New Order for a New World* (1990) esp. 239–52, 'The Self-Conceiving of Modern International Society', also 297–339, 'International Order II: Legal Order'.
55. A. Carty, 'The Japanese Seizure of Korea from the Perspective of the United Kingdom National Archive, 1904–1910' *Asian Yearbook of International Law* 10 (2002/3) and all the references cited therein, particularly to the works of Oppenheim.

human consciousness of law. At the same time, while the romantic, internal, hermeneutical approach to normativity is unsympathetic to the abstract, transcendent moralising of natural law, it by no means excludes the idea that practice can be qualitatively judged as good or bad. This underlay Wharton's view of American adherence to customary international law, as expressed in his *Digest*. To search for the legal conscience of States and nations means that one can distinguish conscience from its absence. One does this through historical analysis, while exercising a judgement the same as the natural lawyer does, when determining which conduct is genuinely normative and to be followed. This is clear in the example given by Parry from Wharton's *Digest* of US State practice to explain the doctrine of the incorporation of general customary law into American law.[56] It is interesting that Parry criticises Wharton as being predominantly interested, in compiling his digest, not as evidence of the conduct of the United States as a source of law, but as evidence of the writings of peculiarly well-qualified (American) publicists, that is, a number of distinguished Secretaries of State.[57] He goes on to note Wharton's view that their opinions have established a jurisprudence for the civilised world. This jurisprudence, quoting Wharton, 'as is the case with all true law whose continued existence depends on its responsiveness to popular conscience and need, adapts itself, in its own instinctive evolution, to the contingencies of each social and political juncture that occurs'.[58] Again, the historical and the normative combine.

This is where also one can return to Allott's critique. His critique is historical and deplores that democratisation of the international order has not accompanied the democratisation of the national order, the reason for 'sécret de l'état'. It may be possible to try to argue theoretically, following Jurgen Habermas's theories of the public space, for a wider public discourse in which the international lawyer could participate effectively in the normative argument both preceding the actions taken by States, and reflection upon those actions afterwards, actions that eventually become international legal practice.[59] Perhaps

56. C. Parry, 'The Practice of States', 1958–9 Transactions of the Grotius Society, 145, at 145 quoting from Wharton's *A Digest of the International Law of the United States*, 2nd edition (1887) 149–50.
57. Ibid., 151.
58. Ibid., 152.
59. This idea is explored in the author's critique of general customary law in his *Philosophy of International Law* (2007) esp. 51–9 and for what follows in the text.

the original idea behind the Institute of International Law, at its foundation, in 1873, was that international lawyers could effectively participate in an international legal discourse along with leaders of world opinion inside as well as outside States. However, this belies the continuing, for Allott, Vattelian structure of inter-State relations. The individual doctrinal writer has no international status other than that accorded to them by his own State, and remains marginal to great issues of international affairs.

Hence it may be more sound, in trying to ground effectively representational functions for doctrine, to explore more systematically the difficulties underlying the absence of authority for a doctrine that purports to rest upon some normative legal philosophy such as natural law. Yet it is precisely here that one must say it is only the science of international legal history – positivist in its craving for sources and hermeneutic in its understanding of them – that can explain the loss of a critical role for doctrine. Historically, at least one strand of doctrine, the natural law as distinct from the positivist approach, was supposed to offer a transcendent standard against which the practice of States can actually be judged as nugatory. Whether one uses the contemporary technical terms *null and void* to describe the effects of this doctrinal activity, it does definitely claim that there is a human responsibility to resist and disregard offending State practice. Strangely, a primary obstacle in the way of a natural law style doctrine comes from within the liberal, democratic paradigm of law and not just from the theory of positivism that denies any transcendent source for legal obligation. The view appears to be shared by almost everyone that the metaphysic underlying natural law has vanished. For liberal, democratic theory, Law is what the States' representatives decide following agreed constitutional procedures, and if they have not spoken, there is simply no law. The most vital distinction is then between *lex lata* and *de lege feranda*. International constitutionalists imagine that the 'way forward' internationally, is to reproduce agreed law-making procedures at the global level, when these are clearly consented to by the international community.

However, it is precisely a challenging of the contemporary doctrinal frames for the practice of States, especially the official ones designated by the Council of Europe and through a completely fresh inter-action with alternative theoretical constructions of modern international history (from the sixteenth century to the twentieth-first), that is, *intellectual frames and constructions entirely beyond the contemporary discipline of and doctrine of international law,* which can afford the international lawyer the opportunity to engage once again much more profoundly with the historical significance of the actual practice of States. Then the international lawyer may find a way to re-establish the once close relationship between a critical natural law theory and a judgement of the quality of State practice in the light of a normative standard – itself not necessarily easily distinguishable from the historical-positivist search for the presence or absence of legal conscience in the actual practice of States. What this necessitates is a leap outside the usual confines of the international law discipline itself, that is, doctrine in the narrower sense, into a wider intellectual work that is engaging as much with actual State practice as the German School (including the authors for the www.mpepil.com and also Steiger, Grewe and Nussbaum) could want.

This venture into the history of ideas or intellectual systems is precisely not a concentration upon the history of international legal doctrine, but virtually the opposite. It is a search for alternative intellectual frames that allow one to bring to life the true normative experience of modern peoples, nations and States in their relations to one another – a life that has become elided out of view by a desiccated form of historical legal positivism in its approach to State practice. In fact, this is the very sentiment that drives the German School to deplore both the exclusive concentration on the history of international law as a history of ideas and, alternatively, history of the peculiarly Western history of international law as it has developed since the modern construction of the State and the Westphalia Peace of 1648. The difficulty remains that the firm, orthodox holding to the doctrinal view of customary international law is not going to change overnight as a consequence of these attempts at new theoretical reflections. Despite the inaccessibility of the materials needed to judge the practice of States and despite the fact that this is largely attributable to the secretive structure of international relations, it is still possible to look to new frames for understanding the present development of this international structure with a view to drawing once again on the more critical, independent aspects of the international law tradition.

The Present Crisis of Doctrinal Construction of Customary International Law from the Founding of the Institute of International Law (1873) until Today: Legal Doctrine within a Framework of a Sociology of Knowledge

When the present form of the subjective element of customary law came to be established in international law doctrine, international lawyers do not appear to have had a legal understanding of the State primarily as a corporate entity. It is the Swiss jurist Alphonse Rivier who is given the honour of being the first to employ the modern concept of *opinio juris* as an essential psychological element in his definition of general customary law. This was at the end of the nineteenth century, in 1896. Rivier's own manual is based on a more extensive review of sources and methods of law that he undertook with von Holtzendorff (first published in Berlin in 1884 and translated into French in 1887).[60] Both Rivier and von Holtzendorff fit firmly within the tradition of the historical school of law. The life of peoples is more powerful than written laws or legal doctrine, and the supreme goal of law is to return to custom, which provides a foundation beyond the disputations of treaties and doctrine.[61] In themselves treaties are usually diplomatic means to resolve particular uncertainties. They can be instructive as precedents, but they do no more than reflect on historical development and, as such, they are a poor reflection of the historical consciousness of peoples.[62]

Rivier was one of the founders of the Institute of International Law in 1873 and he succeeded Rolin-Jaequemyns as its second Secretary General. His *Principes du droit des gens* was not, in his view, a digest of material but a guide to politicians and diplomats that aimed to draw out of the multiplicity of facts certain general and dependable principles and rules of law universally and habitually respected 'de façon á faire ressortir ce qu'il appelle "la consience juridique des nations"'.[63] In the preface to the Serbian edition of his work, Rivier defined the task of the international jurist in terms that Jürgen Habermas has described as the classical liberal public space.[64] The juridical conscience of nations was precisely a liberal space of political rationality that independent academic lawyers could influence and help to direct. The task of jurists was:

> de controller les actes des politiques et de les juger, non d'après un code arbitraire, mais du point de vue le plus élevé du juste et de l'injuste; il

60. F. von Holtzendorff and A. Rivier, *Introduction au droit des gens* (1887). The reliance of the textbook on this work is quite explicit, for example, 27, 31 and 37.
61. Ibid., 140–1.
62. Ibid., 142–3, 145.
63. Obituary of A. Rivier by M. E. Lehr, *Annuaire de l'Institut de Droit International*, XVII (1898) 415, 429.
64. J. Habermas, *L'Espace public* (1986). This part of the argument draws upon what the author has already written in his 'Changing Models of the International System', in *Perestroika and International Law*, W. E. Butler (ed.) (1990) 13–30.

> proclame que c'est abaisser le droit des gens envisagé comme science que de lui assigner le role passif d'un simple enregistrement et classification des faits internationaux; il affirme qu'il doit constamment s'inspirer des principles supéreurs de la morale, de la justice et de la fraternité.[65]

The founders of the Institute said that without the support of public opinion even the unanimity of men of science would be ineffective. That is not to say that they relied upon public opinion alone. There was a law of progress and there were the imperfections of human nature.[66] This means that jurists have to state the juridical opinion of the civilised world as clearly as possible, so that it can be accepted by States as regulating their relations.[67]

So, for the founders of the Institute, the notion of general custom itself had to be understood in the wider context of liberal legality, which it was the function of jurists to uphold by their power of reasoning in public debate. In spite of the vicissitudes of politics, the society of fact existing between nations is becoming a society of law, because it is difficult for an individual or a State to confine its activities to its own territories. In these circumstances the rules of law are not merely a moral and scientific necessity, but also a political necessity of the first order.[68] Rivier says that States are independent, but that, in their autonomy, they adopt certain rules and submit to certain principles, whose necessity they recognise, this voluntary consent expressing itself in custom and treaties.[69] However voluntary it may be, the positive law is not merely changeable and relative. It is not arbitrary: 'Ses principes découlent des relations effectives des peuples, de l'ordre universel, tel que Dieu l'a créé et continue a le créer.'[70] In other words, peoples, nations or whatever are the centre of international legal activity. Rivier is preoccupied with a law of peoples, a *droit des gens*, who exist in a morally significant global order created by God.

---

65. Cited in E. Nys, 'Alphonse Rivier, sa vie et ses oeuvres', *Revue de droit international* XXXI (1899) 342, 344.
66. Speech of M. Mancini, in G. Rolin-Jaequemyns, *De la necessité d'organiser une institution scientifique permanente pour favoriser l' étude et le progrès du droit international*, *Revue de droit international*, V (1873) 463 at 706.
67. Ibid., 705.
68. Ibid., 463.
69. *Principes du droit des gens*, I, 27.
70. Ibid., 29.

The international system is not a world federation. Nations retain their autonomy but must submit to the laws of justice. The Institute was set up by academic lawyers 'to serve as an organ for the legal opinion of the civilised world on the subject of international law'.[71] The ambition was to avoid the national bias that was possible with the continued independence of States, and to give expression to the elevated sentiment of law and to the conscience of humankind, which is not simply a product of the conduct of diplomats. The latter must respect first the instructions of their sovereigns. Thus, they will not necessarily be able to direct themselves to an absolute rule of law beyond the particular interest of the nations that they defend.[72] It is a liberal internationalism that assigns to the academic international lawyers the task of exploring the ethical sense of humankind. They must discover and make precise the rules of justice, morality, and fraternity that they recognise as having to be the basis of the relations that peoples have with one another.[73]

It may be wondered, even at this ascendant point of liberal internationalism, how international lawyers thought that they could hope to direct or regulate the activities of powerful, centralised States. Even in the most democratic of States, the Foreign Offices and Diplomatic Services continued to be staffed from a minute section of society. Parliament and public opinion were not important, although they exercised influence at certain intervals. Foreign affairs were still the prerogative of a largely pre-bourgeois aristocratic class. They were reputedly still honourable men who really experienced a conflict of loyalties between the defence of their country and the claims of a common heritage and unity in the civilisation of Europe.[74] What is incongruous about the growth of a bourgeois or liberal middle-class perspective on international law at this time is that the most distinctive feature of a continuing *ancien regime* was the secrecy with which international affairs were conducted.[75]

Nonetheless, the picture is clear. Habermas explains that classical liberal political space was not the sole prerogative of State power, but belonged as well to civil society, which enjoyed the public interest as an 'affair' to which it could contribute with a public use of its reason-

71. R. P. Dhokalia, *The Codification of International Law Less* (1970) 63.
72. Note 66 above, Mancini in Rolin-Jaequemyns, *De la necessité d'organiser une institution scientifique* 704.
73. Ibid.
74. R. Albrecht-Carrie, *A Diplomatic History of Europe* (1967) 152–3.
75. A. J. Mayer, *The Persistence of the Old Regime* (1981) 79–127.

ing powers.[76] This capacity for reasoned public debate was seen as rooted in the untrammelled subjectivity of the individual, protected by his economic independence and by the emotional privacy of his family.[77] For this notion of debate each participant is taken as a simple person without hierarchy or status, equality is assumed, and the laws of the market are suspended, to achieve a detachment beyond mere competitiveness.[78] Ideas of public reasoning were intimately related to the notion of conversation or dialogue. The independence of the individual conscience was decisive.[79] The very idea of 'humanity' in this liberal sense rested on free will, the intimacy of the family (that is, free of compelling social constraints), and an independent intellectual culture.[80]

Such a notion of liberal political rationality is tied to a substantive view of legality. The constitutional State has to guarantee the connection between law and public opinion. The rule of law signifies the representation of the people. However, law is not simply an expression of the will of a particular group of people, but also a guarantee of a *ratio* that puts aside a dimension of domination, precisely because it is the outcome of a continuing spirit of public debate. Insofar as law is an expression of agreement based upon rational public discussion, the inevitable arbitrariness of actual laws has to be submitted to the constant pressure of public debate, so that a positive legal order cannot be seen as a static phenomenon. There must be a constant pressure to turn *voluntas* into *ratio*.[81] Clearly, there is presupposed the possibility that each person can attain the independence of property and culture that will permit a detached concern for the general public welfare. Once this public transforms itself into a dominant class, reason will become dogma and opinion will become command. Nevertheless, the bourgeois idea of legality remains that truth, not authority, makes law, and that liberal political rationality is able to untie the dominant force of group interest.[82]

Thus, a critical spirit of Enlightenment does depend upon an intellectual class. They must be independent vis-à-vis the State and elaborate critical principles for their own sake. In Habermas's view it is to philosophy that one must look and not to law as such, in a

76. Note 64, at 34, 38.
77. Ibid., 39.
78. Ibid., 47.
79. Ibid., 53.
80. Ibid., 56–7.
81. Ibid., 91–3.
82. Ibid., 96–8.

narrower sense, or theology and medicine, all of which rest upon authority, erudition, and a certain supervision by the State.[83] There is by definition no hierarchy of rational authority, nor are professional demarcations clear. The general principles of bourgeois legality in question have to serve to remove, or at least to assuage, the element of command and domination in public life. This means a conflation of law and morality.[84] The task of public instruction then falls to what Kant calls, in his *Critique of the Faculties*, 'Professeurs de Droit libres', which really presupposes an underlying pre-statist natural law.[85]

Where international lawyers style themselves on the intellectual class of the time of the founding of the Institute (1873) it is possible to imagine them engaging with issues such as foreign military invention (Nicaragua), nuclear deterrence, immunity of State officials for war crimes, and so on. In ordinary common-sense thinking or language one may say that States are in fact nations or peoples, with representatives who are bound by human laws of justice and fairness, the meaning and implications of which could be elaborated in concrete terms. The procrustean bed of the State need not appear and the international lawyer need have no connection with the State. This could allow the international lawyer as critical intellectual to ask about the history of US relations with the Samoza and then Sandinista regimes in Nicaragua. One may explore concretely the nature of the Contras who fought the Sandinistas. Again, who are the elements within the US political system who want to see a change in Nicaragua? What are the pretexts that the Sandinistas give for not holding elections? Principles of democracy, political independence, equality of peoples, human rights, freedom from arbitrary violence, the right to life of non-combatants, and so on could be discursively developed by a critical, reflective intellectual class, which, by definition, remains open and non-hierarchical. The same could be said of the dilemmas of nuclear defence, of the moral confusion of an international political class steeped in political violence, and of the desperate conflict between the Palestinians and Israelis. These controversies can be made concrete, conceptualised, and, most of all, be attributable to particular individuals and groups, through a history of their motives, intentions, and actions.[86]

83. Ibid., 114–15.
84. Ibid., 118.
85. Ibid., 125–6.
86. Cases before the International Court of Justice discussed exhaustively in the first edition, and see further chapter 3, p. 117 et seq.

Instead one appears to be faced with a paralysis of reflective intellect and moral sense in the work of the International Court of Justice. The court is an inter-State institution, and only States and UN bodies can appear before it, and its judges are State nominated. Of such elements Habermas suggests a not very promising political sociology. These are very hard words, but it is high time to stop being surprised at the hopelessness of the deliberations of the ICJ and look in other directions. The symbiotic relationship of the 'State' lawyer to inter-State law is well up summed by Habermas in his assertion that the loss of independence of the intellectual is rooted in both the loss of a private, interior life and in the exclusion from active, in the sense of spontaneous, participation in public life.[87] A process of 'disinteriorization' is the converse of the social absorption by an all-embracing State regulatory apparatus.[88] An independent critical standard becomes inconceivable as a matter of the sociology of knowledge. Habermas draws a sharp contrast between the private culture of the traditional bourgeois, who engages in independent integration of material, and the 'ready-made' debate furnished by the mass media, in which the vast majority can participate only at a voyeuristic level that cannot possibly unpack the rigid social structures of modern society. Such public debate becomes one more form of production and consumption, which will inevitably obey its own laws of the social market, without necessarily having any impact on the rest of the system.[89] Public discussion takes the form of fabricating an acclamatory consensus as a passive social response and is a far cry from the Enlightenment ideal of civil society as the foundation for independently directed criticism of public power. Such a picture cannot survive the totally integrative function of the production–consumption cycle of the social market.[90]

Power is now transferred to groupings, whether public or private, whose interests are reflected in attitudes, and that use publicity, the mediation of pre-digested views, as part of a bargaining process, where 'consensus' reflects what a traditional liberal rationalist would regard as a stalemate or a standoff. If there is a 'real' debate, it is secretive and takes place within these groupings.[91] The public sphere is refeudalised by formalistic acts of self-representation by these groupings, struggling for prestige and reputation.[92] It is precisely

87. Habermas, *L'Espace public*, 165.
88. Ibid., 167.
89. Ibid., 170–2.
90. Ibid., 203.
91. Ibid., 208.
92. Ibid., 209.

these groups, for example, Israeli State security interests, nuclear deterrence States, communist regimes in Central America, which produce, in the public domain, standoffs in terms of struggling self-representations, that the State officials who are judges, or advocates of States, can merely reproduce, select arbitrarily, or allow to cancel out against one another.

A way out of the impasse, which Habermas considers, is to create further institutions, which may undertake the task of publicising and popularising the opinions of an elite, qualified by a special level of intelligence and information. This is openly to sacrifice universality in order to retain rationality,[93] a form of government by expert opinion or 'doctrine'. Such institutions could embrace governmental commissions, the secretariats of unions, and the 'quality' press. The difficulty is that they do not amount to public debate in the classical liberal sense because there is no relationship of reciprocity between them and the general, unorganised mass of the population. They owe their profile to a prior conferring of privilege by institutions.[94] The only fragmentary public debate that is still possible is between people who are 'private' intellectuals in the classical liberal sense and the members of those social groups or institutions that are willing to permit their internal structures to function on a basis of democratic discussion.[95]

Translated into the terms of international law and doctrinal or judicial reflection, this programme means that one will have to confront and attempt to enter into dialogue with a variety of quasi-official, readymade discourses, rather than imagine that there is a single 'State' discourse that is authoritative and that can influence or even merely absorb and reproduce. The orthodox criteria for the identification of law – general custom and treaty practice – cannot yield the type of objective, critical legal standard set by the founders of the Institute. There is no single authoritative monologue to which the legal profession can listen, any more than that there is a possibility of universalised rational public discourse. All that remains of the classical paradigm of the Institute is the illusion that the methodology of international law can refer to a single, global, thinking public, with a conscience to which appeal can be made in the form of rational debate and, through a scientific distilling of the essentials of the debate, one can recover single, authoritative legal answers still somehow addressed by everyone to everyone.

93. Ibid., 248.
94. Ibid., 257.
95. Ibid., 259–60.

As has already been noted, the issue of sources is acutely interrelated to that of the subject of law, primarily the so-called Statehood in international law. This will become the theme of the next chapter. However, here an outline, by way of conclusion, is necessary to demonstrate where the international lawyer actually finds himself. The classical analytical-empirical definition of the State as a territory, with a population and a government in control, which is seen as a corporate entity capable of engaging responsibility, has its uses, as already indicated. However, it needs to be completed with a historical understanding of how concrete, namely particular, States have been constructed and also, vitally, there is a need for a dimension of self-awareness and self-understanding of such collective entities, however limited. This means abandoning abstractions of Statehood for a political sociology of democratic, historical nations – at least for the West and much of Asia – that function as collective systems of epistemological reference. They have inherited traditions, prejudices, strivings, and so on, which all contribute to the style and content of their behaviour. There can be no search for a unitary State-will, but rather an at least heuristic acceptance of a psycho-social collective as a framework in which to pursue concrete individual behaviour in both reflective and unreflective forms.

At most, the 'State' may be regarded as an institutional framework for the numerous subordinate institutions within which individuals, including international law officials, work with – and against – others to achieve certain aims with more or less conscious intentions.[96] The conclusion, in terms of Habermas's theory of institutional rationality, is that the most that exists for international law and lawyers is the international law departments of States, their interaction with the academic community and with the judiciary, both national and international. They are limited forms of government by expert opinion that sacrifice universality (vital to democracy) for a limited expression of rationality. While they will suffer all the constraints already identified, they do provide material for analysis and reflection.

It is worthwhile to ask, in a particular case, whether a State's actions are motivated by legal considerations among others. Whether this is the case is simply a matter of assessing whether significant State officials acted in terms that were understood subjectively to be

96. See further, A. Carty, 'Scandinavian Realism and Phenomenological Approaches to State and General Customary Law', *EJIL* 14 (2003) 817–41.

formulated legally.[97] That is to say, the officials considered they were acting as they were legally entitled or bound to do. This is a matter of evidence and the evidence is in the archives, the internal history of various State institutions. If States have, as collective entities, an idea of obligation, it can only come from an ethnological background, a common historical, by its nature almost entirely unreflective, consciousness. Much more will have to be said about this later.[98]

The actual practice of inter-State international law is bound up, ethnologically, with a closeness to particular national institutions, which determine the meaning of obligations, which need interpretation. It is too simple to say that States, as sovereigns, give words meanings that suit State interests. However, a political sociology, following Habermas, does not deny any dimension of institutional intentionality or any measure of normative behaviour at any levels within the State. The latter is seen here as a framework for numerous subordinate sub-institutions providing textual or interpretative communities within which international law officials work with others towards certain aims. It may be that in a particular case the lawyers are the determining voice, so that to understand the outcome as human action it is only necessary to trace the intentions of the lawyers and how they came to be adopted. However, more usually the work of the international lawyer officials will be entwined in a complex of attitudes and expectations also held by those who are not lawyers. It is the sheer complexity of the relationships that exist that make it so difficult to be categorical that the language of legal duty is the most appropriate way to describe action eventually agreed upon.

In ethnographic terms, the assumption is being made that law really exists within a web of tacit understandings and agreements among and within a number of States whose meaning cannot be unravelled without regard to the interaction of the intentions and expectations of diplomats, politicians, and lawyers. The international law practice of a State, so far as any of the State's institutional practice has a rational, consciously thought-out dimension, will exist alongside other standards, ethical, political, or whatever, which together make up the ethos that permeates the context in which all

97. A. Carty and R. Smith, *Sir Gerald Fitzmaurice and the World Crisis, a Legal Adviser in the Foreign Office 1932–1945* (2000) 25 ff.
98. See the use of ethnographic theories of Clifford and Rouland in A. Carty, 'Critical International Law: Recent Trends in the Theory of International Law,' *EJIL* 2 (1991) 66–96.

of the State officials, including elected politicians, work. This much can be studied with the tools of diplomatic history relying primarily on archives and with the tools of contemporary history and investigative journalism, which are also capable of extensive penetration of the corporate veil of the State.

With these qualifications, it is possible to give intellectual credibility to the empirical study of State practice to see whether and how far it has been motivated by the desire to observe or to create law. The historical school's approach to law becomes an ethnography of, for the most part, sub-institutions of the State. This leaves intact theoretically Habermas's critique that the State, taken as a collective entity, cannot be studied simply in terms of the normative significance of its actions on the assumption that they have a unitary source. An international law, rooted in practice, must have a much more comprehensive picture of the nature of the State as an expression of brute force, unconsciously exercised tradition and prejudice, as well as blind, fragmented confusion. The boundary line between the reflective/rational – in which law may play a part – and the rest is always problematic and should be the object of the idealist international lawyer to contest.

FURTHER READING

Allott, Philip, *Eunomia, New Order for a New World* (2001).

Carty, Anthony, 'Visions of the Past of International Society, Law, History and Politics', *Modern Law Review* 69(4) (2006) 644–60.

Carty, Anthony, 'The Practice of International Law', in *Routledge Handbook of International Law*, David Armstrong (ed.) (2009) 81–100.

Carty Anthony, *Doctrine versus State Practice in International Law* in *Oxford Handbook of the History of International Law*, Anne Peters and Bardo Fassbender (eds) (2012) 972–96.

Anthony Carty and Richard Smith, *Sir Gerald Fitzmaurice and the World Crisis: A Legal Adviser in the Foreign Office* (2000).

Habermas, Jürgen, *The Structural Transformation of the Public Sphere: An Inquiry into a Category of Bourgeois Society* (1989).

Parry, Clive, 'The Practice of States', *Transactions of the Grotius Society* 44 (1958–9) 145–86.

Parry, Clive, *Sources and Evidences of International Law* (1965).

Perreau-Saussine, Amanda and James B. Murphy (eds), *The Nature of Customary Law: Legal, Historical and Philosophical Perspectives* (2007).

Scharf, Michael P. and Paul R. Williams, *Shaping Foreign Policy in Times of Crisis: The Role of International Law and the State Department Legal Adviser* (2010).

Second Report on Identification of Customary International Law, Michael Wood, Special Rapporteur, International Law Commission A/CN4/672 22 May 2014.

2

Towards a New Theory of Personality in International Law

THE ILLUSORY CORPORATE NATURE OF STATE PERSONALITY

There has to be a fundamental rethink of the concept of personality in international law, given the dysfunctionality of an approach that takes Statehood, based on the principles of effectiveness and declaratory recognition, as a starting point. Such an approach may be useful for the judicial verification and regulation of business transactions and personal relations in private international law and international commercial law, but it cannot address the defects of international order attributable to a State sovereignty not subject to compulsory international adjudication. It is always open to each State to put its own unassailable unilateral interpretation on any legal standard.

Some analytical framework has to be found to challenge and take further such autistic behaviour. Unilateral interpretations are rooted in the consciousness of the communities that underlie them and some legitimate way must be found for international lawyers to penetrate through to these communities to understand the contradictions that their relations with other communities cause. As has already been seen, there is no hope whatsoever in going down the pathway of traditional doctrine of international customary law. The majority view of international lawyers is that it makes no sense to search for the subjective dimension of an institution. So, the first task has to be to show, conversely, that it makes equally no sense to regard the State as a corporate entity. In fact, this is itself a fiction driven by a delusion of liberal democratic theory, especially at the level of constitutional law.

Scandinavian realism has already exposed the illusory natural law fantasies underlying the unitary formalism of the positivist view of the State. The Swedish philosopher Axel Haegerstrom deconstructs, as a natural law myth, the argument that one can speak of the will of the State as an organised authority within society. That is to say, he begins the sociological task of trying to unearth the whereabouts of the structures, which are the figments of the legal and political formalist imagination. Empirically, no organised authority in a society can be so centralised that it is confined to a single person. Any system of law is merely maintained by a majority of the population for an infinite variety of motives, so long as they have no sufficiently focused motives for breaking with that system of law – the idea that a society governing itself implies a unitary willing, in turn implying a unitary subject is perhaps habitual. However, it can only mean that certain rules relating to a group are supposed to be applied by specifically appointed persons, somehow 'through forces operative within the group'. In the end it is a judge who declares a legal principle in litigation.[1]

If law understood as an imperative is called the will of the State, one will still not be able to look to an identifiable group maintaining the system of rules within the group. The reason is that all sorts of factors make up the social forces that maintain the impact of the rules. This medley of factors includes the habits of people to obey decrees, popular feelings of justice, class interests, the lack of organisation among the discontented and the positive acquiescence of the military. Even if each person wishes to conform to the law that does not imply a unitary will in all those individuals participating, that they have a common end as a unifying focus. The force of a law never depends merely upon the fact that a certain section of people within a group desire it to be obeyed. The concept of a unitary will, as a supposed real will of the community, is in fact a continuing spectre of natural law. So supposedly positivist estimates of the sources of law, for example, custom, will, in fact, be imbued with natural law illusions.[2]

The idea that there must be a supreme rule of law, which is a principle of validity of all legal systems, translates into the idea that every group is a corporate entity with a supreme holder of power whose ordinances must be followed. This proposition is supposed to be a necessity of thought but rules are applied in practice, as applications of law, in consequence of the already mentioned medley of general extra-legal factors. There is no factual continuity or coherence in

1. A. Haegerstroem, *Inquiries into the Nature of Law and Morals*, K. Olivecrona (ed.), C. D. Broad (trans.) (1953) 36–8.
2. Ibid., 39–42.

legal rules other than what is stated by the judges. Authority is not in fact clearly attributed to individuals in a corporate hierarchy if one is to look to rules and practices actually followed. Such a way of thinking is in fact all a part of the already mentioned naturalist myth of contractarianism, supposedly legitimising politically and validating legally every decision taken in a way that can be traced back, purely hypothetically, to individual consent. So the belief of positivist international lawyers that there is an identifiable State 'complete with will' is a natural law (contractarian) fantasy. There is now absent the classical natural law association with a supposed objective justice, but the obsession with legal validity has simply replaced that idea of justice with a concept of legitimacy based on a fictional individual consent. Haegerstrom's basic point is that this approach to law fails to regard legal systems as actual social-psychological phenomena. Indeed, he appears to go so far as to argue that any theory of the sources of law will presuppose naturalist fantasies of unitary harmony, when in fact the very idea of the existence of laws supposes a continued application of them, which is as difficult to unravel sociologically, in terms of actual driving forces, as the idea that one can unravel the intentions behind any original declaration of the laws.[3]

As a heuristic device Haegerstrom's so-called sociological realism is immensely helpful in deconstructing the intellectual apparatus with which the formal and particularly French tradition of international law works. Traditionally, a legal question is usually a variant of the theme: whether the sovereignty of the State is limited by some international rule, willed explicitly or implicitly by itself alone or in conjunction with others or by the international community as a whole, which has, equally, expressed its will if only implicitly. The international or national judge is set in search of valid rules. Thereby national sovereign space is either limited or extended as a result of the judgement reached as to the whereabouts of the international legal rule. To accomplish all of this, international lawyers at present think with the formalist triangle of sovereignty, international law and community, without any regard for the concrete factors, which are peculiar to the evolution of nations and their relations with one another. Formal logic does not express the reality of actual social movement and so the society of nations, the so-called international community,

---

3. Ibid., 43–5, 48–51. Of course, Haegerstroem applies his views only to the contractarian theory of the State. I endeavour to elaborate their international law consequences.

has a form as unitary as the so-called sovereign State (the organised nation), hiding as much profound difference as exists within States. The UN Charter, in this 'objectivist logic', rediscovers its conclusions at its point of departure. For instance, the international conditions the national, modifying it or abrogating it ipso facto. Indeed, the two cannot logically conflict, because the trio State, international society, and legal order are uni-dimensional elements of a formal equation. For instance, municipal law cannot overrule or be invoked against international law. Equally, the principle *rebus sic stantibus* cannot, in promissory commitments, override the principle *pacta sunt servanda* and so on, effectively the same as the principles either of the priority of the international community or of the inevitable harmony of the international and national communities.[4]

Critical legal studies are correct that the illusory search for any of these national or international 'legal wills' is merely a projection of the interpreting judge, who never undertakes what Haegerstrom, or any sociologist, may remotely recognise as a realistic, empirical search for the actual intentions of concrete people. However, the difficulty with the critical school, is that it leaves matters there. It recognises, in very vague and general terms, the contingency of the social reality, or at least what it may call, 'that which lies beyond the purely projected legal forms', but it does not attempt to reach out beyond these forms. And indeed, it cannot, for it accepts Haegerstroem's radical critique of the subjective premises of the contemporary dreamy legal formalism. So, Haegerstrom rejects the Kantian idea that human reason can introduce an 'ought' into human behaviour, because subjective attitudes in terms of feelings are reduced to, or explained in terms of, the outcomes of social upbringing and tradition. A clash of subjective attitudes has no moral significance and cannot be resolved. The idea of normative judgement tries to retain the element that something is true because it springs from our will as intelligence and so from our proper self. However, this merely refers to feelings with which, in Humean terms, the person assumes a certain attitude to what is given. If the person lacks the appropriate attitude of feeling and volition, the feeling of attachment to obligation vanishes. Any search for external authority is illusory, which means that any search for 'objective standards for normative judgement'

4. This style of critique of particularly French international law formalism is set out by C. Apostolids, *Histoire du Droit International, Doctrines Juridiques et Droit International, Critique de la connaissance* (1991).

will be authoritarian and produce fanaticism.[5] Hence, the critical legal scholar will treat any essential search for 'objective normative foundations' as fanatical, hegemonial or whatever. Instead, he will preach to the judicial interpreter the virtues of modesty and conversationalism, while still supposing, quite inexplicably, that somehow the international legal enterprise, and particularly its judiciary, should continue to function.[6]

It has, therefore, to be appreciated that the so-called corporate character of the State is really a liberal democratic ideology of contractarianism. The corporatist way of thinking about the State resolves the problem of political legitimacy through a theory of representation that has its roots in various forms of contractarianism. All of these theories suppose that legitimacy arises through the consent of the individual and this can be supposed – here enters the mythical character of contractarianism – to be given because of an original contract whereby he can be taken to have consented to the institutional framework whereby he is politically represented. Political legitimacy will be the equivalent of legal validity. If decisions are taken by corporatively authorised representatives, then they will be legally valid and binding. The formalist lawyer's self-appointed task will be to assess whether decisions taken by supposed authorised representatives have been so taken. I say self-appointed task, because the most dominant theory of contractarianism applied by international lawyers is the Hobbsean variety, whereby the representor and represented are subsumed into one person, so that issues of invalid State actions, at least at the international level, are difficult to imagine. Of course, State representatives accuse one another readily, of having committed invalid and illegal acts, but as there is not yet a world State, a world corporate entity, that could resolve the validity of these allegations, it is precisely this type of mutual abuse that States find so frustrating and leads them to behave violently towards one another. So, whatever limited function the international lawyer may have as an external relations lawyer, a branch of constitutional law, at the international level he has no impartial third party or otherwise objective legal standards with which to make judgments about legal validity. Nonetheless, his conceptual framework for approaching international legal personality bars him

5. See J. Bjarup, 'Reality and Ought: Haegerstroem's Inaugural Lecture Re-examined', *Scandinavian Studies in Law* 40(11) (2000) 57–68.
6. This is the very vague conclusion of M. Koskenniemi, *From Apology to Utopia* (1988).

from more productive avenues, such as the development of international legal dialectic.

It is proposed here to reiterate this argument by means of a close reading of contemporary French doctrine on international law, also because French is the second language in which international courts work. While by no means every country follows French doctrine, it is sufficiently sophisticated, in terms of awareness of the background of political theory underlying international law, to be taken as a genuine challenge for my project. The French State as a corporate entity in the formalist legal imagination is incapable of recognising any internationally significant dialectic, because it is, at the internal, domestic level, unitary and uni-dimensional. This primary international law understanding of corporatism is Hobbsean. It requires a unity of the represented and the representative in the latter. The essence of the State as a subject is a single will, which projects itself externally. There is quite simply no place for inter-subjectivity within the State and inter-State meeting is confined to a formal convergence of wills that represents a thoroughly statically conceived fettering of otherwise sovereign State discretion. This Hobbsean approach recognises that at the international level, there is no world corporate entity.

It is the actual corporate character of the State that counts. A State as a structure is inconceivable[7] if it does not have a constitution, which treats a group of persons as organs of the State. As Combacau says, the apparition of the State is inconceivable if the collectivity does not give itself the organs by means of which the actions of fact of the social body that it, presumably the collectivity (les agissements du fait du corps social) constitutes already, can be imputed to the legal corporative body (corps de droit) that it claims to become.[8] The co-author Sur says of the relation State/nation that the coincidence of the two is a delicate matter. The national composition of a State is a social reality and not a juridical matter. International law attaches to the idea of sovereignty and sees in the State a stable element and foundation. Sovereignty itself signifies a power to command. As Combacau says,[9] sovereignty signifies the power to break the resistance as much of one's own subjects as of one's rivals in power. It has to subordinate both. The beginning of

7. J. Combacau and S. Sur, *Droit International Public,* 1st edition (1993) 268.
8. Ibid.
9. Ibid., 226.

the institutions of the State is a matter of fact because, by definition, the State does not pre-exist them, that is, the institutions have not come into being by a constitutional procedure. They may claim a legitimacy from a struggle that the collectivity has led against a State that it judges oppressive, but international law is indifferent to the internal organisation of collectivities. Nothing requires that organs be representative, but merely that they have power 'de quelques moyens qu'ils aient usé pour le prendre et qu'ils usent pour l'exercer'.[10]

This obliteration of the social body or community as against the corporate character of the State itself is reproduced across the whole spectrum of French international law textbooks, regardless of their ideological tone. In *Droit International Public* by Nguyen Quoc Dinh, Patrick Daillier and Alain Pellet, the authors say that for the definition of the elements of a State, among the terms 'population', 'nation' and 'people', only the first is accepted. Disagreement is total on the meaning of the term 'nation'. The spirit of this analysis is the same as with Combacau and Sur. The effect of a right of secession, vindicating a right of self-determination of peoples, would be unlimited territorial claims. So any recognition of the material substance of the social body is seen by Daillier and Pellet as an immediate recipe for international social chaos. Once a State is created it confiscates the rights of peoples.[11]

In the collective volume directed by Denis Alland, *Droit International Public* (2000), Hervé Ascensio provides a very lucid third chapter on the State as a subject of international law, which makes rather explicit the philosophical and ideological foundations of French formalism. Using virtually identical metaphors to Daillier and Pellet he speaks of the right of self-determination of peoples as a matter that may be exercised at a particular historical instance, *after which the people effaces itself once again behind the State.*[12] The sociological approach recognises that no international law order is strong enough to control or regulate the coming into existence of States. A juridical definition creates only the illusion that such a legal order is much stronger than it really is.[13]

10. Ibid., 269.
11. Nguyen Quoc Dinhp Dailler and A. Pellet, *Droit International Public,* 6th edition (1999) 407–8.
12. D. Alland, *Droit International Public,* 1st edition (2000), in the chapter by Herve Ascensio, 'Etat', p. 99 et seq. at paragraph 91.
13. Ibid., paragraphs 73–5

It is only in the work of Dupuy, arguably the most purely technical, in the international law sense, that the inherent confusion of the whole French approach is brought to light. In his *Droit International Public*, Pierre-Marie Dupuy gives extensive attention to the relationship between the classical definition of the State and *the right of self-determination of peoples*, saying that '*the problem is difficult because the latter is accepted as legal and as applying in all situations, if one follows the letter and the logic of the international legal texts*'.[14] He looks to international recognition as a solution, with the qualification that there are not clearly objective criteria to identify what is a people. While international law is no longer indifferent to issues of legitimacy and human rights, it will still be a question whether the traditional elements of the State, which express effectiveness, are reunited in a particular case.[15] This position more accurately recognises the confusion that international law does experience, between corporatist and ethnic or other social concepts of the personality of the main subject of international law.

Once constituted the State appears to exist in an immaterial world. It is said that the State as a corporate body is detached from the elements that compose it. This reasoning allows Combacau to say that the moral personality of the State, in the sense of corporate identity, removes the significance of the identity of the persons and the groups that make it up materially. This has the consequence that the greater or lesser modification of the spatial basis or the population of this territorial collective that is the State do no more than draw in another manner the contours of the object with respect to which the international competences of the State are recognised.[16]

The historical significance of the corporatist approach (effectively Hobbsean in the French case) for the impossibility of a hermeneutic of inter-State traditions is made clear in the work of Jens Bartelson who describes the rupture with the past more contextually. The late medieval tradition, which included Vitoria and especially Grotius, started from the premise that Man is still embedded in a universal society and in the Cosmos. As Bartelson puts it, '[T]he question was not how to solve a conflict between conflicting sovereigns over the foundation of a legal order, but how to relate concentric circles of

14. P. M. Dupuy, *Droit International Public* (1998), 4th edition paragraph 133; emphasis mine.
15. Ibid., paragraphs 30–4, 130–2.
16. J. Combacau and S. Sur, *Droit International Public,* 219–20.

resemblant laws, ranging from the divine law down to a natural and positive law'.[17] Whether Vitoria or Grotius, they would look to the resemblance of episodes and events by drawing upon an almost infinite corpus of political learning recovered from antiquity, whether legendary or documented, 'because it is assumed that they (modern rulers) share the same reality, and occupy the same space of possible political experience'.[18] Neither Grotius nor Vitoria would countenance any opposition between the kind of law that applies between States and within States, since this would imply an absence of law.[19]

The break with the Medieval-Renaissance picture comes with the modern State arising out of the wars of religion of the sixteenth and seventeenth centuries. The conception of this State broke with any attempt to ground its existence in a transcendent order. The new State had to self-ground itself in the absolute, unquestionable value of its own security, as defined and understood by itself. The science of this State was Hobbsean, concerning the sovereign who obliges, but is not obliged, to whom everyone is bound, but that is itself not bound. Territorial integrity is an aspect of the security, which rests in the already established territorial control. This control of territory comes to be what the so-called law of territory has to authenticate and validate. The extent of the territory of one sovereign is marked by the boundary of the territory of other sovereigns. The actual population of each sovereign territory is limited to the extent of power of the sovereign, measured geopolitically. *The populations of other sovereigns are not unknown 'others' in the modern anthropological sense, but simply people beyond the geo-political boundary of the State.*[20]

The purpose of law is no longer to re-establish resemblances in a fragmenting medieval Christian world, but to furnish dependable information about the limits, as boundaries, of the sovereign State, whose security rests precisely upon the success with which it has guaranteed territorial order within its boundaries, regardless of whatever is happening beyond these boundaries. Mutual recognition by sovereigns does not imply acceptance of a common international

---

17. J. Bartelson, *A Geneology of Sovereignty* 128; emphasis in the original. See above, p. 5 note 10.
18. Ibid., 110.
19. Ibid., 130–1; Bartelson applies these remarks to Vitoria.
20. Ibid., a summary of the whole of Bartelson's chapter 5, 'How Policy Became Foreign', 137–85; my emphasis.

order, but merely an analytical recognition of factual, territorial separation, which, so long as it lasts, serves to guarantee some measure of security. However, as Bartelson puts it, *the primary definition of State interest is not a search for resemblances, affinities of religion or dynastic family. Instead interest is a concept resting upon detachment and separation.* The rhetoric of mutual empathy or sympathy between peoples is, in a logical or categorical sense, inconceivable. International society is composed of a collection of primary, unknowable, self-defining subjects, whose powers of detached analytical, empirical observation take absolute precedence over any place for knowledge based on passion or empathy, whether oriented towards sameness or difference.[21]

This structure of sovereign relations remains the basic problematic that international lawyers face today. The origin of the State is a question of fact rather than law. One may not enquire into its composition or nature. Law is whatever the sovereigns choose to define as such through their will. The instability of this supposed legal order is patent. The status of mutual recognition as a means of assuring security is unstable. There is no agreement about the legal significance of recognition. Fundamentally, the problem is that while there is plenty of what all the State parties are willing to identify as law, there is auto-interpretation of the extent of legal obligation.

So, law has come to be defined unilaterally by the Sovereign (of Descartes and Hobbes). The meaning of legal obligation has no communal sense. It merely attaches spatially to a geo-politically limited population. Sovereigns, detached and separate from society, can determine meanings by legal fiat, by using words to reflect their exclusive monopoly of physical power and the capacity to coerce. It has always been my wish to argue, since *The Decay of International Law* (1986), that international legal concepts have been embedded in political theory, that is, probably long forgotten projects to give meaning to public life. The corporativist project rests upon a contractarian myth, expressing the belief that all political legitimacy, *and with it legal validity,* must rest upon being able to draw a contractual chain, however implicit or supposed, between the consent of the individual and the act of the State. Thereby, the State act has a legally and politically representative character. If the chain is clearly broken at any point, both the lawyer and political theorist will say that legal validity and political legitimacy have vanished. That is all either of

21. Ibid., my emphasis.

these two would-be professionals have to do or indeed can do. They do not have to recognise or understand anyone, or indeed engage in any material argument, dialectical or otherwise, with anyone. Formalism is a matter of chasing after the imaginary contractual chain.

The most penetrating criticism of contractarian theory known to me comes from political theology, which has a perspective sufficiently broad to appreciate the mythical character of the theory and how it blocks the way to a legal politics of cultural identity. Oliver O'Donovan points out how any community identity rests upon historical provenance.[22] He objects, contrary to the Hobbsean and other contractarian myths, that contractarian theory as a way to political authority cannot actually constitute a people.[23] A State structure, the outcome of a successful argument for political authority, serves for the defence of something other than itself. O'Donovan makes the vital claim that contractarianism, as a mythical foundation for political authority, offers no theory of identity that could support the moral unity of a people.[24] He affords a brilliant insight into the extraordinary violence of self-styled Western democracies, when he goes on to argue that this huge deficiency in contractarian theory leads its proponents into a compensatory compulsion to impregnate the shell of their societies with an ideological self-consciousness from the very start. For instance, Rawls' language distinguishing liberal from so-called decent peoples is abstract political invention, not rooted in ordinary life. The narrative myth of constitution has to perform the task of political analysis.

O'Donovan has also understood the inevitable path that contractarian theory will follow at the global level and makes the point that the theory will be self-driven to think globally of a single world government, reigning over a non-existent world people, since the theory has no place for identity. The theory makes impossible any material, mutual dialectic of identities, because contractarianism ignores any moment or place for recognition, conceiving the representative relation as achieved by a once and for all act of the human will,[25] that is, in the founding Hobbsean contractarian myth, which combines the representative and the represented in one entity. As there are no possibilities of mutual recognition – given the once and

22. O. O'Donovan, *The Ways of Judgement* (2005) 140.
23. Ibid., 150.
24. Ibid., 155–6.
25. Ibid., 163.

for all expression of a single unified will – whether of Hobbes or Rawls – the newly constructed entity, whether national or global, cannot be self-reflective or exist in relationship. A government of a people without internal relations of mutual recognition can have no identity.[26] So, at the global level, contractarianism can only jump to a theory of world government, once again striving forcefully to reproduce globally a single world people, just as the single State produces ideologically its own people.[27]

Again, a crucial insight into contractarianism that O'Donovan provides, is that the single global people reproduced by a global constitution ignores the idea of a people as a subject in a world of reciprocating others. This is why it inevitably happens that schemes of world government cannot be distinguished from the realities of imperial-colonial enterprise, given that they work with an abstract idea of a government of a people with no internal relations of mutual recognition.[28] In whatever their claims to universality, all empires need strong boundaries – empires are driven, metaphysically to recreate the I–Thou relationship, for instance as Rome did through Byzantium.

The brutality of contractarian universalism can be seen so clearly in the solipsist argument of Robert Kagan's *Paradise and Power*, where, as O'Donovan would lead us to expect, an ideologised concept of American democracy, as an objective value, is projected on to the global scene, whose violence is above all a failure of cognition, rooted in a two-fold failure of both internal and external self-recognition and mutual recognition. As O'Donovan has pointed out,[29] a people must have internal relations of mutual recognition to have a capacity for identity and hence external relations of recognition. The ideological aspiration of a single State to be a global government – anyway only ideologically implicated – ignores the idea of a people as a subject in a world of reciprocating others. It may not be fashionable in academic scholarship to pinpoint a particular country and a particular personality, but the issue of imposition of a constitutional order, outside American policy, is purely academic. I agree with Kagan 'that EU foreign policy is probably the most anaemic of all the products of European integration'.[30]

The challenge of global liberal constitutionalism, effectively, comes only from this American source. Of course, the irony is that it is not

26. Ibid., 214.
27. Ibid., 219–20.
28. Ibid., 214.
29. Ibid., 214.
30. R. Kagan, *Paradise and Power* (2003) 65.

conceived in terms of multi-lateral institutionalism, but, as O'Donvan warns, it depends upon a confusion of the self with the global. It is best to quote Kagan, as paraphrasing of Kagan's delirious script will risk the accusation of anti-American bias in anaemic European academic circles:

> The United States *is* a behemoth with a conscience . . . Americans do not argue, even to themselves, that their actions may be justified by *raison d'etat*. They do not claim the right of the stronger or insist to the rest of the world that the strong rule where they can and the weak suffer what they must. The United States is a liberal, progressive society through and through, and to the extent that Americans believe in power, they believe it must be a means of advancing the principles of a liberal civilization and a liberal world order.[31]
>
> Americans have always been internationalists, but their internationalism has always been a by-product of their nationalism. When Americans sought legitimacy for their actions abroad, they sought it not from supranational institutions but from their own principles. That is why it was always so easy for so many Americans to believe that by advancing their own interests they advance the interests of humanity.[32]

This perspective will not change, in Kagan's view, and it has long been the American position. Both the Clinton and Bush administrations rested on the assumption of America as the indispensable nation.[33] Kagan continues: 'Americans seek to defend and advance a liberal international order. But the only stable and successful international order Americans can imagine is one that has the United States at its centre.'[34] This is not described as an expansion of international law, because supranational governance means, for Kagan, working with other nations.[35] Instead, Kagan means actual government of the whole world by the United States. So he says:

> Just as the Japanese attack on Pearl Harbour led to an enduring American role in East Asia and in Europe, so September 11, which future historians will no doubt depict as the inevitable consequence of American involvement in the Muslim world, will likely produce a lasting American military presence in the Persian Gulf and Central Asia, and perhaps a long term occupation of one of the Arab world's largest countries. Americans may be surprised to find themselves in such a position . . . But viewed from the perspective of the grand sweep of American history, a history marked

31. Ibid., 41; emphasis in the original.
32. Ibid., 88.
33. Ibid., 94.
34. Ibid.
35. Ibid., 95.

by the nation's steady expansion and a seemingly ineluctable rise from perilous weakness to the present global hegemony, this latest expansion of America's strategic role may be less than shocking.[36]

A MINORITY ETHNIC VIEW OF THE STATE AS AN EXPRESSION OF THE SELF-DETERMINATION OF PEOPLES

The textbook *Universelles Völkerrecht* (1984 edition) by Alfred Verdross and Bruno Simma is widely regarded as a most authoritative statement of German/Austrian international law doctrine during the Federal Republic of Germany of 1949–89. It is at present not a dominant textbook in use in German law faculties, partially because as a source of reference it is sharply dated. Much greater place is given to two important collective works, *Völkerrecht,* edited by Ipsen, and *Völkerrecht,* edited by Vitzthum.[37] In the text by Verdross and Simma there is a commitment to the distinctively German view of the nature of the nation/*Volk* and its relationship to the State. This is an ethnic nation, which, at the time, did not enjoy full self-determination because of the partition of the country. The discussion of the relationship between State and nation is distinctive in European terms. Verdross and Simma argue (paragraph 380) that a State is not simply an association of people for individual goals, but is, once again, a *civitas perfecta* of those belonging to it, which provide the State the primary basis of its authority, a personal rather than a territorial jurisdiction. A population of a State must be a permanent association of people tied together by blood.[38] The State territory is not simply the spatial dimension of the jurisdiction of the State, but the secured space (*den gesicherten Raum*) of the people, which has organised itself into a State (paragraph 380). The root of the authority of the State is the *personality principle* of Germanic law, whereby every member of the tribe (*Stamme*) is under the authority of the legal order of its community. The authority of the

36. Ibid., 96.
37. *Völkerrecht*, 4th edition, Knut Ipsen (ed.) (1999), and *Völkerrecht*, Wolfgang Graf Vitzthum (ed.) (1997), with a second edition in preparation. Throughout the paper, account will be taken of the positions presented in these works, bearing in mind, at the same time, both their collective and reference (informational) character.
38. 'Bei einem Staatsvolk muss es sich um einen dauerhaften Personenverbund handeln, der in der Geschlechterfolge fortlebt.' Different from standard British and French definitions. The authors cite a German court case that refers to the celebrated strong concept of the population as a *Schicksalsgemeinschaft* (a community of destiny).

State over everyone on its territory is becoming more important but *it cannot push into the background* the personal dimension, which is the most important to the State, an association of persons based upon personal loyalty between the State and the nation (*Staatsvolk*) (paragraph 389). The authors stress sharply exactly what they are saying. Naturally, it would be possible to have a purely territorial view of the drawing of the boundaries of the world, but then there would be no *Heimatstaaten* and no *Staatsangehörige*, both concepts that suppose attachment of particular people to one another and to a place. Without this dimension the State would not be the organisation of a people but an administrative region of a world State.[39]

This concept has profound implications for the detail of principles and rules of international law. A direct consequence is that a change of government does not touch the identity of the State. It is 'in der Geschlechterfolge fortlebende Bevölkerung', which provides the material element of the State, that the continuity of the State is grounded. While Grotius is cited, the authors are really thinking of the German situation. They have also in mind the continuity of the German State from 1937 to 1990. This analysis leads into the most difficult subjects of contemporary international law. A discussion of associations without territorial authority (paragraph 404) focuses especially on movements of national liberation (paragraph 410). In the case where a power does not recognise its duty to allow a people that it dominates illegally to go free, this people has the right to realise its freedom through the use of force. This is affirmed in the 1974 General Assembly Resolution on the Definition of Aggression (Res. 3314/29). How can one justify this argument in the light of Article 2/4 of the Charter, and the objects of the Charter itself? It is a question of an international war and not a civil war as the majority of Western jurists believe. One can no longer suppress a revolt on the part of national liberation groups.

Much later in the manual (paragraph 509) there is an extensive consideration of the principles of respect and promotion of the right of self-determination of peoples. In terms of a common European history the oppression of one people by another begins with the

39. It is here that the collective and reference character of the other textbooks present problems. In Ipsen's work, chapter 2, on the State as the normal subject of international law, stresses the unity of a State not in terms of language, culture or religion, and so on, but simply their living together under a common legal system (paragraph 5). However, the long chapter 6 on peoples (*Völker im Völkerrecht*) by Hans-Joachim Heintze is much closer to the main text, especially paragraph 27.4.

Dutch and the Spanish in the early seventeenth century. Oppression by one people of another leads to the latter insisting on withdrawing from the political community that it constitutes with the former. When India claimed in its ratification of the Covenant of Civil and Political Rights, with respect to Article 1 that refers to the right of self-determination of peoples, that it applied only to people under a foreign jurisdiction and not to countries already independent, the Federal Republic replied formally in August 1980 that the right of self-determination is valid 'für alle Völker und nicht nur für Völker unter Fremdherrschaft'.

Any restriction is contrary to the clear expression of the Covenant (paragraph 510). The central idea is that where a people (*Volksgruppe*) suffers discrimination, with the result that the people is no longer represented fully, the sense also of the 1970 Declaration of Friendly Relations among States applies. There no longer exists a government that represents the entire people in an equal manner. Examples are Bangladesh and Northern Ireland. Article 1/4 of the 1977 1st Protocol to the Geneva Conventions of 1949 reaffirms the right of military resistance on the part of discriminated peoples. The only restriction the authors seem to allow in their argument is that it can happen that certain peoples are so small that they will, in any case, only seek autonomy (paragraph 512). They accept that the UN practice opposes what they are saying. Once exercised, the right of self-determination is exhausted in the UN view. However, such a perspective ignores the well-known history of how the post-colonial States were constructed in disregard of ethnic distinctions. More fundamentally, the notion of the exhaustion of a right, once exercised, has no scientific basis.[40]

---

40. This has remained a virtually standard German position if one considers the whole chapter by Heintze, *Völker im Völkerrecht*, cited above, which is a systematic forty-plus-pages treatment. While Heintze regards appeal to an external right of self-determination as exceptional, compared to the preservation of the territorial integrity of states, he gives general grounds for the exercise of the right. In contrast, in Vitzthum's work in chapter 3, Kay Hailbronner in *Der Staat und der Einzelne als Völkerrechtssubjekte* dismisses the legal character of a right to self-determination in less than a page (3.24–5). At the same time, he recommends a practical conflict-prevention strategy in the face of demands of collective groups. Appropriate autonomy measures can anticipate conflict between a State and its minorities (3.26–9). This approach is grounded in a functionalist assumption that stable State structures should ensure a Law of International Relations that guarantees individual and, where appropriate, minority group rights (3.4–6).

Remaining within the contemporary German context, it is proposed to present Karl Döhring's views of the right of self-determination of peoples in his *Völkerrecht*.[41] While the latter text, written by an international lawyer, takes the form of a manual it provides a much more exhaustive and penetrating analysis of the implications of an ethnic grounding of the State. The central aim of the work is to provide a systematic account of the legal implications of the self-determination of ethnic peoples.

Döhring offers a rigorous logic to his defence of the right to self-determination of peoples as a human right. It is possible for a majority within a State to coerce into submission a minority, as a matter of empirical fact. However, this power brings with it no compelling authority. There is no force in the argument that every life in common requires acceptance of rules because this leaves open the question of whether any particular life in common is necessary. That is, the presence of two ethnic groups in one State does not have to persist. Contemporary revolutions and wars show that continuing to live in peace together is not always desired. The people of a State (*Staatsvolk*) does not have to be homogeneous, but if it is not, the State must be able to postulate values that can hold together the cultural differences of its peoples. Those States that are not able to will not endure (they are *nicht überlebensfähig*).[42]

The starting point of this analysis is that the greatest threat to security of a State is from within, not from other States. The greatest cause of this threat is the unrepresentative, coercive State that oppresses its large ethnic minorities. Döhring treats the UN, a framework of collective security, as largely irrelevant to the types of problems caused by internal repression of one ethnic group by another. Döhring defines ethnic groups as distinguished by language, religion, race, and culture and as situating themselves on a distinct territory. Döhring, like Verdross and Simma, has already defined the population element of a State as a *Schicksalsgemeinschaft* and he treats the right of self-determination of peoples as a fundamental principle of *ius cogens*. Since the people are the essential substrate of a State, it is not surprising that it can survive the collapse of the State (for example, the Somalis and Somalia). The right of self-determination of peoples is not confined to the colonial world and it is clear both that a right must bring with it the means to defend it – or it is not a right – and that collective self-defence must mean the right of another

41. K. Döhring, *Völkerrecht* (1998).
42. Döhring, *Volkerrecht* 3–4.

to come to one's assistance, whether it is an individual or group right that is violated.[43]

If one returns to Döhring's starting point, he has placed the active obligation on a multi-national State to ensure a value framework to bridge cultural difference. He recognises the dangers of his approach in considering the defensive right of self-determination in the context of the definition of aggression. In 1974 the relevant UN resolution makes an exception to the illegality of the use of force that effectively exempts the typical conflicts of the time.[44] Equally, a State that suffers a revolt by a minority claiming a right to self-determination will resist its dissolution by making the same claim. There will be a collision of norms as in constitutional law and the principle of *ius cogens* will give no direction.[45] Nonetheless, for Döhring the starting point remains that the empirical coercive power of the majority within an existing State is merely that. The democratic aspect of self-determination means, in Döhring's view, that the State has a duty to give a minority the institutional possibility to express itself, in order to be able to determine the will of the minority group.[46] One cannot escape from ethnic conflict and violence into the illusion that the fiat of the State, as a matter of legal epistemology, can resolve such conflict.

BEYOND STATISM AND ETHNICITY

As we have already seen, and Bartelson has brilliantly explained,[47] Hobbesean, statist thinking has its roots in a Renaissance politics of conspiracy and espionage of sovereign princes. States, in this model, do not approach one another as comparable institutions retaining their character as moral persons, in the municipal law sense. Bartelson has explained how the modern State, born of the wars of religion, wants to forget the birth that has traumatised it. This is the real meaning of the desire of Combacau to argue that one need not look to a theoretical origin of the State because its concrete foundation preceded the emergence of the concept of the State, the birth of which remains non-justiciable (p. 265). The State has become, as a subject of French public law, the subject of the

43. Ibid., 28–9, 71–3, 197–8, 242–6, 330–7.
44. Ibid., 240–2.
45. Ibid., 324.
46. Ibid., 335.
47. Bartelson, *A Genealogy of Sovereignty*.

distinction made by Descartes between the immaterial subject and the material reality, which it observes and analyses. In this scheme knowledge supposes a subject and the subject is the Hobbesean State that names but is not named, observes but is not observed, a mystery for whom all has to be transparent. It is the first problem of this theory of knowledge to find security, which lies, in a one-way rational control and analysis of others by itself.

In other words, the violent Hobbesean State of nature is self-justifying, made inevitable by its own theory of knowledge. There is no place for a reflexive knowledge of self, save for an analysis of the extension (spatial) of the power of the sovereign (that is, geopolitically) up to the frontier. Other sovereigns are not unknown in an anthropological sense, but they are enemies with interests in contradiction, whose behaviour has to be measured and calculated. The mutual recognition of sovereigns does not imply the acceptance of an international order in common, but simply a recognition of what is similar but territorially separated, an according of reputation and a limited security.

One comes back, inevitably, to the need for some theory of natural law, some grounded humanism. Lejbowicz tries to deconstruct and reconstruct the French Hobbesean perspective. The State as such has to be left behind. It is because States confront one another as *facts*, and not as corporate bodies or *moral persons*, that the identities of the persons who compose them are fundamental. So Lejbowicz argues that where these brute facts confront one another, one must return to the natural State of fraternity, which makes it impossible for humanity to be captured by one person alone. The inspiration of the *ius naturale* is that we return to recognise the other as similar, as reflections of the self, images of the self to be found in others because we have a common origin. It is the forces of exclusion that found State particularism, the opposite of mutual comprehension. The enemy is not on the outside but within the self, an evil that each has to rework. State law creates frontiers but without a human space between them. It is the confusion of languages that God has created that ensures an inevitable anthropological distance among peoples and engages them in a perpetual quest for mutual understanding. 'L'imaginaire du relationnel se construit avec le *ius* naturalisme de la *societas amicorum* sur le présupposé d'un milieu de communication déjà ouvert.'[48]

---

48. Lejbowicz, *Philosophie du droit international* (1999) 407–16, quotation at 416.

Lejbowicz thereby provides a wider context of the Western humanist tradition in which the arguments of Bartelson need not appear so alarming. Bartelson suggests the inevitability of accepting peoples, not States, as a starting point for the definition of international society. Since the revolution of linguistic nationalism of Herder and Vico there is no point of return. The exercise of giving a name, of which juridical recognition is only a part, refers directly to language and, with it, to the history of the nation. As we have seen, Bartelson has argued that there are no mysterious powers, detached from society, which can determine a signification by decree, by the employment of words that reflect their monopoly of power and their capacity to coerce. In this sense Döhring is stating the obvious in distinguishing the power from the authority of the majority controlling a State apparatus. Instead of the State, it is man who emerges from the subordination to the prince to become the sovereign of his own representations and of his concepts. The words are not *there*, as they were for Descartes, to represent passively, functioning as a mirror to reflect something external to the subject. It is the activity of the subject itself that creates its own world of experience and that gives itself the words with which to express itself. So language is a reflection of the experience of the individual and of the collectivity to which it belongs. Thus, it is language that becomes the subject of interpretation. Language in its dense reality can explain the history of the institutions, which are rooted in that language. The world of institutions is made by men and thus one can arrive at a comprehension of them *through a knowledge of the self.*[49] (emphasis in the original)

WHAT IT MEANS THAT THE STATE IS A FACT AND NOT A PRODUCT OF LAW

The assumption of a positivist international law of personality is that there has to be some kind of distinction between the factual existence of a State and its acceptance as part of a normative order, that the State is somehow a 'legal fact'. The mainstream, even liberal and interdisciplinary wings of the discipline, for instance represented by the late Antonio Cassese, think they do provide such as distinction. However, major protagonists against international law, such as Hans Morgenthau and Raymond Aron, do not agree. The view taken here is that the latter are correct and that international lawyers are left chasing after brute force and

49. Bartelson, *A Genealogy of Sovereignty* 188–201.

blessing it unintelligently. They are unable to show any normative pull attaching to brute facts and this can be illustrated most easily with the absence of any credible international law of territory and with no convincing framework in which to encompass the issue of self-determination of peoples. However, it is necessary to go beyond these deficiencies, to accept some measure of the alternative visions of nation state and other internationally significant collectivities, such as offered by Aron and Morgenthau and then to take the true task of an international law of personality to be to correct, develop, modify and otherwise accept their theses.

To the larger question of whether international law as a system has any answer at all concerning international legal personality, especially as it affects States, the answer appears to be that it pragmatically accepts States as the primary subjects of the system, in accordance with a more or less explicit principle of effectiveness. Cassese provides an outstandingly exhaustive and authoritative exposition of this view, much more historically grounded and reflective than is usual in the profession. He has said that there is no international legislation setting out detailed rules, but that '*it is possible to infer* from the body of customary rules granting basic rights and duties to States that these rules presuppose certain general characteristics in the entities to which they address themselves'.[50] These general characteristics confirm a principle of effectiveness.

Cassese explains that the principle of effectiveness permeates the whole body of rules making up international law.

> New situations are not recognised as legally valid unless they could be seen to rest on a firm and durable display of authority. No new situation could claim international legitimacy so long as the 'new men' failed to demonstrate that they had firmly supplanted the former authority. Force was the principal source of legitimation.[51]

Cassese says this applied essentially to the traditional setting of the international community.[52] However, it continues to provide the central structural framework, followed in practice, also by Cassese, with a ragbag of inconclusive exceptions. It is still the case that the concept of statehood rests on the principle of effectiveness. The rules granting basic rights and duties to States suppose two elements.

---

50. A. Cassese, *International Law* (2001) 47.
51. Ibid., at 13.
52. Ibid.

> The first is a central structure capable of exercising effective control over a given territory. The bodies endowed with supreme authority must in principle be quite distinct from and independent of any other State that is to say endowed with an original (not derivative) legal order. The second element needed is a territory that does not belong to or no longer belongs to, any other sovereign State, with a community whose members do not owe allegiance to other outside bodies. Territory may be large or small, but it is indispensable if an organised structure is to qualify as a State and an international subject. International law always requires *effective* possession of, and control over, a territory . . .[53]

It may be argued that the concept *international law* and the *principle of effectiveness* are splintered, absent *voices of authority* on to which an author such as Cassese projects what I would consider are the forgotten sediments/experiences of diplomatic and national constitutional history. Cassese explains (paragraph 16) that the word *State* marks a unitarily closed-up entity in which all authority is granted only by the State itself. Underlying it is a shift in loyalty from the family, local community, or religious organisation to the State. It is such loyalty patterns, essentially a social process, which mark the legal supremacy of the State. However, there is a special quality to this entity. Following Strayer, Cassese notes that it persists in time and is fixed in space, permanent and impersonal, although underlying it is simply agreement on the need for an authority that can give final judgements. Once again what Cassese stresses is *closure*. The concept of State excludes any authority above or below it. This excludes any possibility that there could be any interpenetration of such States, that one could set in motion a process of cultural translation from one entity to the other. As Cassese puts it, each country (his choice of word) 'increasingly regarded each other as separate and autonomous entities, and each struggled to overpower the other' (paragraph 16). This would seem to grasp best the reality of the concentration of authority in the State in the seventeenth century, at least as Cassese describes it. Beyond the Church and the Empire, remembering that the Protestant Churches are purely national, all signification is concentrated in the State. This allows Cassese to say (paragraph 11) that the lack of strong political, ideological, and economic links between States (as Christian principles were not allowed to override national interest) resulted in self-interest holding sway.

53. Cassese, *International Law* 48; emphasis in the original.

What is missing from the theory of international law is a detailed account of the significance of Hobbeseanism for the absence of international legal structures. In fact, the absolutist State has had to mean the disappearance of a universal international legal order. In the period of transition from the medieval-feudal system of public authority over land and population to the modern absolutist State in the course of the sixteenth century and early seventeenth, the focus of public lawyers was on the terms of submission of subjects to rulers. The tradition that the central legal concept should be jurisdiction (of a lord over his vassals in his court) gave way to the more nebulous notion of the limits of the supreme power (*potestas suprema*), in effect, of an unconstrained executive. A fatal development was that, among public lawyers and political theorists of the State, all interest in the justification of the historical legal title to territory of individual States was abandoned. Instead, attention was devoted simply to the capacity of the prince to exercise power over subjects. For this power to have sought or found justification would have meant looking to a law of the Holy Roman Empire or of the Papacy, as this was the traditional sense given to the existence of a higher authority. The authority of the prince was given a rationale by political theorists such as Bodin.[54]

The very idea of absolute authority had to mean its separation from any argument of legitimacy of the relationship of ruler to ruled. The legal development marked a separation of the governing power from concrete legal relations, where primary importance was given to the concept of frontier as the means of delimiting the territorial scope of the prince's power.[55] Territory came to be defined merely as the areas of command of the prince, with a supposedly unquestioning duty of the subject to owe submission to the prince. The difficulty, from the late seventeenth century to the twentieth, and particularly in the eighteenth, was that the territorial princes of Europe did not obtain thereby a convincing legal foundation for their possessions, for instance, land and population. The focus was simply on the advantages of order that would follow from a generalised submission. As a result, there were ever harsher territorial conflicts, as the notion of the need for princely authority in political theory was not matched by an international–European consensus on the basis for

54. Dietmar Willoweit, *Rechtsgrundlagen der Territorialgewalt* (1975) esp. 123–5, 126, 129–31.
55. Ibid., 275–6.

territorial title. There had been a sacrifice of political legitimacy, for instance, based on the consent of the population, in favour of the value of public safety. This was understandable, in the context of bloody civil wars, for instance, after the wars of religion. However, safety was conceived of in purely internal, not international, terms.[56]

Cassese fully outlines further relevant material for the significance of the principle of effectivity. Where frontiers were extended outside Europe there was just as little conviction brought to bear on the legitimacy or illegitimacy of territorial expansion. There is, first (paragraph 19), the remarkable withdrawal of European States in the nineteenth century to a position of ethnocentric dominance, in which they treated the non-European world as, in principle, not within the international society of States in the sense (borrowing Hedley Bull's terminology) that 'a group of States, conscious of certain common interests and values, forms a society in the sense that they conceive themselves to be bound by a common set of rules in their relations with one another'. This notion of community was based upon a sense of cultural superiority that is also reflected still in the notion of general principles of law recognised by civilised countries (see Cassese, paragraph 94). It is Cassese who explains that this led to two distinct classes of relations with the outside world depending upon whether they consisted of States 'proper' such as the Ottoman Empire, China, or '[were] instead made up of communities lacking any organized central authority (tribal communities or communities dominated by local rulers, in Africa or Asia)'. Detailed case studies of these two categories will reveal that the dichotomy is not accurate, that in both cases the so-called principle of effectiveness operated. The definition of a State, in terms of defined territory and a population subject to effective governmental control, provided the conceptual framework for the subordination of non-Western countries to the West, above all in the period 1815–1960. The so-called principle of effectiveness is, by its nature, impervious to intercultural *translation*, dialogue, and so on. The reason is that it served an *incorporative* function. The concept of culture, in the sense that Hedley Bull has spoken of a society of States, becomes, in the hands of nineteenth-century European States, a notion of civilisation that served to accommodate European perspectives on how international society should function.

This is the context in which M. F. Lindley, in *The Acquisition and Government of Backward Territory in International Law* (1926),

56. Ibid., 306–7, 349–50, 360–1.

said that the requirement of a civilised State was political organisation. The latter meant 'a considerable number of persons who are permanently united by habitual obedience to a certain and common superior, or whose conduct in regard to their mutual relations habitually conforms to recognized standards'.[57] In other words, the conditions of statehood in general international law, of which Cassese speaks, were also elaborated in a colonial context. Any entity not capable of providing security for persons and property, in terms identical to what Westerners could expect in their own countries, indeed any entity that was not able to resist penetration by Western States anxious to provide this security for themselves, could expect to be incorporated into the territory of a Western State. The two categories represented by Cassese – subjection to unequal capitulation treaties, and incorporation of supposedly *res nullius* territories – merely reflect in simplistic terms a wide variety in the measure of penetration and control of non-Western societies necessary to ensure a Western-style world order.

The discourse of civilisation is one of *modernisation*. Since the time of Vitoria there was a European expectation that certain inalienable rights were associated with the freedoms of trade, travel, and proselytising.[58] The process of modernisation was increasingly coercive in the course of the nineteenth century. This is the true meaning of the so-called principle of effectiveness. As Gong puts it:

> While positive international law sanctioned the selective use of force against the 'uncivilized', and defined such countries as 'uncivilized' – partially for the circular reason that they were unable to defend themselves against military attack – the effect of such doctrines did not depart that radically from what Vitoria's natural law philosophies had countenanced in the past.[59]

The 'need' continued for the same universal freedoms of Vitoria. Positivism itself (the philosophical foundation of 'effectiveness'), as a belief in the science of progress and physical achievement, on analogy with the natural sciences,[60] will favour effectiveness.

---

57. G. W. Gong, *The Standard of Civilisations in International Society* (1984) 16.
58. Ibid., 36.
59. Ibid., 43.
60. Ibid., 47.

A close examination of the jurisprudence usually presented as material for a law of territory shows that it concerns mainly relations with non-Western peoples. The prime example is the *Island of Palmas Case*.[61] The language of the arbitrator shows how far he was concerned with ensuring a globally *efficient* organisation of territory. With respect to title by occupation, arbitrator Huber says:

> The growing insistence with which international law, ever since the middle of the 18th century, has demanded that the occupation shall be effective would be inconceivable, if effectiveness were required only for the act of acquisition and not equally for the maintenance of the right.

He points out how effectiveness, insisted on with respect to occupation, is, in fact, already there 'with territories in which there is already an established order of things'. Indeed, the concept is supposed to precede international law. For Huber alleges that

> before the rise of international law, boundaries of land were necessarily determined by the fact that the power of a State was exercised within them, so too, under the reign of international law, the fact of peaceful and continuous display is still one of the most important considerations in establishing boundaries between states.

The reason for this perspective is quickly provided. Territorial sovereignty has a corollary: the duty to protect within the territory the rights of other States, together with the rights that each State may claim for its nationals in foreign territory. 'Territorial sovereignty serves to divide between nations the space upon which human activities are employed, in order to ensure them the minimum of protection of which international law is the guardian.' The analogy is drawn with abstract rights to property in municipal law, which do not need to be exercised. In the absence of a super-State the same licence cannot be tolerated in international law. One may ask what evidence Huber offers for the following proposition, which seems to suppose an independent subject – *international law* – just as does Cassese with his principle of effectiveness:

> International law, in the 19th century, having regard to the fact that most parts of the globe were under the sovereignty of States members

61. (Perm Ct Arb1928) 2UNRep.Int.Arb Awards 829.

> of the community of nations, and that territories without a master had become relatively few, took account of a tendency already existing and especially developed since the 18th century, and laid down the principle that occupation, to constitute a claim to territorial sovereignty, must be effective, that is, offer certain guarantees to other States and their nationals.

As for the original inhabitants of the island they are referred to in the context of the type or amount of exercise of sovereignty required. Indeed, Huber says that some exercise of sovereignty 'over a small and distant island, inhabited only by natives, cannot be expected to be frequent' so that one need not go back very far. Nonetheless, 'a clandestine exercise of State authority over an inhabited territory during a considerable length of time would seem to be impossible'. In my view there is not a hard distinction between lands inhabited by 'natives' and lands inhabited by non-Western States in the development of 'international law' in the nineteenth century. This is because States such as the Netherlands did conclude contracts with 'native chiefs' that were taken as evidence of consolidation of sovereignty in a context in which the 'natives' were not entirely without rights. Their land was not *res nullius*. At the same time Huber describes how State sovereignty evolved in the context of more complex organisations in the nineteenth century.

> It is quite natural that the establishment of sovereignty may be the outcome of a slow evolution, of a progressive intensification of State control. This is particularly the case, if sovereignty is acquired by the establishment of the suzerainty of a colonial Power over a native State, and in regard to outlying possessions of such a vassal State.[62]

This superficial jurisprudence has to be put in a wider context. There is a crucial gap in the so-called international law of territory that was noticed by Carl Schmitt in his work, *Nomos der Erde* (1950).[63] The extension of the concept of State territory from Europe in the great colonial seizures of the late nineteenth century separated the idea of the territory of a State from being the home of the State's population. In Schmitt's view this hollowed out the very

---

62. Island of Palmas Arbitration, 829.
63. A. Carty, 'Carl Schmitt's Critique of the Liberal International Legal Order, 1933–1945', *Leiden Journal of International Law* 14 (2001) 25–76.

idea of international law as an order of States, because it hollowed out the idea of the State itself. Virtually every European major State extended itself as a State over vast territories with which it had no organic connection. This was possible because the concept of the State with which they worked was the French Hobbsean State and not the ethnically rooted 'Schicksaal Gemeinschaft' of which Verdross and Doehring write.

Raymond Aron is withering in his disdain for a law of territory that has as its main preoccupation what he calls empty spaces. He says that there are or should be practical implications in regarding the State as a fact and not a so-called legal fact. It can close its frontiers against others, boycott whom it pleases, destabilise its neighbours, and so on. Yet, most of all, there is no agreement on the basic point of a constitutional order, the distribution of territory. The international law on this subject, the rules on the acquisition of territory, is quite banal, as the concern of the engaged political analyst is not with empty spaces. The problem to be faced is the attachment of populations to one State rather than to another or the desire of a population to constitute an independent State. History offers few examples of peaceful disintegration of a national or an imperial State.[64]

Aron explains that what is provoking crises in international relations is the continuing dispute about the legitimacy of States. Strangely, the crises of Islamic terrorism and tidal waves of immigration across Europe from the Middle East see an absence of any wide-profile or high-level discussion of the legitimacy of the States of Israel, Iraq, and Syria, not to mention the Gulf States and the Arabian Peninsula. No discussion of the so-called international law on the use of force that does not take account of the contested legitimacy of the States usually at the centre of violence can make any analytical sense.[65] What is happening now in the second decade of the twenty-first century is much as it was when Aron was writing in the 1960s. There is a collapse of the previously self-evident legitimacy of whatever was an established power, usually a military-based monarchy, in a world that is now increasingly dominated by nationalism

---

64. A. Carty, 'The Continuing Influence of Kelsen on the General Perception of the Discipline of International Law', *European Journal of international Law* 9 (1998) 344, at 351, drawing on R. Aron, *Paix et Guerre* (1962) at 712–15.
65. Of course the historical research on the origins of these states is bountiful and well known in literate circles, but still not part of the public debate. See further, later in a chapter on the use of force.

and democracy. In the face of these real tensions, in Aron's view, the normativist approach to the State – that it is a legal order whose existence, scope and competence is determined by a hierarchically superior international order (the Kelsen hypothesis) – is nothing but a play on words. Kelsen and his disciples will not distinguish a juridical order and a State order, or they reduce the latter to a larger juridical order. That is, they think the concept of sovereignty is useless because, according to the Pure Theory, it means only the validity, within a certain space, of a certain system of norms. A realist approach appreciates that States are a law unto themselves and do not bow to external authority.[66]

In this particular respect Aron is supported strongly by Morgenthau in his critique of the normativist approach. Morgenthau insists that the notion that norms enjoy validity through a process of delegation must have an empirical dimension.[67] For Morgenthau a juridical norm that delegates to another cedes to that other a part of its own strength, while for Kelsen delegation concerns merely an epistemological criterion.[68] Yet this controversy touches acutely upon the question of whether it means anything to say that international law delegates to States the validity of their legal orders. The legal order of the State takes from within the power of the State itself the reality of its normative order. It is empirically observable that the State exercises the highest concentration of power that exists over a specific territory.[69]

For Morgenthau, normativism must include a criterion whereby one can identify whether a legal order can determine the will of another.[70] How can international law penetrate State territory that is, by definition, already subject to the highest, strongest power.[71] Kelsen's theory of law should require that sanctions are above their objects. It may well be possible to say that the nature of a sanction, such as blockade or intervention, is determined by a rule of international law, but the normative determination of the means of realisation remains entirely with particular States.[72]

66. Ibid., Aron at 724.
67. Ibid., at 349, drawing on H. Morgenthau, *La Réalité des Normes* (1934) 171.
68. Ibid., Morgenthau 174–5.
69. Ibid., Morgenthau 176–7.
70. Ibid., Morgenthau 183.
71. Ibid., Morgenthau 214.
72. Ibid., Morgenthau 225.

To return to Aron – the nature of actual collectivities about which Morgenthau also has much to say – the centre of a responsible political theory of international society has to be concern with the composition of its basic political entities. For Aron these are a historical mixture of several elements. As a cultural historical nation an entity will have its own hierarchy of values and, however subjective these may be, in a democratic world they will be held on to and will lead to resistance against patterns of domination that are historical leftovers.[73] The frontiers between allegiance based upon historic tradition and allegiance resting upon participative nationalism remain fluid and unstable. Yet even if they were resolved, in favour of the latter, states would still pursue a rivalry of national cultures, each claiming superiority and a right to dominate.[74]

Where does this leave international law? Aron remarks that the concepts of its multi-lateral treaty law, such as the right of self-determination of peoples, collective security, and so on, are very vague and in need of interpretation. These are formulae that require a mediation between positive law on the one side and ideologies and philosophies on the other,[75] precisely the task that Kelsen and his formalist, positivist followers wish to deny the lawyer. One may speak of the principle of *pacta sunt servanda*, but treaties represent a balance of forces, they are rarely signed freely and a stable *juridical* order is not possible unless all the parties judge it to be equitable. [76]

SELF-DETERMINATION, THE STATE AS FACT OR 'LEGAL FACT' THE ABSENCE OF AN INTERNATIONAL LEGAL ORDER

The mainstream approach as to whether there is a right of self-determination of peoples should look to whether a rule of general customary international law has developed requiring states to grant it or giving specified groups automatic entitlements. The argument so far in this chapter has at least two dimensions. The more fundamental is that the coming into existence of states is not regulated at all by an international legal order. Neither states nor so-called peoples have any legally significant right to existence, apart from the prohibition on the use of force in the UN Charter and supposedly

73. Ibid., Morgenthau 251, Aron 296–9.
74. Ibid., Aron 294–9.
75. Ibid., 352, Aron at 116.
76. Ibid.

customary law – of which more in a later chapter. The international community or legal order, so-called, is not strong enough either to constitute states or to prevent their disintegration. The second dimension is that the traditionally German ethnic notion of the nation state is *theoretically, but not necessarily as a part of political practice,* open to the granting of a right to self-determination to a people within an existing State where there is sufficient ethnic difference and a corresponding conscious will for separation. In contrast, the traditionally French 'Hobbsean' State cannot pose the question at all because of the belief that the identity of the people within a State is absorbed in the unity of the represented and representative in the unitary State.

This latter dimension is not dismissed here for being theoretical. Quite the contrary, it is ideas about social and political organisation that shape States both domestically (internally) and in their relations with one another. The ideas have both qualities of traction in a scientific sense and also integrity in an intellectual and moral sense. In other words, there is a positivist, in the sense of contextual, significance in arguing the merits of self-determination in countries as varied as France, Germany, the United States, China and the United Kingdom, not to mention Africa, South Asia, or Latin America.

It is unlikely that one can formulate any universal principles or rules about a right to self-determination of peoples. What is intended in the concluding section of chapter 3 is merely to suggest that there is some traction in the general critique of the State coming from within American liberal political theory. Opposition to the sanctity of the principle of effectivity is realistic at the present time, given the fragility of most states. So it is useful to explore the manner in which this school challenges the analytical positivism of the effectivity principle. The two are inter-related and so there is some measure of coherence in contrasting them. However, this is not to grant any exclusive priority to this liberal political theory. It is merely to take advantage of the fact, from a heuristic perspective, that it has directly deconstructed the effectivity principle.

The mainstream jurisprudence and doctrine are very firmly restrictive of any right to self-determination of peoples that can come in conflict with the territorial integrity of existing states. More precisely, it seems to go as far as to say that secession is not legally permissible without the consent of the State of which the people is already a part. In the *Case Concerning a Frontier Dispute* (Burkina Faso and the Republic of Mali) the International Court of Justice noted that, given the acceptance of the principle of *uti possidetis juris* (reliance upon former colonial administrative boundaries) in the case *by both* parties, it was not necessary to show that the principle was firmly established in international law where decolonisation was involved. Nevertheless, the Court insisted that *uti possidetis juris* is a general principle of international law that exists to prevent the stability of new states being endangered by fratricidal struggles, themselves provoked by the challenging of frontiers following the withdrawal of the administering, colonial power. This is not just an administrative procedure in Africa but a rule of general scope.[77]

One may note indeed the oblique way the issue of self-determination of peoples is side-stepped by such turns of phrases as that African states have been induced 'judiciously to consent to the respecting of colonial frontiers and to take account of it in the interpretation of the principle of self-determination of peoples'.[78] This is a euphemism for the suppression of secessionist movements in African states.

This African decision has been applied by Europe's international lawyers in the context of the break-up of Yugoslavia. The Conference on Yugoslavia's Arbitration Commission, in its Opinion No. 3 (11 January 1992), had to answer the question of whether the internal boundaries between Croatia and Serbia and between Bosnia-Herzegovina and Serbia should be regarded as frontiers in terms of public international law – a question put by the Republic of Serbia. The Opinion of the Commission was that once the break-up of Yugoslavia led to the creation of one or more independent states, except where otherwise agreed, the former boundaries between the Yugoslav republics should become frontiers protected by international law. The principle of respect for the territorial status quo and the principle of *uti possidetis juris* meant that these boundaries were not to be altered, except by agreements freely concluded. The alteration of existing frontiers or boundaries was not capable of producing any legal effect.[79]

Another intimately related question was put by the Republic of Serbia. Does the Serbian population of Croatia and Bosnia-Herzegovina, as one of the constituent peoples of Yugoslavia, have the right to self-determination? The answer of the Commission, in its Opinion No. 2, was negative. It held: (1) Not all the implications of self-determination were clear under contemporary international law. Nevertheless,

77. *ICJ Reports* (1986) 554 and especially paragraph 20.
78. Ibid.
79. *International Law Reports* 92 (1994) 170.

the right of self-determination must not involve changes to frontiers at the time of independence, except by agreement between the states concerned – the principle of *uti possidetis juris*. (2) Ethnic, religious and language communities within a State had the right to recognition of their identity under international law. One possible consequence of this principle may be for the members of the Serbian population in the two republics to be recognised under agreements between all the republics as having the nationality of their choice.[80]

This jurisprudence is endorsed in the doctrine by Antonio Cassese and James Crawford. It is remarkable that both authors concentrate primarily on the period of world history from 1918, and, indeed, in Crawford's case, even more so in the post-1945 period, although that is also the primary time of reflection for Cassese.

The first major event that international legal theory should have faced came after the French Revolution, with the linguistic nationalist upsurge against Napoleonic France. This was fundamental because it was to provide an entirely alternative foundation to statehood, through linguistic or ethnic national self-determination, replacing military-grounded dynasties. In this view, expressed concretely in the theory of Mazzini, each nation had a right of self-determination, to form its own State. Here is where the modern idea of secession first arose, with the desire of one ethnic group to break away from what would usually be a multi-ethnic empire, united under a monarchical principle of legitimacy. Virtually the whole map of Europe has been rewritten on the basis of this principle. Perhaps it has not had the same significance in other parts of the world, such as Latin America. Perhaps, there it was simply a quasi-democratic principle that motivated the original revolts, which then depended on the actual recognition of accomplished facts, thereby not disturbing the classical view that the origin of states was a mere matter of fact.[81] However, European newcomers were usually acknowledged by some form of the Public Law of Europe, to have caused a legitimate disturbance of the existing order, for example, the unification of Italy or the breakaway of the south-eastern European provinces from the Ottoman Empire, for example, The Congress of Berlin in 1878.

---

80. Ibid., 167–8.
81. See the classic work of Hersch Lauterpacht, *Recognition in International Law* (1948), which considers the nineteenth-century State practice and especially the independence of the Latin American states.

The difficulty for international legal doctrine was that it has not tried to absorb these developments into a new framework of an international legal order. The newly independent states still came into existence largely through measures of force, through obtaining patronage of a major power that supported their nationality claims, for example, France for Italy, Russia for Romania and Bulgaria. Germany had no patron and appeared to use an ideology of conquest to justify its unification. Legal theory, in the view of the German international lawyer August von Bulmerincq, writing in 1874, could still say that it would be impossible to talk of a legal right to self-determination, if that were to mean a people had a legal right to independence that a confederation of states could and would use force to assert against the multi-national, monarchical State holding on to that people. The independence of nations such as Italy, Belgium, and Greece did not change anything of the structure of the international legal order.[82]

The international law position was not considered – by international legal doctrine – to be modified by the Treaty of Versailles and the other Peace Treaties. These Treaties attempted to implement a right of self-determination according to the nationality principle. It may be asked again: why did international legal doctrine not respond to this development by saying that now the principle of self-determination was clearly a part of international law? Probably it was again the difficulty of implementation. A Minority Rights regime was imposed on a number of powers, but there was no insistence that as a general rule a generic type of entity could claim the right of self-determination. Yet now it must surely be becoming extremely serious that international legal doctrine was continuing to fail to respond reflectively to the total transformation of the political map of the world. A fundamental and quite arbitrary consideration is that legal doctrine has never assessed the significance of a parallel doctrine of the Public Law of Europe as devised through the general peace treaty settlements, such as Westphalia, Utrecht, Vienna, and Versailles. In fact, the Congresses and Conferences concluding these Treaties did function in a quasi-legislative fashion and did operate according to principles, legitimacy in 1815 and nationality in 1919.[83]

82. Carty, *Philosophy of International Law,* at 88, and references cited therein.

83. See the standard work by Antonio Cassese, *Self-determination of Peoples: A Legal Reappraisal* (2005 [1995]), especially at 27 et seq. He insists that at this stage self-determination remains a political postulate.

In my opinion it has to be appreciated that present arguments about whether there is a legal right to self-determination, and ultimately a right of secession, have to be seen in the face of this immensely complex history that has not been taken into account by international legal doctrine. This is completely clear from Cassese's *Self-determination of Peoples: A Legal Reappraisal,* already referred to. As has just been noted, Cassese claims that the right of self-determination remained a political postulate at the 1919 Peace Treaties. The argument about the meaning of the legal right to self-determination is taken to have arisen only in the context of post-colonisation and the question is whether those states that have now acquired independence, that is, since the 1950s, are bound to submit in their turn to demands from their own minorities to become independent. Needless to say, when asked, they deny any such obligation.[84]

Cassese's reference to the history described above is that, in spite of these nineteenth- and early twentieth-century European Congresses, self-determination remained a political postulate.[85] He argues, rather oddly, that the political character of the principle was affirmed in the *Aaland Island Case* 'even before the principle of self-determination had taken on the status of an international legal standard',[86] thereby ignoring the whole legal history of international relations. He is referring back to the *Aaland Island Case* of 1920, where a report of a committee of three jurists to the League Council affirmed that 'it pertains exclusively to the sovereignty of *any definitely constituted State* to grant to, or withhold from, a fraction of its population the right of deciding its own political destiny by means of a plebiscite, or in any other way'.[87] The argument of the committee shows a failure to integrate doctrine around one of the most problematic aspects of international law, the failure to regulate the coming into existence of states. Cassese goes on to say that in the particular Finnish case – thereby reducing the above quotation to the status of an *obiter dictum* – 'the principle of self-determination of peoples was called into play not

84. Ibid., 122–4.
85. *Self-determination of Peoples*, the sense of chapter 2, of the book, self-determination as an international political postulate. The reasoning is simply to treat the grounds or motives of the decision makers at these conferences as political, rather than as legal principles to which they were giving institutional form.
86. At 123.
87. Ibid., 29; my emphasis.

because the population of the Islands had a right that superseded State interests, but because Finland was purportedly in a state of flux'.[88] In other words, Cassese, in the 1990s, is not taking the matter any further than von Bulmerincq in the 1870s. He does not even show the latter's awareness of the procedural dimension of the question of whether there is a right of self-determination of peoples.

James Crawford argues how State practice demonstrates the extreme reluctance of states to recognise or accept unilateral secession outside the colonial context.[89] He points out how no new State formed since 1945 outside the colonial context has been admitted to the UN over the opposition of the predecessor State. This remarkable proposition is demonstrated by the extreme example of Bangladesh, which was not admitted to the UN until 1974 after its recognition by Pakistan.[90] This contradicts the classical view, first enunciated in the case of Latin America in the early nineteenth century, which then depended on the actual recognition of accomplished facts by third states, thereby not disturbing the classical view that the origin of states was a mere matter of fact.[91] There may have been in play simply a quasi-democratic principle that motivated the original revolts in Latin America, but the completeness of the separation and the certainty that the mother country would not overcome it was what counted with the celebrated English Foreign Secretary, George Canning.

This very recent history may appear consistent. However, secessions have continued, for example, Bangladesh, Eretria and the latest example being Kosovo. The very way the law is formulated shows that the longer historical dimension is left aside. Starting with the UN practice, Crawford says that the UN has never recognised and admitted to UN membership any State seceding unilaterally, for example, Bangladesh, until the metropolitan State accepts this.[92] Yet his formulation of quasi-law runs so completely contrary to the classical international law that still governs the coming into existence of states. Bangladesh was recognised by major countries such

88. Ibid.
89. James Crawford, 'State Practice and International Law in Relation to State Secession' *BYBIL* 85 (1998) at 114.
90. Ibid., at 95 and 115.
91. See the classic work of Hersch Lauterpacht, *Recognition in International Law* (1948), which considers the nineteenth-century State practice and especially the independence of the Latin American states.
92. James Crawford, 'State Practice and International Law in Relation to Secession', 95 and 113.

as France and Britain within weeks of the Indian army driving the Pakistani army out of East Pakistan in December 1971, before even there was clear evidence – whatever that could amount to – that Bangladesh would be stable without Indian support.[93] This practice accommodated the very traditional international law of recognition first formulated in the context of the Latin American secessions from Spain after 1810. The classical criterion has always been the viability of the new State and not the recognition of the old one. It was always obvious that the latter had a political interest in withholding recognition.[94]

So the formulation of the question by Crawford needs to be considered again. It accepts as conclusive, as a legal value, the standpoint of existing states, that international law does not require them to accept their own dismemberment without their consent. Hence, Crawford defines secession as 'the process by which a particular group seeks to separate itself from the State to which it belongs'. The value judgement-laden character of this proposition is quite clear. Crawford could simply have spoken of existing states and changing the status quo. This he distinguishes 'from a consensual process by which a State confers independence upon a particular territory and people by legislative or other means' – language that is equally value-laden.[95] Since international law is supposed to rest on the consent of states, Crawford is saying that states cannot be taken to have consented to their dismemberment without their consent because they have not consented to their dismemberment without their consent.

This interpretation of the event goes much further than just to deny the right of self-determination of peoples against the territorial integrity of existing states. It asserts the sole authority of the 'mother country' to deny the international legal personality of its wayward child, regardless of what principle the latter is asserting. This goes against the classical doctrine.

A remarkable example, which Crawford gives detailed treatment, is Eritrea. It represents a settlement of colonial territory by colonial powers, which subsequently was disputed. The Italian and then British colony was federated with Ethiopia under UN auspices and the latter did not react when the federation was abolished in 1962. There followed thirty years of political violence until a new Ethiopian government, which received Eritrean military support

93. See UK National Archive, Bangladesh, Recognition 1971.

94. See Lauterpacht, *Recognition and International Law*.

95. Ibid., 85–6.

in coming to power, recognised the right of the Eritreans to self-determination. While the agreement between the latter referred to the principle, no UN resolution did so. It may be argued that what counted was the agreement between the parties rather than the entirely passive and irrelevant UN. It is also clear that the agreement was the outcome of a history of enormous violence.

Crawford is carrying forward a tradition in doctrine that has existed since the beginning of the self-determination national movements in the nineteenth century.[96] As has been noted above, then the German international lawyer August von Bulmerincq, in his *Praxis, Theorie und Codification des Völkerrechts* (1874), was anxious to argue that the precedents of Italy, Belgium, and Greece are not enough to show the existence of a rule of international law that there is a right of peoples to self-determination. They do not provide precise evidence of who in general is a subject of the right and how it is to be exercised. Indeed, this would necessitate a congress of states that would have to assemble and decide that a particular entity enjoyed the right; these states would then have to award the right against a particular State, which of course already existed. The question would then arise as to whether a war to enforce this right would be justified. Law consists of a system of rights guaranteed by force. von Bulmerincq concludes that any right to self-determination in those terms would run counter to a legal order that already guaranteed the integrity of states.

The heart of Crawford's argument is the exhaustive list of instances that he gives in which the struggles for secession, whether violent or not, have not been successful. These instances all concern post-colonial independence and whether there can be further breakaways from newly independent countries. It is certainly the practice that all such states have fiercely resisted any further secessions. He lists twenty-nine that have actuality. They cover areas where there are most serious human rights and humanitarian concerns, such as South Sudan, Sri Lanka, Kurdistan, and Chechnya. He argues correctly that all of these cases have one feature in common. Where the government of the State is opposed to secession, such attempts have gained virtually no international support or recognition, even where other humanitarian aspects of the situations have triggered widespread concern.

Acute conflicts in Africa in the 1990s do appear to show a continuing reluctance of the international community to countenance boundary

96. Ibid; also A. Carty, *The Decay of International Law* (1986) 55–6.

changes following ethnic lines. In Africa the Congolese civil war involving most neighbouring African states has had and continues to have ethnic implications. The Great Lakes Region encompasses the stalemate between Rwanda and Uganda in Eastern Congo. So also the conflicts in Senegal and Sierra Leone threaten to dissolve West African boundaries. As *The New York Times* (29 January 2001) put it, with particular respect to the Congo conflict: 'No Western government likes to admit that Africa's awkward colonial borders are finally dissolving.' This has proved a premature judgement. However, at present, the boundaries of Middle East States, such as Iraq, Syria, and even Turkey are questioned by ISIS, which is well able to mount a significant destabilising effect on Europe, through massive waves of immigration and commando-style terrorism, factors that should count with Cassese's so-called principle of effectivity.

In this context it is probably too optimistic to expect that classical-style peace treaties will be concluded. There may not be firm parties to conclude them. Yet it is even more irrelevant to ask what the international community wishes – the reference to the so-called international legal order or the UN – because these, however characterised, are simply not active players. This is the correct interpretation to give to the failure of the UN (or whatever) to recognise the legitimacy of this or that territorial change, forceful occupation, or attempted secession.

Instead, what appears to be at stake is the weakening of the State in relation to the ethnic allegiances of its populations. In Western Europe alone Crawford gives ten examples of ethnic unrest involving every existing State, except the Netherlands and Portugal. If one notes as well that, since 1989, about fifteen new ethnic states have replaced two previous multi-ethnic states one may wonder whether the issue of consent of the parties and international recognition may not be as important elements to discuss as the nature of political organisation of community as such. Here apparently the conflict is between the classical State based on the principle of effectivity, and the more recent, if not proven to be permanently viable entity, the ethnic nation state.

The legal reasoning of Crawford – and also von Bulmerincq and Cassese – conceals a hidden major premise that there is an international legal order. If there is no such order it will still be true that international law has not evolved rules to define the scope and exercise of a right to self-determination. This is not to deny that *as a matter of fact* – most states are reluctant to countenance the coming into existence of new states through force. Yet clearly this would not mean that there remains an existing legal order to be upheld. The most that a possible legal order could mean is that states in the possession of territory claim that the principle of effectivity with respect to their territory has legal character. This is all that analytical jurisprudence can say. Those groups that wish to dismember existing states will dispute the claim. The outcome will depend upon which party is the stronger. In fact, this logical discontinuity of argument reveals the huge vacuum in the theory of legitimacy – a corpus of argument by lawyers about justification of territorial title – to which reference has already been made.[97]

This is hardly satisfactory if one takes a global view of the contemporary State system. The conceptual point remains, as it was made by von Bulmerinq in the late nineteenth century, that there is no positive State practice, endorsed by states as general customary law, which says that in certain defined circumstances the community of states will compel a recalcitrant individual State to cede a right of secession to a part of its territory. However, this is merely to restate the unwillingness of states, or their incapacity to act collectively, to regulate the origin of states generally, and not particularly in connection with a limited right of secession. In no case involving the right of a people to self-determination can this enfeebled community of states act. Kashmir, Palestine, Tibet, the Western Sahara, Taiwan, and so on, are all just as much neglected as the Kurds, the Basques, or whatever. What can the community of states do to China over Tibet, to India over Kashmir, to Israel over Palestine? The international legal community has no enforcement mechanisms. On rare occasions, in times of acute crisis, usually at the end of world wars, this community does act fairly collectively and then the principle of self-determination does receive application. Otherwise, no matter how grave the consequences of not implementing the principle may be – and for Kashmir and Palestine the implications are very serious indeed – nothing is done. This failure is of no legal significance and cannot be taken to constitute evidence of a so-called State practice grounded in a so-called legal conviction or *opinio juris*.

Where two nations separate voluntarily, such as with Czechoslovakia recently, or Norway and Sweden at the beginning of the twentieth century, or Singapore and Malaysia in the 1960s, there was no hue and cry that such fragmentation of states constituted

---

97. Willoweit, *Rechtsgrundlagen der Territorialgewalt* esp.123–6, 129–31, 306–7, 349–50, 360–1.

a threat to international public order. The realisation of pragmatic international lawyers is simply that in many circumstances, if not always, attempted, unilateral secession will meet with armed resistance and therefore this particular form of the exercise of the right of self-determination is discouraged. The hesitation thereby evidenced does no more than indicate the harsh fact that where a secession is attempted no second country will usually be ready to wage a war against the first in order to help a part of it to break away. Where such a second country is willing to assist, that country, for example, India with Bangladesh, will not be condemned internationally as an aggressor, and will in turn have usually nothing whatsoever to fear from yet a third country intervening against it. It really is entirely in order for the reflective non-international lawyer to wonder about qualifying these reflections on international practice as an international legal jurisprudence, and it will be seen shortly that harsh reflections on international law do come from many liberal political theorists, particularly American, who do attempt to construct a philosophically credibly grounded system of international law, based upon principles of human rights and democracy.

SELF-DETERMINATION AS A HUMAN RIGHT AND THE DEVELOPMENT OF LIBERAL POLITICAL PHILOSOPHY OF INTERNATIONAL LAW

It is precisely the continued lack of an institutional framework to regulate disputes about self-determination peacefully that leads international lawyers to work pragmatically to resolve such questions through the mechanism of what they call internal self-determination, a right of peoples to make choices that stop short of changes of State boundaries, such as minority group rights and forms of internal autonomy. Even this process must be seen for what it is. It is not an internationally accepted normative framework for implementing a right of self-determination – as a matter of binding customary law – but merely a mechanism that progressive international lawyers try to use to persuade states to accept as a least bad option, and that many states are still refusing to accept in all parts of the world.

The one exception to the prohibition on secession that has some weight among international lawyers comes from the 1970 Declaration on Principles of Friendly Relations among States. This exception itself shows the confused thinking of international lawyers about the relationship between norms and institutional implementation. Severe exclusion from democratic participation in the institutions of the

State and grave and persistent violations of basic human rights are supposed to make possible a claim of a right to secession. The 1970 Declaration provides a saving clause, that the guarantee of territorial integrity applies to those states of which it can be said that they are conducting themselves:

> In compliance with the principle of equal rights and self-determination of peoples . . . and thus possessed of a government representing the whole people belonging to the territory without distinction as to race, creed or colour.

This is in practice a misleading way to describe a human right to secession. There is almost no prospect that a State that is not behaving in such a way will accept that its victims have a right to secede. If such a right exists in addition to whatever other rights are being disregarded, it will be disregarded as well. Indeed, the prospect that there is such a right could very well intensify the violation of the other rights, to the point of genocide. What the Declaration may well be alluding to pragmatically – but there is no textual basis for saying this – is that where such a situation of massive violations of the rights of a minority is occurring, the State in question will be likely to provoke an intervention from the international community to prevent further atrocities. In other words, the 'victim community' is already indicating a capacity to act and the State itself has already partially disintegrated. It may well be that at this point the international community, or a coalition of engaged states, decide that the most effective way to deal with the situation is to support independence or, equally, to insist upon the granting of much more autonomy than the central government would voluntarily accord. One may say that this is what has happened in Kosovo, where a number of EU Foreign Ministers have appealed to the formula in the 1970 Declaration.[98] The situation of the Kurds in Iraq or the Darfur situation could possibly develop in the same direction.

In other words, international law, law in world society, or the rule of law in international society have to incorporate a pragmatic concern with how generally agreed international principles need to be and can be applied, given the sometimes brutal reality that the origin and continuance of many states rests in violence and in practice world society cannot be mobilised to act in the face of such

98. A press communiqué in the *International Herald Tribune* 18/2/2008.

facts. None of this serves to exclude critical reflection, as a matter of principle, on the nature of the obstacles that actually stand in the way of the exercise of the right of self-determination, that is, the willingness of the dominant central State to use force to suppress the right.

Once the question is posed in this way, one can see immediately that the reasons for the absolute exclusion of the right of secession, by international lawyers as a matter of doctrine – *but supposed to be a matter of general customary law, which is of course a construction of doctrine and merely a particular way of interpreting international events* – do not apply at all in so-called Western democracies, bound by the rule of law, also of international law, which has as its most central principle, the prohibition of the use of force. As a positive law principle the prohibition of the use of force applies formally to relations among states, but as a substantive and material principle of law, it must apply to any concentrated use of military force to resolve differences a State has with any collective entities whether inside or outside of its territory, with the qualification of the right of self-defence against armed attack in the terms of Article 51 of the UN Charter. This is to distinguish concerted military operations of a certain level of intensity from security operations, for example, in response to individual acts of sporadic or terrorist violence. It would be inconceivable that a Western democracy would now respond to a unilateral declaration of independence from a subordinate territorial unit in the manner in which the military dictatorship in Nigeria did to the Biafran declaration of independence in 1967, or the Pakistan government did to East Pakistan after its elections in 1970, not to mention the US Union government to the Confederacy Secession of 1861. Whatever the ambiguity of the democratic credentials of some of these historical examples of candidates for secession, it is inconceivable that a Western liberal democracy would wage all-out war on the seceding territory that had not attacked it.

In other words, progressive or creative reflection on basic principles of international law must leave out of account that the origin of states is a matter of violent fact in much recorded history. It must also leave out of account that no enforcement mechanisms exist for the implementation of a right to self-determination of peoples, to compel the implementation of a so-called unilateral right of secession. Instead, the boundaries or limits to a unilateral right to secession are to be sought within the general system of collective and individual human rights, as these are understood in democracies that are generally committed to observing human rights.

This way of thinking jars profoundly with the analytical theory of international law that starts from the principle of effectivity, the juridification of established facts, *by virtue of the fact that they have become established.* It is particularly difficult within the discipline of analytical jurisprudence, which takes its inspiration from Hart's *Concept of Law,* to pose effectively the question of whether international law makes up a legal system. Analytical jurisprudence supposes the priority of whatever happens to be the dominant (that is, general or community) perspective of the chief officials of a legal order as against recalcitrant minorities or dissident members. This community priority is inevitable given the value scepticism that underlies the analytical approach. One can only understand obligation from the internal perspective of those submitting themselves to it. One can only take language at face value, asking how it is actually used in society.[99] Therefore, dissidents and minorities will be treated as outside the international legal order, terrorists, rogue states, or otherwise to be marginalised. There is no possible dialectic between the dominant legal opinion (in German, die herschende Meinung) and minority opinion. Sanctions may not be immediately effective, but the only meaning that can be given to international order is that the majority tries to impose it anyway. The need for consensus or unanimity in international law is 'saved' by the need for law to have an object against which it can assert its will. That object can easily be characterised as non-legal or anti-legal in some sense, but primarily in the sense that its opinions will receive no consideration.

For instance, H. L. A. Hart's *Concept of Law* (1994 [1961]) supposes the priority of whatever happens to be the dominant (that is, general or community) perspective of the chief officials of a legal order as opposed to recalcitrant minorities or dissident members.[100] This rigorous dichotomy is essential: either legal officials or outlaws (or 'bad sports' in more discrete versions of the story). The acquiescence of 'the rest' completes the picture. This curiously defined community (read: coalition) priority is inevitable given the value scepticism that underlies the analytical approach to law. That is, if all values are a matter of subjective preference, the only objectivity possible will come from a formal consensus of a majority, or of dominant key figures representing a majority. In this dominant analytical approach one understands legal obligation from the internal perspective of those applying

99. Hart, *The Concept of Law*, 116–17.
100. Ibid.

the law, namely the legal officials, especially the judges. What these officials have internalised as the demands of norms will be eventually enforced. Hart makes impossible any direct reference to human rights as attaching to a 'person as such'. This would be to treat rights as facts, as directly derived from a situation, that is, the condition and needs of a person. Instead, Hart praises Bentham for realising that the statement 'You have a right' has to refer to the existence of a law imposing a duty on some other person, 'and, moreover, that it must be a law which provides that the breach of the duty shall be visited with a sanction if you or someone else on your behalf so choose'.[101] Such an approach is effectively to eliminate all the elements from the idea of law except the use of force. The subject is dissolved into an addressee of norms, which destroys any possibility of human rights as real. Man exists as an artificial construction of the State. Values incorporated in norms cannot be true or false but only valid or invalid, because they rest on a social power that is capable of compelling the individual to behave in a certain way. This can only be group power, the contagion of custom.[102]

For Hart the problem has been confusing the explanation of the definition of law with the correspondence theory of truth. He praises Bentham for realising this.

> By refusing to identify the meaning of the word 'right' with any psychological or physical fact it correctly leaves open the question whether on any given occasion a person who has a right has in fact any expectation or power.

While Bentham puts the emphasis on punishment in a system of rights, Hart sees that many would prefer to speak of remedy: 'But I would prefer to show the special position of one who has a right by mentioning not the remedy but the choice which is open to one who has a right as to whether the corresponding duty shall be performed or not.'[103]

All of this sacralisation of the actual is anathema to liberal philosophy of international law. Given a picture of contemporary international society, which is dominated by the US, the question arises as

101. H. L. A. Hart, 'Definition and Theory in Jurisprudence', *LQR* 70 (1954) 37 at 48.
102. Michael Schooyans, *La face cachée de l'ONU* (2000) 136–41, with reference to Kelsen.
103. Hart, 'Definition and Theory', 48–9.

to how to understand the same subject as it is presented by contemporary American scholars, both lawyers and political philosophers. Such authors as Allen Buchanan and David Golove,[104] Fernando Teson,[105] and, of course, John Rawls himself,[106] present a closely reasoned agenda for what they call the democratisation of international society, setting out conditions for the legitimacy of states, which are marked by human rights standards that can themselves trigger grounds for forceful intervention by other states. The central point of these reflections on the need for a morality of international law is that a critical reflection is made of the State's claim to legitimacy in international law by virtue of the mere fact of control. As Buchanan and Golove put it,

> according to some normative views, including Rawls's in the *Law of Peoples*, only those states that meet the requirements of transnational justice, understood as respect for individual rights, are entitled to enjoy the rights and privileges of members of good standing of the international community.[107]

There are nuances in this debate as to whether so-called illiberal regimes should be tolerated, or whether pragmatic considerations should weigh against democratic regimes declaring war on authoritarian regimes.[108] There is no doubt that this school of thinking is very pertinent and stimulating for international law. It is probably based upon the single critical charge that it is not enough to assume, as traditional international law does, that officials and regimes of states are representative simply because they are in effective control.[109] Rawls himself puts it very clearly. He distinguishes international law from a 'law of peoples' that is a family of political concepts, including principles of law, of justice, and of the common good, all of which stem from a liberal concept of justice that is to be applied to international law.[110] This is not a blank check to use force

---

104. *The Oxford Handbook of Jurisprudence and Philosophy of Law* (2002), chapter 21, 'Philosophy of International Law.'
105. *A Philosophy of International Law* (1998).
106. *The Law of Peoples* (1999).
107. *Oxford Handbook*, 887.
108. See Teson, *Philosophy of International Law*, chapter 4, 'The Rawlsian Theory of International Law' esp. 115 and 120.
109. Ibid., 116.
110. John Rawls, *Le Droit des gens*, intro. Betrand Guillarme (1996) 51.

against non-democratic, non-liberal, or whatever, states, but it does mean that the only constraint is one of prudence, not law. So Teson says, quite frankly, 'Even in cases where the regime is overtly tyrannical (as in present-day China) waging war would be wrong because of the impossibility or prohibitive cost of victory.'[111] Teson's conclusion is that 'the relationship between liberal and illiberal states can only be a peaceful *modus vivendi* and not a community of shared moral beliefs and political commonalities.'[112]

These Americans' reflections on a need for a morality of international law are impossible for classical international law, with its doctrine of effectiveness, to resist intellectually. They force a radically new approach to the issue of effectivity as the principle of the international legal personality of states. In the United States, reflections among American liberal political theorists have given rise to a particular understanding of what may be called *The Philosophy of International Law.* This school will recognise only as legitimate, states that are constituted by democratic, representative institutions, that is, ones whose governing bodies are subject to regular and contested elections. In addition, such states should and normally would respect the rule of law and human rights. This is in contradistinction to the classical international law principle of efffectivity as the ground of the State, which this school rejects.[113] Such essentially analytical political theorists provide intellectual tools with which it is appropriate for Western European democratic states, operating within the framework of the Council of Europe, to approach the right of self-determination of peoples. Because of the blockage in classical international legal theory around the questions of institutional forms for and enforcement of human rights generally, it may be possible to look instead to liberal political theory for elaborations of the complexities of the right of self-determination of peoples, the manner in which it has to be reconciled with other human rights and, indeed, any inherent limits attaching to the right.

Democratic theory does recognise, as did the Canadian Supreme Court, in the *Reference re the Secession of Quebec,* that there are difficulties in recognising automatically the right of a territorial entity

111. Teson, *Philosophy of International Law*, 120.
112. Ibid.
113. See, in particular, Allen Buchanan and David Golove, 'Philosophy of International Law', chapter 21 of *The Oxford Handbook of Jurisprudence and Philosophy of Law* (2002); Fernando Teson, *A Philosophy of International Law* (1998); John Rawls, *The Law of Peoples* (1999).

within an already existing State simply to declare unconditionally a right of secession. First, it is still a matter of historical fact that most existing territorial boundaries are not demonstrably a matter of actual individual or collective choice. Equally, democratic theory does not assert the absolute principle that it must be actively shown that at some point in time the particular governing powers in existence territorially in a State have been the product of formal consent. Democratic theory, in this view, does not insist that every State must be able to point to an original social contract. Contractarian theory makes for an idealist heuristic principle and not for a historical fact.[114] This is a point at which democratic political theory is taking some account of the international law principle of effectiveness. Democratic theory has to recognise that the constellations of territorial communities actually existing are generally historical accretions that no one tries to justify systematically on the basis of individual or collective choice. The issue of secession is nearly always exceptional and arises in particular circumstances that call for involved historical explanations.

Nonetheless, the principle of democratic legality requires, as already argued, that its application should not be cut short by such a pragmatic consideration as that a central territorial entity – the dominant State – may be willing to resort to military force as a coercive measure to resolve its conflict with a subordinate territorial entity within its State territory. However, this does not exclude the central State authority from arguing that in a particular case no democratic principle requires recognition of a right of secession. This is where the true weakness of the claim to secession arises and not in the so-called customary international law that does not recognise a right to secession.

The difficulty is reflected in one aspect of the 1970 Declaration on Principles of Friendly Relations among States (DFRAS). It has argued that where there is a right of democratic participation – within boundaries in which one has been born anyway, that is, without choice – there is no rational argument that can justify a purely formal exercise of an unrestricted group right of self-determination. That is, normally a democratic State will never see secession as a way of exercising a democratic right, since all the members of the State are formally indistinguishable from one another. Arguments for national self-determination have traditionally been that there are

---

114. See especially, Allen Buchanan, *Justice, Legitimacy and Self-determination: Moral Foundations for International Law* (2004) esp. 234 et seq.

serious distinctions among groups. Indeed, some liberal political theorists argue that the right to self-determination arises from membership in an encompassing group. 'It is a group right, deriving from the value of a collective good, and as such opposed in principle to contractarian individualism approaches to politics or to well-being.'[115] The right of self-determination of peoples is a right of national self-determination. Liberal political theorists argue passionately for the collective group right to self-determination, precisely on the ground that a member of such a national group that is not able to exercise collective political rights in the collectivity into which he is born, will suffer severe human deprivation, risk loss of respect, and be politically vulnerable.[116] Hence the group itself is the best judge of what it needs and, consequently, it need hardly have to prove oppression.[117] The authors conclude:

> [T]he interests of members of an encompassing group in the self-respect and prosperity of the group are among the most vital human interests. Given their importance, their satisfaction is justified even at a considerable cost to other interests.[118]

So for the sake of national self-determination one would have to move beyond the claim of a formal right to democratic expression of will for a group and argue that a minority group has a specific ethnic or cultural identity, which it can only exercise effectively through resort to the full institution of an independent State. This is to go back to the historical origin of most European states, which, as has been noted already, international law doctrine has not integrated into its construction of an international legal order. There has been a sea change of an epistemological nature in the understanding of the State that the burden of the classical period – that is, until the French Revolution – still appears to impose upon doctrine. In the classical epoch Law, as also any other significant political meaning/symbol, was defined by the detached, mysterious Sovereign (of Descartes and Hobbes) in an exclusive, authoritative fashion.

---

115. Avishai Margalit and Joseph Raz, 'National Self-determination', *The Journal of Philosophy* LXXXVII(9) (September 1990) 439 at 456–7. Of course, the adjectives 'legal' and 'political' are not terms of art at the level of philosophical reflection. For instance, Joseph Raz holds a chair of legal philosophy.
116. Ibid., 443–4.
117. Ibid., 457.
118. Ibid., 461.

This is the perspective that Cassese reproduces in laying down the dogma that it is for the State to determine the scope of the right of self-determination.[119] Now it is recognised, following Bartelson's stress on the early nineteenth-century revolution of language, that the exercise of naming – of which legal naming, the acceptance of obligation, is merely a part – is directly related to language and the history of the nation. It is no longer a matter that mysterious sovereigns, detached and separate from society, can determine meanings by legal fiat, by using words to reflect their exclusive monopoly of physical power and the capacity to coerce. Instead, man emerges himself as the sovereign creator of his representations and his concepts. Words are not there, as with Descartes, to represent passively, as if mirroring, something external to the subject. It is the activity of the subject itself, which creates its own world of experience and gives words to it. Language reflects the experience of an individual but also of the tradition of a collective political being. Therefore, language becomes subject to interpretation. Language in its dense reality is able to tell us the history of the institutions signified by the words. The world of institutions is made by men and therefore can be reached as a mode of self-knowledge.[120] The agenda of this escape of meaning from the sovereign State at the international level is something of which international lawyers have been conscious for a long time, even if they cannot give the change a clear theoretical focus.

The implication of Bartelson's distinction between the language of State security and the situation that followed the early nineteenth-century revolution in national languages, is that now *we all become responsible ourselves for the meaning of the language we use.*[121] Bartelson suggests the inevitability of accepting peoples, not states, as a starting point for the definition of international society. Since the revolution of linguistic nationalism, of Herder and Vico, there is no point of return. The exercise of giving a name, of which juridical recognition is only a part, refers directly to language and, with it, to the history of the nation. As we have seen above, Bartelson has argued that there are no mysterious powers, detached from society, which can determine a signification by decree, by the employment

---

119. Supra, *Self-determination of Peoples* 122. Territorial integrity and sovereign rights are of paramount importance, 'indeed they have been considered as concluding any debate on the subject'. Cassese then cites post-decolonisation literature and practice.
120. Jens Bartelson, *A Genealogy of Sovereignty* (1995) 188–201.
121. See already Carty, *Philosophy of International Law* 16.

of words that reflect their monopoly of power and their capacity to coerce. It is obvious that one can distinguish the power from the authority of the majority controlling a State apparatus. This is because, instead of the State as an abstraction or even fetish, it is man who emerges from the subordination to the prince to become the sovereign of his own representations and of his concepts. The words are not *there*, as they were for the absolute monarch, for example, the Bourbons, to represent a reality that remains passive, the language remaining as a mirror to reflect something external to the subject. It is the activity of the subject itself that creates its own world of experience and that gives itself the words with which to express itself. So language is a reflection of the experience of the individual and of the collectivity to which it belongs. Thus, it is language that becomes the subject of interpretation. Language in its dense reality can explain to us the history of the institutions, which are rooted in that language. The world of institutions is made by men and thus one can arrive at a comprehension of them *through a knowledge of the self*.[122] It is this world of institutions unified by language that gives rise to a right of *national* self-determination of states.

It is precisely this sea change in the legal epistemology of nation and State to which international legal doctrine can react with no better than Cassese's opinion that the paramount importance of the State 'concludes any debate' on the right of national self-determination. In other words, international lawyers have no ingenuity whatsoever with which to resolve the contradictions that may arise between the new nation state paradigm and the old classical State.

Perhaps given the inevitability of serious conflict when the question of secession is posed, even in the 'democratic West', one may speculate that autonomy or secession movements are now wary of using 'ethnic' or explicitly nationalist arguments. Ethnicity comes merely from the idea of *ethnos,* that a group has a particular way of 'doing things' and that if an individual in such a group cannot exercise an effective right of participation in such a group then in practice all of the other rights of the individual are hollowed out and the individual person seriously loses the possibility of respect and dignity. However, the prospect of serious conflict where the issue of secession is posed, argues for a theory of legitimacy to ground it that should be as inclusive and as formal as possible. The paradox, recognised on

---

122. Carty, *Philosophy of International Law* 105, and Bartelson, *Genealogy of Sovereignty* 188–201.

all sides of the argument, is that claims of legitimacy when they are now rooted in ethnicity are difficult to prove in absolute terms and have the potential to be socially and therefore politically very divisive within the subordinate territorial entity. This makes it all the easier for a central State to oppose a secessionist national self-determination argument with the cosmopolitan liberal argument that the most desirable form of democratic-liberal human rights theory is that all existing territorial entities should work towards ensuring the maximum participation and welfare within existing State boundaries, while always working to reduce the significance of these boundaries, through inter-State co-operation, as far as possible.

Nonetheless, a further radical or purely formal democratic response to the *ethnos –cosmopolitanism polarisation* is to insist that the most basic principle of democracy is that there is no political or legal authority that can stand over a territorial entity in order to question the wisdom or even the usefulness of its exercise of its democratic choice. The entity may choose to include for itself the most extreme option of external self-determination, subject to its continued duty to respect basic human rights and probably also an equal right, in turn, of any subordinate group within that seceding entity, to exercise, in turn, its right of full, external self-determination. In other words, in the radical or purely formal democratic perspective, to exercise a right, in a free vote, of secession a territorial entity does not have to demonstrate a prior density of cultural/ethnic distinctiveness. This may in fact exist and may, as a matter of political sociology, explain why the entity wishes to have the opportunity to express its will democratically, for secession. However, in terms of democratic theory, all that is necessary is a significant expression of regional institutional will, that they wish to vote for options that logically at the most extreme, include the right to declare a unilateral secession.[123]

Obviously, this position includes the much milder option of a claim to independence that is conditional upon negotiation to take account of the various conflicting interests of the central government or other provinces. However, it does not include lesser options such as modified forms of association with the central government, which the latter does not prefer to enter into, as that is, by its nature, an attempted violation by the subordinate territorial entity of the right

123. This line of argument is most clearly presented by Harry Beran, 'A Liberal Theory of Secession', *Political Studies* XXXII (1984) 21–31 and 'More Theory of Secession', *Political Studies* XXXVI (1988) 316–23.

of self-determination of the central government. The latter cannot, in turn, be obliged to enter into any different type of association with the subordinate territorial entity.

This radical, purely formal concept of self-determination of peoples is reflected in the actual and relevant recent practice of Western democratic governments, and, arguably, in normal circumstances, everywhere. It was, as already noted, the choice of the Canadian Supreme Court to say that where there was a clearly expressed wish of the Quebec people to negotiate independence, there was a constitutional duty on the part of Canada, as a liberal, federal democracy bound by the rule of law, to negotiate with Quebec, and if, in good faith, no agreement could be reached, that greatly strengthened the expectation of Quebec to be sympathetically received into the international community.

In this view, the option given to the people of Northern Ireland could be treated as part of a process of decolonisation. Equally, the solution to the Northern Ireland question was to give Northern Ireland the right to choose by referendum whether to remain part of the UK or to join the Irish Republic. However, it has to be remembered that the official UK position has been that the North of Ireland was an integral part of the United Kingdom, predominantly inhabited by UK citizens of the same ethnic origins as the mainland British. The UK was giving the population of the territory the option to decide that they were now, or always had been, Irish. In other words, the UK was giving a part of its own population the option of leaving the State if they chose to do so in a clearly expressed wish in a referendum.[124] It is now accepted by both the UK and Ireland in the 1998 Agreement, that the resolution of the status of the regional entity of Northern Ireland is a matter of its choice, just as its association with either the UK or the Republic of Ireland is also a matter of their choice. It cannot become a part of the Republic of Ireland unless its people also vote for this solution.

The Kosovo independence dispute has characteristics that may appear to put it beyond the parameters of the democratic international polity. The EU Foreign Ministers supporting independence have justified it on the grounds of the serious human rights violations in Kosovo

---

124. Ibid. In this view Ireland had always until 1922 been in a perfect political union with the UK and its citizens also full UK citizens. After 1922, when the Free State became virtually independent, the Northern territory retained the status that the whole of the island had enjoyed up until then.

by Serbia, which made continuous association of the two entities untenable. A press communiqué, in the *International Herald Tribune* of 18 February 2008, reported the lead being taken by Britain, France, and Germany, that 'Kosovo served as a rare exemption from international law, saying its unilateral declaration was justified by Belgrade's oppression and Serb leaders' rejection of a negotiated final status for the region'. That statement made it possible for some EU nations to recognise Kosovo's independence as an exception to the rule of 'territorial integrity' of nations under international law. In turn, Spain said that it would not recognise Kosovo's declaration of independence, because it was a unilateral act that does not respect international law.

The difficulty with the argument of the EU Troika may well be the one of authoritatively determining levels of guilt on the part of Serbia, either in the short term, since 1989 or in the history of the region since, for example, 1941, when the population of Kosovo was 50 per cent Serbian ethnically. Nor is it easy to see how objectively one could determine who, between Kosovans and Serbs, would be responsible for a failure of negotiations between them. It seems much more compatible with democratic principle to argue that where a historically easily defined territorial entity chooses its independence this must be accepted. There would evidently be a duty as well as a right on every side, to negotiate the modalities of independence and to ensure equitable resolution of the inconveniences following from independence, but it is the right to independence that remains paramount, and not some archaic monarchical doctrine of territorial integrity, left over from the time of the Bourbons and the Hapsburgs.

It may be added, as a personal caveat or comment, that I see no intellectually convincing point or even political likelihood of a regional territorial entity claiming or exercising a right of external self-determination, unless it is motivated by some kind of belief that it incorporates a nation in the traditional ethnic, historical, or cultural sense of which Margalit and Raz write. Such a nation must want to set up the full institutions of a State because it considers this much to be necessary for it to find full expression of its particular identity as a nation. Of course, the formal democratic aspect of the expression of nationhood must also be satisfied and, of course, it is not open to outside powers to dispute a subjective self-consciousness of nationhood that is thought to exist and is formally expressed, but where the region is altogether without the national argument, the teleology of the exercise becomes unclear. Without the solid identity of the nation, there is no objective need for the institutions of statehood and probably also no prospect of convincing the regional population – when it comes to the crunch – that independence is necessary in an otherwise post-modern, globalised world. It is the marks of nationhood that distinguish the regional population from that of the rest of the State and from the central government. Without such objective and relevant characteristics, there is no need for the region to obtain independence.

FURTHER READING

Allott, Philip, *The Health of Nations: Society and Law Beyond the State* (2002).

Aron, Raymond, *Peace and War: A Theory of International Relations,* with a new introduction by D. J. Mahony and B. C. Anderson (2003).

Buchanan, Allen, *Justice, Legitimacy and Self-determination: Moral Foundations for International Law* (2004).

Carty, Anthony, *Was Ireland Conquered? International Law and the Irish Question* (1996).

Cassese, Antonio, *Self-determination of Peoples: A Legal Reappraisal* (2005).

Chomsky, Noam, *Who Rules the World* (2016).

Crawford, James, *The Creation of States in International Law* (2006).

Hägerström, Axel, *Inquiries into the Nature of Law and Morals,* Karl Olivecrona (ed.), C. D. Bond (trans.) (1953).

Hart, H. L. A., *The Concept of Law,* 2nd edition (1997).

Johns, Fleurs (ed.), *International Legal Personality* (2010).

O'Donovan, Oliver, *The Ways of Judgment* (2005).

Rawls, John, *The Law of Peoples* (1999).

Teson, Fernando, *A Philosophy of International Law* (1998).

3

The Existence of States and the Use of Force

INTRODUCTION

As the existence of states has been traditionally seen as a matter of fact, a meta-legal fact, and since states depend first on themselves for their security, and second, on collective security that cannot be universal, reflection on the sources of international law on the use of force cannot be confined to a so-called customary law, State practice, or even the UN Charter. The question remains, then, what should be the purpose of a chapter on the use of force in a book of the philosophy of international law. A philosophy of the subject can ask why the use of force occurs and how it could, or even should, be limited. The starting point has to be the nature of the personality of the collective subject, its internal dynamic, especially propensity to conflict. The standard theory of personality from Hobbes, through Vattel and Hegel to the present, provides a conceptual framework within which the present idea of the State as a legal fact, within an international law order, is embedded. Therefore, the task of international legal philosophy, assuming it is not happy with this framework, is to reflect upon how this jumble bag of security neurosis, following the collapse of the medieval European Christian order, can be pushed in the direction of a less neurotic view of world society.

There is inbuilt into the very idea of the State a propensity to violence, because of its ontological lack of grounding. This expresses itself in the domestic–foreign dichotomy, rendering the very possibility of global bonding problematic. Hobbsean amoralism and Vattelian solipcism render the crisis ever more acute. Finally, the Hegelian master–slave dialectic shows the inevitability of incessant rivalry-driven struggle for supremacy. This rivalry spills over into the economic sphere.

It is possible to tackle the issue of the use of force as a personality-based problem both at a general and a specific level. At the general, purely theoretical level, it is a matter of attempting to reconstruct the theory of the State as a matter of the history of ideas. The direction taken here will be for an ethical phenomenology of personality, based primarily on the work of Paul Ricoeur, but considering also James Der Derian. At a more specific level it is a matter of engaging with innumerable offshoots of the neurotic world order in terms of concrete historical developments. In this chapter, on this occasion it is intended to deal with several: the Liberal International Legal Order as inherently aggressive, the History of Western Engagement in the Middle East and Islamic Jihad, the Role of Lawyers in Advising Targeted Killing and a Return to Classical Legal Reasoning. The purpose of the last illustrative specific topic is to show the essential transparency of the problem of the use of force in terms of personal, individual human responsibility.

However, before one proceeds to these two further stages, it is intended to press home the point that there is little to be gained from continuing to place the jurisprudence of the International Court of Justice at the centre of intellectual concern of international lawyers. That jurisprudence is itself trapped in the structure of a discipline that does not understand or accept that there is no functioning international law method of penetrating State practice. In addition, the mistaken view of the State as a legal fact, rather than a meta-legal fact, means that international lawyers simply do not understand how the so-called international community of states, by its very nature, cannot devise unconsciously, customary rules of law to deal with their existential crises, where their State of panic makes the prospect of unity of vision inconceivable.

AUTO-INTERPRETATION AND THE POSITIVE INTERNATIONAL LAW ON THE USE OF FORCE BY STATES

The Jurisprudence on the Use of Force before the International Court of Justice

A number of recent landmark cases in the jurisprudence of the ICJ illustrate these difficulties. In the 1986 case *Certain Military Activities Concerning Nicaragua* the ICJ affirmed a formal principle with respect to sources of law. The mere fact that states declare their recognition of certain rules does not make these rules customary law without the essential role required by Article 38 of its Statute, played by general practice.[1] This means that there should be a practice to confirm a legal discourse. There must be conduct of states consistent with rules, or at

1. *ICJ Reports* (1986) 1, paragraph 184 of judgment.

least inconsistent behaviour should generally be treated as breaches of the rule.[2]

The difficulty facing the Court was fundamental. There appeared to be a general rule, recognised in numerous declarations, that intervention in the internal affairs of states is illegal. However, interventions are frequent, especially by the US – in this case, in Nicaragua. The Court decided, first, that the rule existed, and then asked whether exceptions had been recognised.[3] Then, it changed the object of analysis away from actual practice, in the sense of externally observed conduct, to the delicate subjective element, declarations of opinion concerning conduct. The principle of intentionality is introduced as decisive, although the starting point of the Court's analysis was that it could not be given separate analysis.

So how did the Court treat 'actual practice'? The US authorities clearly state grounds for intervening in a foreign State for reasons

> connected with, for example, the domestic policies of that country, its ideology, the level of its armaments, or the direction of its foreign policy. The Court converted these statements into what it called statements of international policy, and not an assertion of rules of existing international law.[4] [In this case] . . . the US has not claimed its intervention, which it justified in this way on the political level, was also justified on the legal level . . . [where it] has justified its intervention expressly and solely by reference to the 'classic' rule involved, namely collective self-defense against armed attack.[5]

Here the Court is speculating about State intentions that are not completely transparent. The Court can freely classify as political/insignificant, or legal/significant, what it likes about the intentions of states, which the Court, is, in any case, projecting on to the states. States are unwilling to give formal, principled declarations in favour of their actions. The US is in fact giving substantial material support and training to armed bands that are attacking a foreign State. The US was claiming the right to come to the aid of an opposition group (the Contras) in a country led by a one-party communist regime (the Sandinistas), which had undertaken to hold free elections at a meeting of Organization of American States (OAS) Foreign Ministers. It had not done so. The Court, as it were, declassified this undertaking

---

2. Ibid., paragraph 186.
3. Ibid., paragraph 206.
4. Ibid., paragraph 207.
5. Ibid., paragraph 208.

as itself political/insignificant, a pledge made not only to the OAS, but also to the people of Nicaragua. However, 'the Court cannot find an instrument with legal force, whether unilateral or synallagmatic, whereby Nicaragua has committed itself in respect of the principle or methods of holding elections'.[6] Only legal force, as characterised by the Court, is significant.

How far can the Court take its investigation into the *real intentions of states, or other collective entities*? The Court puts its position modestly: 'nor has it authority to ascribe to states legal views which they do not themselves advance'.[7] This limitation is particularly important when the Court is in fact equating the State of Nicaragua with the national *junta* of reconstruction (the Sandinistas). A US Congressional finding was that the Nicaraguan government has taken significant steps towards establishing a totalitarian communist dictatorship. The Court responded:

> [A]dherence by a State to any particular doctrine does not constitute a violation of customary international law; to hold otherwise would make nonsense of the fundamental principle of State sovereignty, on which the whole of international law rests. Consequently, Nicaragua's domestic policy options, even assuming that they correspond to the description given of them by the Congress finding, cannot justify on the legal plane the various actions of the respondent complained of.[8]

Normally, legal intention (that is, seriousness) can be inferred from action in an area or field, which is itself taken to be serious. Where the US gives military support to opposition parties to overthrow a communist regime in a Latin American State, it can only be supposed that it is extremely serious about what it is doing. It is difficult to see what is gained by the Court treating some State intentions (whether of the US or of Nicaragua) as political and others as legal. This appears to be a 'head in the sand' approach, which denies the international law profession the analytical framework to grasp fully the *intentionalities* of the parties engaged in a conflict, thereby penetrating beyond the corporate veil of the State to find the subjective elements within it.

The ICJ was faced with an issue of high politics. This should provoke reflection upon the question of whether the traditional analytical tool of general customary law is suitable for the elements of idealism and realism, altruism and State egotism that are at play in

6. Ibid., paragraph 261.
7. Ibid., paragraph 207.
8. Ibid., paragraph 263.

the legal phenomena of international relations. The US determines that its interest or national security cannot tolerate the close proximity of a new neighbour (Sandinista Nicaragua) dedicated, in its view, to an irreconcilably hostile ideology. It is very problematic for the legal positivist to ask himself categorically, in each atomistic instance, whether the State has or has not acted on the basis of a legal conviction. Yet it is inevitable that a State will form some ideal view of what it needs to undertake for its own security. Is there no analytical framework within which one can assess critically how the State attempts to do this?

It is logically conceivable for the Court to define a particular framework as legal – an absolute prohibition of the use of force to intervene in a civil war (a rule that certainly does not exist) – and then to assert that the intentions of the State violating the rule evidence policy rather than law and are therefore not legally relevant, that is, to the issue of whether this key State is engaging in a 'State practice' that is legally significant. In this case it is not necessary for the Court to *understand the State as a collective phenomenon.* Nor is it necessary for the Court to be concerned with the effectiveness of the legal norms that it considers are being violated. It need not reflect upon the destabilising effects of cold war ideology on the State system, because it is not concerned with the question of whether international law is actually taken into account in the foreign policy of a superpower. These are not *legal considerations.* However, a philosophy of international law is concerned directly with the actual use of force in international society, its logic or root causes and whether there is any possibility of constraining it. The Court's judgment in this case is part of the picture and it is also appropriate to explore whether the judgment had any impact on State conduct.

A later landmark case, *Legality of the Threat or Use of Nuclear Weapons* (1996), shows, to an acute degree, the intensity of contradiction between realism and idealism in analysis of what is, above all, the State practice of liberal, democratic Western states. The difficulty with this case was how to square the commitment of states to principles of humanitarian law and, at the same time, their reliance upon nuclear deterrence as a central part of their strategic defence policy. The aim of the latter is the elimination of large centres of enemy population, indeed the elimination of entire enemy societies, while the basic principle of humanitarian law is that there is a distinction between combatants and non-combatants, that war must remain limited to military defeat of the enemy.

The majority opinion of the Court provides further evidence of the distinct coyness with which positivists grapple with 'the realities' of the 'practice' of contemporary states. From the beginning, the Court was aware that the question existed of whether the present international law system had relevant rules on the issue of threat or use of nuclear weapons. It responded that its function was not to legislate, but to state the existing law. Somehow it could also say, 'An entirely different question is whether the Court, under the constraints placed upon it as a judicial organ, will be able to give a complete answer to the question asked of it. However, that is a different matter from a refusal to answer at all' (paragraph 18). What the Court may mean by such a promise of self-restraint became clear in its consideration of the exercise of the right of self-defence. Quoting itself in the *Certain Military Activities in and against Nicaragua Case,* it said that self-defence 'would warrant only measures which are proportional to the armed attack and necessary to respond to it, a rule well established in customary international law' (paragraph 41). Certain states argued that the very nature of nuclear weapons and the high probability of escalation of nuclear exchanges mean that there is an extremely strong risk of devastation. Then the Court went on to make a remarkable statement about the sharing of responsibilities between a reviewing Court and sovereign states, in the post-Vattelian subjectivist international legal order:

> The risk factor is said to negate the possibility of the condition of proportionality being complied with. The Court does not find it necessary to embark upon the quantification of such risks; nor does it need to enquire into the question whether tactical nuclear weapons exist which are sufficiently precise to limit those risks: it suffices for the Court to note *that the very nature of all nuclear weapons and the profound risks associated therewith are further considerations to be borne in mind by states believing they can exercise a nuclear response in self-defence in accordance with the requirements of proportionality.* (paragraph 43; emphasis added)

That is, the Court recognises, as would Combacau and Sur, that the issue of self-defence of a 'modern' State in the context of a nuclear threat (now immeasurably enlarged by the prospect of such weapons falling into the hands of 'terrorists') is a matter lying entirely within its discretion and not reviewable by a Court. This is all the Court has to say about the compatibility of the strategy of nuclear deterrence with the principles of the UN Charter, that is, whether as a means of self-defence the threat or use of such weapons 'would necessarily violate the principles of necessity and proportionality' (paragraph 48).

The Court is on stronger ground when it says that the illegality of the use of certain weapons as such does not result from an absence of authorisation, but, on the contrary, is formulated in terms of prohibition (paragraph 52). In the past two decades a great many negotiations have been conducted regarding nuclear weapons, but they have not resulted in a treaty of general prohibition of the same kind as for bacteriological and chemical weapons (paragraph 58). A key issue is the legal significance of the Treaty on the Non-Proliferation of Nuclear Weapons. Those states supporting the legality of the use of the weapons say that the very logic of the treaty is on their side. The treaty evidences the acceptance of the possession of nuclear weapons by the five nuclear weapon states. '[T]o accept the fact that those states possess nuclear weapons is tantamount to recognising that such weapons can be used in certain circumstances' (paragraph 61). The Court concludes that such treaties 'could therefore be seen as foreshadowing a future general prohibition of the use of such weapons, but they do not constitute such a prohibition by themselves' (paragraph 62).

Surprisingly, the Court distinguishes this interpretation of treaty practice from customary law, which it gives the usual definition of actual practice and *opinio juris* of states (paragraph 64). Some States refer to a consistent practice of non-utilisation of nuclear weapons since 1945 as an *opinio juris* that such non-use evidences a conviction that use would be illegal (paragraph 64). Other States invoke the doctrine and practice of deterrence as showing that States have 'always reserved the right to use those weapons in the exercise of the right to self-defense against an armed attack threatening their vital security interests'. So, non-use merely means the circumstances that may justify their use have not arisen (paragraph 66). There follows an extraordinary pronouncement of the Court, which shows that the doctrine of positivist customary law can hardly work to register virtually universal unconscious consensus in situations of existential crisis:

> The Court does not intend to pronounce here upon the practice known as the 'policy of deterrence'. It notes that it is a fact that a number of states adhered to that practice during the greater part of the Cold War and continue to adhere to it. Furthermore, the members of the international community are profoundly divided on the matter of whether non-recourse to nuclear weapons over the past fifty years constitutes the expression of an *opinio juris*. Under these circumstances the Court does not consider itself able to find that there is such an *opinio juris*. (paragraph 67)

It is, as Habermas has pointed out, a matter of the sociology of knowledge, that judges, State-nominated officials, will not be able to afford a critical, reflective view of their State's practice. Judge Schwebel, a former US Department of State Legal Adviser, gives a separate opinion, also on the significance of the 'history' of diplomatic and military practice. Schwebel argues, pointedly but in general terms, that State practice demonstrates that nuclear weapons have been manufactured and deployed by States for fifty years. In that deployment inheres a threat of possible use. Nuclear powers have affirmed that they are legally entitled to use nuclear weapons in certain circumstances and to threaten use:

> They have threatened their use by the hard facts and inexorable implications of the possession and deployment of nuclear weapons; by a posture of readiness to launch nuclear weapons 365 days a year, 24 hours of every day; by the military plans, strategic and tactical, developed and sometimes publicly revealed by them; and, in a very few international crises, by threatening the use of nuclear weapons. In the very doctrine and practice of deterrence, the threat of the possible use of nuclear weapons inheres . . . This is the practice of five of the world's major Powers . . . significantly supported for almost 50 years by their allies and other states sheltering under their nuclear umbrellas . . . It is obvious that the alliance structures that have been predicated upon the deployment of nuclear weapons accept the legality of their use in certain circumstances. (pp. 1 and 2)

Schwebel goes on to discuss at length (pp. 9–12) one instance of an implied threat of the use of nuclear weapons that he considers had a positive effect in ensuring international public order in terms of international law. In the case of *Desert Storm*, the 1991 war against Iraq, the US feared that Iraq may deploy chemical and biological weapons against its opponents. The US Secretary of State reported, after the event: 'I purposely left the impression that the use of chemical or biological agents by Iraq could invite tactical nuclear retaliation' (p. 10). Schwebel relies on a further *Washington Post* article for evidence that the Iraqi authorities translated the various ambiguous, but grievous and devastating US threats to mean that it would respond to Iraq's use of chemical and biological weapons with nuclear arms (p. 11). Schwebel concludes that this affords an example of how the UN Charter was sustained rather than transgressed by a nuclear threat. The threat may have made a critical contribution to the UN triumph. This is not a case of the end justifying the means. 'It rather demonstrates that, in some circumstances, the threat of the use of nuclear weapons – as long as they remain weapons unproscribed by international law – may be both lawful and rational' (p. 12).

While everything Schewbel says may be accurate as far as it goes and is much more exhaustive than the Majority Opinion, it is also influenced by the dimension of structures inherited from history, which existing doctrine cannot take into account. The issue of the legality of nuclear deterrence may be different from that of superpower, ideologically driven interventions. However, the existence of nuclear weapons for more than half a century, and the apparent fact that their development cannot be reversed, points in the direction of structures that present generations have simply inherited. The general importance of this fact is that events of the use of force usually form part of wider structures of events in which moral choices are now frozen in time. This is generally the case with the so-called war against terrorism and the entire Western conflict with so-called militant Islam, not to mention the case of the founding and preservation of Israel. Hence, the Nuclear Weapons controversy may not be usefully posed in conventional positivist legal terms. That is to say where X should observe a specific rule at a particular point in time – assuming such a rule to exist – supposes a level of freedom that does not exist in reality. For instance, the question of whether targeted killing by drones in the Middle East is legal is too late to pose if the departure of Western states from the Middle East is not even a matter present in Western consciousness.

So the following deliberations are of general relevance to discussions of the use of force. How can liberal democratic Western states embark upon security strategies that include a willingness to obliterate entire societies, as a way of ensuring one's own security? The answers lie in historical processes. The foundations for total war waged with nuclear weapons, bringing with them the complete destruction of one's enemy, were firmly laid by 1945. They amount to nothing more or less than the continuation of strategies used during the last war, resting upon an ideology of total war. Doctrines associated with nuclear deterrence come later and have not modified the essential strategic assumptions or what the armed forces are actually organised to do. Questions of the credibility of the deterrence, the morality of a conditional threat to carry out an act in itself admitted to be immoral, and so on, are raised when there is already a commitment to a type of warfare in which the absolute destruction of one's opponent is regarded as normal. Certain strategic practices have become institutionalised. One has still to trace out historically and recognise exactly where responsibility for this institutionalisation rests.[9]

---

9. T. Carty, 'The Origins of the Doctrine of Deterrence and the Legal Status of Nuclear Weapons', in *Ethics and Defence,* H. Davis (ed.) (1986) 132.

It is inherently difficult for a judiciary to consider anything other than individual, or collective, responsibility of contemporary actors. Yet the law has to find some way of facing issues of historical responsibility. It is not enough to start from where we are now. Nuclear strategies are embedded in wider, institutionalised military-economic strategies. It is simplistic to say that one has to balance considerations of humanitarian law with legitimate claims to use certain instruments of self-defence, when it was decided long ago that the most economical way to wage war is to bring it to the enemy civilian population. No piecemeal reversal of policies is conceivable. We are faced not so much with individual, present moral dilemmas as with the baleful consequences of wrong actions. The extent of the crisis is expressed by the American sociologist Robert Nisbet. He concludes his study of what he calls the lure of military society thus: 'that only events presently unforeseeable in nature and scope . . . could possibly arrest the present drive of militarism in the Western world'.[10]

The complexity of the issues includes the following two elements. First, there has been a remarkable lack of concern in the West about the scale of casualties that nuclear deterrence could cause, suggesting a general public denial psychosis that a judicial process could hardly be a suitable forum to penetrate. Second, one needs to understand the responsibility that German and Japanese aggression bears for a dehumanisation process in which the allies, in turn, implicated themselves when they undertook total war. Garrison captures this dimension in the provocative remark that the conflagration with Germany was the outcome of psychic conditions that were universal 'only while the Germans threatened a single people with genocide'; the 'nuclear arms race threatens the entire human race with extinction'.[11]

Schwebel come closer than the Court to facing the implications of nuclear deterrence in State practice. Yet his own historical approach lacks the moral perspective that reveals how moral choices are already frozen in practice. The balance of humanitarian law and the law of self-defence has long ago been decided in favour of the latter. A legal analysis, which is to challenge or even understand this, requires a dimension of *opinio juris* in State practice that recognises the contextual and structural dimension of states as historical communities.

---

10. R. Nisbet, *Twilight of Authority* 191, quoted in T. Carty, 'Legality and Nuclear Weapons: Doctrines of Nuclear Warfighting', Davis, *Ethics and Defence* 152.
11. J. Garrison, *The Darkness of God: Theology after Hiroshima* (1982) 29–33 quoted by the author in Davis, *Ethics and Defence* 153.

The final general issue that needs to be clarified with respect to the Advisory Opinion concerns its unreflective reception of the Vattelian radically subjective notion of State sovereign. At first, it looks as if the Court accepts objective humanitarian constraints on states. The Court puts a large weight of argument on the compatibility of nuclear weapons with the principles of humanitarian law. It says that it has not found a conventional rule of general scope or a customary rule specifically proscribing the threat or use of nuclear weapons (paragraph 74). However, the fact that humanitarian law pre-dates the advent of nuclear weapons, and that its development through conventions did not explicitly take the weapons into account, does not preclude the application of the law to the weapons. Any other conclusion, says the Court,

> would be incompatible with the intrinsically humanitarian character of the legal principles in question which permeates the entire law of armed conflict and applies to all forms of warfare and to all kinds of weapons . . . In this respect it seems significant that the thesis that the rules of humanitarian law do not apply to the new weaponry, because of the newness of the later, has not been argued in the present proceedings. (paragraph 86)

However, when the Court came to consider how the principles would be applied, it observed that none of the states advocating legality in certain circumstances had indicated what would be the precise circumstances justifying such use, nor whether such limited use would not tend to escalate into all-out-use of high-yield nuclear weapons. Once again the Court restrained itself: 'This being so, the Court does not consider that it has a sufficient basis for a determination on the validity of this view' (paragraph 94). Conversely, the Court would not make a determination that the use of nuclear weapons would be illegal in any circumstances due to their inherent and total incompatibility with the law applicable to armed conflict. The weapons would scarcely seem to be reconcilable with the law. Nevertheless, 'the Court considers that it does not have sufficient elements to enable it to conclude with certainty that the use of nuclear weapons would necessarily be at variance with the principles and rules applicable in armed conflict in any circumstances' (paragraph 95).

In fact, it is the subjectivity of liberal, post-Vattelian international law that is determining the Court's conclusion. The Court cannot lose sight of the fundamental right of every State to survival, and thus its right to resort to self-defence, in accordance with Article 51 of the Charter, when its survival is at stake. Nor can the Court 'ignore the practice referred to as "policy of deterrence", to which an appreciable section of the international community adhered for many years' (paragraph 96). This leads the Court to say, effectively, that because it cannot penetrate the meaning or significance of State practice, it cannot say whether the use of nuclear weapons would be illegal where states are actually going to invoke the right:

> Accordingly, in view of the present state of international law viewed as a whole, as examined above by the Court, *and of the elements of fact at its disposal, the Court is led to observe that it cannot reach a definitive conclusion as to the legality or illegality of the use of nuclear weapons by a state in an extreme circumstance of self-defence, in which its very survival would be at stake.* (paragraph 97; emphasis in the original)

This statement is not a *non-liquit*. The Court is saying that the highest purpose of international law is that each individual State in world society should be the final decision-maker where it considers its existence at stake.

Judge Higgins comments that at no point does the Court engage in a systematic application of the relevant law to the use or threat of nuclear weapons. 'It reaches its conclusion without the benefit of detailed analysis. An essential step in the judicial process – that of legal reasoning – has been omitted' (paragraph 9). Yet Higgins is equally operating within the Vattelian principles of subjectivity. She objects to the idea that the Court is implying that states could justifiably use nuclear weapons to ensure their survival, even if that involved a violation of humanitarian law. This goes beyond what nuclear weapons states were claiming, namely they always accepted that they would have to comply with humanitarian law (paragraph 29). What she means is a reference to the same pure subjective belief of sovereign states that prevents the Court itself from penetrating State practice. So Higgins argues:

> If a substantial number of states in the international community *believe* that the use of nuclear weapons might *in extremis* be compatible with their duties under the Charter (whether as nuclear powers or as beneficiaries of 'the umbrella' or security assurances) they presumably *also believe* that they would not be violating their duties under humanitarian law. (paragraph 33; emphasis in the original)

It is the role of the judge to resolve in context and on grounds that should be articulated why the application of one norm (for example, humanitarian law) rather than another (for example, the right of self-defence with nuclear weapons) is to be preferred (paragraph 40).

So Higgins reaches a conclusion identical to that of the Court for exactly the same reason: the systemic character of international law as a liberal (that is, Hobbesean) order of raging subjectivities, none of which can trust one another. It is hardly surprising that a collection of judges can do nothing in the face of such moral chaos. So Higgins herself says:

> In the present case, it is the physical survival of peoples that we must constantly have in view. We live in a decentralised world order, in which some states are known to possess nuclear weapons but choose to remain outside of the non-proliferation treaty system; while other such non-parties have declared their intention to obtain nuclear weapons; and yet other states are believed clandestinely to possess, or to be working shortly to possess nuclear weapons (some of whom indeed may be party to the NPT [Non-Proliferation Treaty]). *It is not clear to me that either a pronouncement of illegality in all circumstances of the use of nuclear weapons or the answers formulated by the Court in paragraph 2E best serve to protect mankind against that unimaginable suffering that we all fear*. (paragraph 41; emphasis in the original)

It is also Higgins who leaves unexplained how states that believe they have to use nuclear weapons in self-defence could not believe that they are violating humanitarian law. This is not only a matter of ignorance of moral history. It is also a matter of the social knowledge that can be possessed by a State-appointed official.

A further case for consideration is the Advisory Opinion of the ICJ (22 July 2010) *Accordance with International Law of the Unilateral Declaration of Independence in Respect of Kosovo*, General List No. 141. It is not directly a case concerning the use of force, but the ethnic-based civil war is a typical use of force context, giving rise to the existence of a new State. So, it is of interest to observe how far the Court goes into the nature of the conflict. Quite simply, it draws a boundary around it.

The issue of Kosovo involves one of the most fundamental in international society at the moment. Where there is a multi-ethnic State and a conflict arises within it, what if the smaller or weaker part wishes to resolve the conflict by breaking away and constituting itself as a new State? The answer is that the coming into existence of a State is a meta-juridical fact. A State is a fact, not a legal fact. So most of the 'use of force' questions at present fall outside the law.

A summary of the Kosovo conflict is bound to be controversial, but the dominant view is that, after 1989 and the fall of communism in Yugoslavia, the Serbs provoked a conflict. They controlled the

Federal and Central Governments in Belgrade and used their domestic legal power to abolish the regional autonomy that the Croat Communist Dictator, Tito, had created for the Kosovo Albanians in Kosovo. The territory had an 80 per cent Albanian majority and a 20 per cent Serbian minority. The history of the balance of populations is different. Before the Nazi German occupation of 1941–5 the balance was about 50 per cent to 50 per cent, and, at one point, historically, before the Ottoman invasions of the fifteenth and sixteenth centuries Kosovo was the centre of Serbia.

Anyhow, the picture after 1989 is that the Serbs, under the leadership of President Milosovic, set about restoring and expanding Serbian influence and power in Kosovo and Kosovo Albanians resisted. Political repression (by Serbs) and resistance (by Albanians) became violent and the Security Council intervened with numerous resolutions calling for an end to violence, respect for human rights and so on. However, Soviet and Chinese vetoes excluded the possibility that the Security Council would authorise the use of force, that is, a military humanitarian intervention. NATO, an alliance of Western powers, decided that military intervention was necessary anyway to protect the Kosovo Albanians. The outcome was the NATO occupation of Kosovo and the withdrawal of all evidences of Serbian sovereign activity. Towards the end of the NATO intervention the Russians also established a military presence in Kosovo. Hence, although the military action was not authorised by the Security Council, there was a Security Council Resolution subsequent to the intervention, in June 1999, SCR 1244, which set up an international authority in Kosovo and provided for a mechanism for a resolution of the conflict.

The Advisory Opinion comes into the above picture. It considers primarily the SCR 1244, which is appropriate for the Principal Judicial Organ of the UN (Article 92 of the UN Charter). The Court is concerned with a resolution that sets up an International Authority to provide a framework for the people of Kosovo to achieve substantial autonomy and have provisional institutions for democratic and autonomous self-government. It should also facilitate a political process designed to determine Kosovo's future status and the transfer of authority from Kosovo's provisional institutions to institutions established under a political settlement.

The Court was asked by a General Assembly Resolution coming from Serbia and its allies (including China, Russia, and Spain) whether the unilateral declaration of independence by the Provisional Institutions of the Self-Government of Kosovo is in accordance with international law. This crucial formulation of the question in a positive form indicates a conviction that the existence of a State has to be seen as a legal fact. The context was the failure of the Kosovo Albanians and the Serbs to agree upon a political settlement. The UN Secretary General's Special Representative, the President of Finland, said that this failure was irreversible and recommended, as the only solution, Kosovan independence. As Russia would veto this, it could not be approved by the Security Council.

The Court makes two moves. It begins the answer to the first question by saying that (paragraph 56) it is entirely possible for a particular act not to be in violation of international law without necessarily constituting the exercise of a right conferred by it. The Court is referring here (paragraph 83) to the questions of whether there are rights to self-determination and secession in international law. The Court says (particularly at paragraph 79) that there is no evidence from the practice of states as a whole to suggest that an act of promulgating a unilateral declaration of independence is contrary to international law. Even where declarations have been made in the second half of the twentieth century outside the context of non-self-governing territories, or cases of alien subjugation, there is no practice of states indicating that such declarations are regarded as contrary to international law. This is to reformulate a positive question into a negative one and turn the issue of statehood from one of legal fact to a meta-juridical fact.

A second part of the first move of the Court is to say that there is nothing in SCR 1244 to prohibit unilateral declarations. It provides a mechanism for a political settlement. It does not address the situation where such a settlement cannot be reached and, specifically, it does not address any specific, substantive instructions to the parties. The Court could see no intention of the Security Council to impose obligations to actors other than the provisional institutions set up under it. Also it did not provide anything for the final status of Kosovo or conditions for achieving it (for example, paragraphs 114–15). At one point it admits that the question put to it by the General Assembly is ambiguous as it appears to envisage that a political settlement must somehow happen (paragraph 118) and a unilateral declaration definitely prevents that happening. However, the Court refers to other SCRs on Cyprus and the Republika Srpska (paragraph 81) where there were specific directions to the Turkish Cypriots and the Bosnian Serbs not to declare independence. It says that there are no comparable instructions to the parties in this case.

The second move concerns the determination of the authors of the unilateral declaration. The question asked of the Court is whether the declaration by the Provisional Institutions of Self-Government of Kosovo is in accordance with international law. It may appear difficult to reach a conclusion favourable to Kosovo from a strict adherence to the question, if one argues that these Institutions owe their existence and powers to processes set in play by SCR 1244, because that resolution does not provide for anyone to declare independence.

What the Court appears to do is make a radical move and say that the authors of the declaration are quite independent of these Institutions and do not owe their existence to them. To justify this assumption, the Court appears simply to take the Kosovans at their word (paragraphs 102–9). So the Court draws from the declaration of independence, that (paragraph 105) the authors did not act, or intend to act, in the capacity of an institution created by and empowered to act within the legal order of the Provisional Institutions (paragraph 105). The declaration does not speak of the Assembly of the Provisional Institutions, but instead 'We, the democratically elected leaders of our people' (paragraph 107). This expression precedes the actual declaration of independence and indicates who the authors are (paragraph 107). The declaration was not forwarded to the Special Representative of the Secretary General. He, in turn, did not purport to oversee and comment on the declaration, as he would have of an act of the Provisional Institutions that had been under his supervision. He was silent (paragraph 108). The President of Kosovo was present at the declaration of independence, and yet he is not a member of the Assembly. This indicates that the Assembly was functioning in a special capacity outside the terms of the SCR. In addition, the UN Secretary General does use language of the Assembly, declaring independence, but says that in fact one is concerned with 'persons who acted together in their capacity as representatives of the people of Kosovo outside the framework of the interim administration' (paragraph 109).

Additional factual background – not stressed by the Court – was that on 17 November 2007 elections were held for the Assembly of Kosovo and this Assembly declared independence on 17 February 2008 (paragraphs 73–4). The declaration was adopted by 109 out of 120 members, including the President, who was not a member of the assembly. The ten Serbian members and one Gorani did not attend the meeting.

It appears to be clear that the Court is following a fundamental aspect of the idea of self-determination, that it is a subjective matter. If the people understand themselves to be conscious of their freedom and wish to have independence that is decisive of their identity. The Court appears to consider that the sense of their own self-consciousness as a People of Kosovo takes priority over the institutions they had been previously accorded and had occupied. The limits contained within these institutions were overcome by the fact that the Kosovo People saw themselves as a distinct people. However, the Court's basic point is that there is no consistent State practice declaring such conduct illegal. At the same time, it is (paragraph 56) entirely possible for a particular act not to be in violation of international law without necessarily constituting the exercise of a right conferred by it. The Court thereby notoriously avoids the question whether there is a right of self-determination of peoples and/or how to balance a principle of self-determination against the right or principle of territorial sovereignty – also not mentioned by the Court. Despite very extensive argument on these issues in many State submissions, the Court appears to be trapped by the lack of any professional, or disciplinary resources to answer such questions.

THE ACTUAL POSITIVE INTERNATIONAL LAW ON THE USE OF FORCE

Jouannet's Interpretation of the Vattelian Heritage

The radical subjectivisation of international law does appear to come with Vattel's concept of sovereignty and it appears to swallow up the legal character of this order. Jouannet does not agree. The State is a corporate entity and as such a legal entity. The fact that there is no global corporate entity merely means that states are left to negotiate their corporate fiats with one another. That is, one is firmly back into controversy about the nature of international legal personality. For Jouannet, Vattel's great achievement was to break with medieval notions of moral responsibility of individual rulers under natural law and place the centre of legal attention with corporate responsibility.

As a historian of international law, Jouannet demonstrates the same continuity of the medieval legal method throughout the seventeenth century and early eighteenth from Grotius to Vattel. All of the major legal figures continue some version of the medieval method. The main figures are Grotius himself and what Jouannet describes as his disciples, Rachel, Zouche, Textor, and Bynkershoek.[12]

12. E. Jouannet, *Emer de Vattel et l'émergence doctrinale du droit international public* (1993) Part II *Autonomisation du droit des gens* esp. 141–7.

The reason why international law had not until Vattel become an autonomous discipline in its modern recognisable form is rather surprising. Jouannet traces how none of the earlier jurists conceived of the State or nation, words used interchangeably, as a corporate entity distinct from the person of the government or the prince. There are traces of the idea of the State as a corporate entity in the writings of Hobbes, which have also exercised an influence on Pufendorf.[13] However, even these two writers remained with the concept of government alone rather than developing a concept of a corporate entity that embraced both the governor and the governed. The elements that would make up the modern State in international law, government, territory, and population, remained the property of the prince. He *had* a territory and a population, in a patrimonial sense. Such a personalised concept of authority directs attention to individuals and favours the retention of the medieval idea of a common law of human beings applied to the leaders of nations. Grotian-style erudition prevails into the eighteenth century to regulate the affairs of princes in their relations with one another, but also in their domestic and even private affairs.

It is with the Vattelian critique of Christian Wolff that one arrives at the modern conception of international law, where sovereignty as a legal concept comes to play a central part. Absolutely central is the notion of the corporate character of the State. As a legal entity, it has to be separate from both government and governed. It is the State, and not the government nor prince, which is subject to international law. It is and can be subject to international law only if it is sovereign, that is, equally independent of all other states.[14] What Jouannet is, above all, anxious to stress is that law should have a dualist character in what she calls the classical form of international law. It is essential to the idea of the corporate character of the State that there should be no relations of individuals with one another across State boundaries. All the relations of individuals, for the purpose of international law, are absorbed into the corporate identity of the State, which then has legal relations with other states. In this way it is the sovereign equality of independent states that defines the object and scope of the rules of international law.

Yet Jouannet sees no difficulty in the Vattelian sovereign being integrated into an international legal order. The lack of difficulty is

---

13. Ibid., 300–24.
14. Ibid., 354–88, esp. 384 ff.

hardly surprising because this new legal order is made by states specifically for their relations with one another.[15] It is because states have no rights over one another that they have need of a law that recognises that they are independent and equal.[16] Jouannet appears to see the entire exercise as a taxonomy of what relates or properly belongs to the rights and duties of nations rather than individuals. The idea that there should be rules specifically designed for the character of sovereign states can hardly pose problems of a legally binding character.[17] The aim of this taxonomic exercise is to register a break with the Roman and medieval tradition of law. The progressive character of this law is that it incorporates the two great principles of liberty and equality of states as the very basis of the society of nations, in place of the *genre humain* (human kind) of the naturalists. Now the nation can govern itself without dependence upon what is foreign to it.[18] The constant theme of this argument is the corporate character of the sovereign. Because sovereign nations deal only directly with one another, they can only see one another as societies of men of whom all the interests are held in common. It is not a law of nations derived from human nature that rules them, but a law derived from the particular nature of the State.[19]

It is interesting to give a prominent place to Jouannet's argument because international lawyers are so little troubled by the concept of sovereignty. She is aware of the problem of subjective appreciation but manages to make it appear that those who stress it misunderstand the structure of international law and lack the technical expertise to understand how it is supposed, following its own nature, to function. Jouannet admits that Vattel keeps the principle of the subjective appreciation of each State in the application of the law,[20] but considers it unjust to make him responsible for the increasing voluntarism of international law. Voluntarism means that the entire body of international law depends upon the continuing consent of states. They can, at any time, cease to accept that a rule binds them, and even cease to recognise other states as subjects of the law. Vattel is not responsible for such a view. He merely introduces the logic of Hobbesean and

15. Bartelson, *A Genealogy of Sovereignty* esp. 137–85, a summary of chapter 5, 'How Policy became Foreign'.
16. Ibid., 194–5.
17. Jouannet, *Autonomisation* 447.
18. Ibid., 448.
19. Ibid., 451.
20. Ibid., 454–8.

Lockean individualism into international law, in terms of the liberty and sovereignty of states as the foundation of international law.[21] A doctrine of the autonomy of states is not a doctrine of absolute or unlimited external sovereignty. It is not a non-submission to a superior juridical order but an autonomy of a political entity vis-à-vis other equally independent entities.

The root of the confusion, in Jouannet's view, is to have made a too rapid combination of the question of the application of international law with the decentralised structure of the community of states. There is no compulsory international adjudication. So states have to interpret for themselves the extent of their rights. She says that the question of the subjective appreciation of the law is not an aspect or logical consequence of voluntarism in international law, a doctrine that all law is a product of State will, but arises from the conditions for the application of the law in a decentralised international legal order. International law is a universal abstract law, but appreciated unilaterally because there is no compulsory international adjudication. It therefore functions in practice as a series of reciprocal and bilateral interpretations given to it by states.

Vattel simply marks a reflection of a change at an international level that had been occurring generally in legal culture – a movement towards the individualisation and subjectivisation of law, combined with a realist vision of international relations where states have a mission to act to assure their security and preserve their interests. It is not Vattel who introduces this subjectivity into international law. It is simply an unavoidable fact of international law in the absence of any supra-State power. So, in the beginning and middle of the twentieth century it is not this subjectivist decentralised appreciation inherent in the structure of the international community that is the problem, but the legitimacy of the use of force that accompanies it.[22]

Mainstream Positivist Doctrine on the Use of Force and the Kelsen Critique

It is particularly difficult within the discipline of analytical jurisprudence, which takes its inspiration from Hart's *Concept of Law,* to pose effectively the question of whether international law makes up a legal system. It supposes the priority of whatever happens to be the dominant (that is, general or community) perspective of the chief

21. Ibid., 458–9.
22. Ibid., 472.

officials of a legal order as against recalcitrant minorities or dissident members. This community priority is inevitable given the value scepticism that underlies the analytical approach. One can only understand obligation from the internal perspective of those submitting themselves to it. One can only take language at face value, asking how it is actually used in society.[23]

So, by way of typical illustration, the present editors of Oppenheim's ninth edition of *International Law* define international law, as any other law, in social terms as rules of conduct accepted in a community by common consent and enforced by an external power (paragraph 3). They rely upon the classical distinction between law and morality (paragraph 17) in terms of the latter applying to conscience and the former being enforced by external authority. A clear weakness of international law, recognised by the editors, is that the enforcement mechanisms of international law continue to be unsatisfactory and the Security Council does not offer an adequate substitute. Yet the same editors treat the controversy about the legal nature of international law as unrealistic (paragraph 4) simply because states recognise that their freedom is constrained by law. This remark is accompanied by the observation, assigned to a footnote, that such a position is not inconsistent with the fact that states may differ as to precisely what rules that law prescribes.

It may be that the editors are not concerned so much about the frequent resort to unilateral action by states in the form of self-help or special interpretations of the right of self-defence and so forth because it must always be possible to have judicial or Security Council review of such decisions if the idea of law is not to be eliminated from the scene (paragraph 127). That is, relevant officials could, conceivably, appear who would apply their internalised norms. The legal observer can, given his lack of status, add nothing. However, the practical implications of this have to be seen in the wider context of 'authoritative' mainstream doctrine as represented in this ninth edition of Oppenheim's *International Law* edited, *inter alia* by a Foreign and Commonwealth Office (FCO) First Legal Advisor, Sir Arthur Watts and Sir Robert Jennings (an ICJ judge and President as well as an academic). They regard the UN as having the potential of a complete legal system, but in the meantime 'we are not that far', particularly insofar as concerns enforcement.

---

23. The seminal study of the influence of this approach on international law is Glanville L. Williams, 'International Law and the Controversy Concerning the Word Law', *BYBIL* (1945) 146 ff.

Using the framework of the 1970 UN Declaration on Friendly Relations among States (FRAS) and superimposing it on the notion of the nineteenth-century fundamental rights of states (Pillet),[24] the editors adopt the rationalistic concept that underlay international law in pre-Charter times. So (para. 119), independence as a legal concept, entails that violation of, for instance, the territorial sovereignty of another State may occasionally be justified on grounds of self-defence or by the failure or inability of the invaded State to fulfil the duties of control over its territory that are the corollary of its right to territorial sovereignty.

The difficulty, of course, is that each State will, in accordance with the legal principle of equality, claim the same right, and thereby cancel out the legal effects not only of all other legal claims, but also its own. The editors, and the mainstream of the profession, have always been aware of this difficulty and believe that they can counter it by making a distinction between the claim of a right to self-preservation and a right to self-defence. While self-preservation as a legal concept is ruled out as illogical, the necessity of safeguarding the integrity of the State may, in strictly limited circumstances, justify acts that are otherwise wrongful (paragraph 126). Article 33 of the ILC draft articles on State Responsibility is the occasion for differing views. But maybe when there is only one means to safeguard essential interests of a State against grave and imminent peril, and there is no serious impairment of the essential interest of another State and no violation of *ius cogens* by using it (paragraph 127), force may be used. In any case, in the view of the editors, self-defence against subversive armed forces can involve crossing the border to deal with intended attackers, and so on. Standard nineteenth-century cases are set out, such as the sinking of the Danish fleet at Copenhagen as well as the sinking of the French fleet at Oran in 1940.

What is more, anticipating an attack is not necessarily unlawful in all circumstances (paragraph 127, continued). In conditions of modern hostilities, it is unreasonable to expect the State to wait. In practice it is for every State to judge for itself in the first instance whether a case of necessity in self-defence has arisen. There are practical difficulties in modern technology, for example aircraft approaching in what appears to be a hostile manner. The editors make no judgements about a number of incidents that they set out in a value-free manner: Suez 1956, Cuba, Aden, South Africa, Vietnam, Iraq, and so on. So, it appears

---

24. Oppenhim's *International Law*, Vol. I. (1992/6), eds A. Watts and R. Y. Jennings 135–6.

that the editors consider that forceful intervention is not necessarily illegal. Justifications have been the protection of citizens, as Britain in Suez, Israel at Entebbe, and so forth (paragraph 131). That is, where national lives are in danger and the territorial authorities are unable or unwilling to protect those at risk, action may be taken that is, in any case, not inconsistent with the purposes of the UN Charter.

A more rigorous journey through Kelsen's positivism will lead to a more correct conclusion that there is no international law on the use of force, at least not in a positive law sense. The war of 1914–18 greatly upset the confidence of international lawyers in the viability of a legal order that left appreciation of violations of rights and methods of vindicating them entirely within the discretion of sovereign states. The response that it is intended to highlight as a reaction to this comes from within the same legal political tradition as Vattel's: theory of social contract. In the first instance, it does not have to be read as a statement that international organisation exists, but rather as a statement of what social contract theory would require at the international legal level.

The fundamental epistemological condition is that law depends upon what the people express through their constitutional organs, that is, through the State. At the international level, this means reproducing the characteristics of a State globally. This is the only possible production of legal meaning. At present, international lawyers are left troubled by the in-between character of an incomplete international institutional order, wherein State sovereignty keeps seeping through.

After the World War, in 1918 Europeans wished to conceive of the rule of law as being capable of defining the spheres of competence of the State. In Austria the *Stufenbau Lehre* (Legal Ladder/Steps) approach conceived of an ideal legal structure in terms of State responsibility. Just as order within the State depended upon the capacity to determine the competences of specific State organs constitutionally, so international order depended upon the existence of an international constitution that could determine the competences of the State in international relations. State responsibility was tied to the notion of executive responsibility towards a parliamentary regime, and to reproduce this regime internationally it was necessary to give priority to international over national law by creating international institutions that could limit effectively the legal competences of states. Such institutions could function as parliaments supervising states.[25]

---

25. B. Stoitzner, 'Die Lehre vom Stufenbau der Rechtsordnung', in *Untersuchungen zur Reinen Rechtslehre*, S. Paulson and B. Walter (eds) (1986) 50 at 76; also T. Ohlinger, *Der Völkerrechtliche Vertrag* (1975).

A chief exponent of the ideal of an international constitutional order was Kelsen. He appreciated the historical perspective that had to be overcome. To argue that State power could look to itself rather than to a constitutional title for its competence to act is to hark back to the spirit of absolutism.[26] The notion that physical, or whatever, State power as such could legitimise an action is to leave the way open to the idea of *raison d'état*, in the sense in which a Renaissance disciple of Machiavelli would have understood this, that is, as the capacity of the prince to put his concept of the public safety of the State above all considerations of law and morality. Kelsen's aim is to construct a barrier between modern constitutionalism, democracy guaranteed by positive law and the historical origin of European states, which was in absolute monarchies.[27] It is the latter who actually consolidated the power that constitutionalism is now supposed to democratise. Kelsen is a theorist of international law who does recognise that there is a danger implicit in the classical notion of the State, whereby sovereignty does create a threat to the obligatory character of international law.

A neo-Kantian epistemological perspective is an essential part of Kelsen's critique of the traditional legal thinking about the State. Power, and hence State power, as an empirical concept has no legal significance. The notion of command has legal meaning/significance only in terms of a normative order that attributes roles: who may command and who must obey.[28] In international terms this implies a break with Vattel, who took the independence and equality of states for a natural fact. For Kelsen the co-existence of States is only legally conceivable on the basis of the existence of an exhaustive association that determines the limits of the validity of competences rather than powers, which are attributed to states. Such a legal framework puts States on the same juridical plane as their own provinces and communities in their own federal law.[29] That is to say, on a par with constitutional-administrative law, the State should be considered not as the highest instance, but as a *relatively high* instance, in a scale of juridical instances – hence the metaphor of *ladder*, or *Stufenbaulehre*.

The difficulty, of which Kelsen was aware, remained that power structures of international society did not automatically conform to his ideal construction for the future. Every legal system must be able

26. H. Kelsen, *Der soziologische und der juristische Staatsbegriff* (1928) 137.
27. Ibid., 138–9.
28. Ibid., 82–3.
29. Ibid., 86.

to say which are its subjects, that is, literally subject to it. A basic, real question is whether states are dependent upon an international order for their existence or whether they create themselves out of their own forces. Kelsen's response has the appearance of a play on words that is left to plague the whole structure of contemporary international law. The only juridical, internationalist way to answer the question is to suppose the existence of an international law norm that posits the acceptance of the legal character of any entity that succeeds to establish itself durably.[30]

Kelsen has to insist that the objectivity of a legal order, in the sense of its validity, has to be independent of acceptance by its subjects, just as the rule of law at a national level cannot depend upon its subjects. This leads him openly into the construction of a *civitas maxima*, a universal international law that stands over against the rules that States have consented to, and that grounds their validity. This is the same *civitas maxima* that Wolff constructed and that Vattel rejected as non-existent. It recognises that the idea of law attaches to the notion of the constitutional State as such, so that the only international legal framework that can adequately encompass the modern State has to be a world constitutional State. This, in the age of modernity, is the only construct that can be a substitute for the medieval notions of the ideas of a continuing Roman Empire, with its tradition of legal naturalism, of a *ius gentium*. Kelsen is not at all committed to claiming that such an order exists, but it is the only conceivable juridical pathway to overcome the absolutist, monarchist Machiavellian State at the international level.[31]

Once this legal ideal is set, the task is to reinterpret the foundations of international law accordingly and to overcome the obvious deficiencies of existing, positive international law, that is merely the legal rules to which states *have consented*, exposed as they are to the dangers of voluntarism. The first stage is easy. One may simply say, almost as a play on words, that treaties are binding, as are rules of general customary law, because there is a basic norm, that is, derived from the idea of a *civitas maxima*, that confers legal validity upon the exercise of State consent that finds expression in such treaties and customs.[32]

---

30. H. Kelsen, *Das Problem der Souveränität und die Theorie des Völkerrechts* ([1920] 1928) 230–1, 239–41.
31. Ibid., 239–41, 249–52, 274.
32. Ibid., 261.

However, the problem is not simply the creation of rules of law, but their interpretation and their enforcement. How does the *civitas maxima* work itself out at this stage? The *Stufenbaulehre* insists upon one simple and new way of looking at states. They are not sovereign entities but organs of the international legal community to which certain competences have been transferred. The difficulty that immediately emerges is that there are, in fact, nothing but states, and that to regard them as organs of the international community is simply an international lawyer's way of speaking. Kelsen is fully aware of this fact. He is merely trying to conceive of the basic logical requirements for the construction of an international legal order. He appreciates that there are problems with the very idea of a legal order, where there are no institutions for the interpretation of the law independent of the states themselves, and equally no mechanisms for the enforcement of legal obligations apart from the states.

So Kelsen embarks upon two important further arguments, concerning the place of war in the international legal order and the place of the judiciary in the interpretation and in the creation of legal norms. The intention at this stage is to explain critically how Kelsen, as a representative international lawyer, develops his ideas. War is a common fact of international life. If international law is to have credibility as a legal order, in Kelsen's view, it must integrate this fact into its interpretative framework. If war is to be evaluated from a juridical perspective, it can only be as a sanction that international law furnishes for the enforcement of law against violators of the law. Traditional doctrine viewed war as permissible. States could wage wars as an instrument of national policy, quite simply to seize territory and resources from other states. Anxious to eliminate such a traditional concept of sovereignty, Kelsen claims that war is regulated by international law.[33] By this Kelsen means that only where a State has suffered an aggression – simply a violation of its rights – has it a discretionary power to react under international law, that is, a discretion to enforce its right. In this sense war is legally objectivised. War becomes an institution created by the law to put the law into force.[34]

To claim that a State is able, at its discretion, to declare war, apart from having suffered a legal wrong, would signify the end of the idea of international law. So Kelsen tries to affirm that a State cannot employ the use of force until there has been first a violation of

33. Ibid., 264.
34. Ibid., 265.

the law. However, the problems of interpretation and application are linked. The lack of an independent instance that can verify objectively whether there has been a violation of law remains. Yet somehow Kelsen believes that such an objection does not prevent a theoretical construction of war being considered as a coercive act, as a sanction, to enforce international law. He insists upon construing the State that has suffered a legal injury, and responds to it through the use of force, as functioning as an organ of the international legal community.[35] In pursuing this line of argument, Kelsen is firmly determined to replace the traditional concept of sovereignty with a procedural approach to law that ensures that the possibility for initiative for states is clearly regulated.

The underlying motive of this approach to international law remains clear. All law must have a democratic foundation in consent. If legal subjects are to be allowed, within an admittedly primitive or decentralised system of law, to use force, this can only be in terms that are clearly agreed in advance by the legal community. Hence, the approach that Kelsen adopts, in order to determine whether the minimum conditions of a legal order exist, has enormous resonance in the profession and indeed can be said to be the only approach that is regarded as conceivable.

Kelsen is able to see that a simple prohibition on the use of force is not enough to settle when states may go to war. Logically, it will provide an answer. Either states use force illegally in contravention of the status quo or they act legally by using force to defend it. However, some mechanism has still to be found to develop and adapt the law in the existing, primitive, and decentralised international society. The solution for Kelsen will be a system of obligatory jurisdiction that would issue judgements that an Executive would be required to implement. This would overcome the obvious fictionality in speaking of states that decide to use force to revenge a violation of their rights as doing anything other than 'taking the law into their own hands'. If a court had to decide whether there had been a violation and could do so in taking a dynamic attitude to the development of the law, the weaknesses of the present system, which favour an easy return to the language of unlimited sovereignty, could be overcome.

It is crucial to such a theory for the development of international law that its corpus consists of a complete system of general principles that can be applied effectively by a judiciary to concrete situations. Hence, the Court will not have to say that, with respect to the issue

---

35. Ibid., 266.

being adjudicated, States have not consented to the development of rules that limit their sovereignty in a particular matter, with the consequence that the Court has to declare that there is no law covering the dispute before it. Such an argument would carry with it the implication that one cannot look to courts to overcome the deficiencies in the corpus of rules of international law that are known to exist, so that there is no alternative to States meeting together as a quasi-legislature to formulate rules of general application to limit and guide their conduct. Kelsen does not see such meetings as a real political possibility, which is why he prefers the option of obligatory international adjudication. Hence, he has to insist upon a strong role for the judiciary. He insists that the application of a general norm to a concrete case is by its very nature an individualisation of the norm. That is to say, '[T]he existing rule is a framework of several different rules. By choosing one of them the law applying organ [the judiciary] excludes the others and thus creates, for the concrete case, a new law.'[36] The conclusion that Kelsen and the profession generally draw from this argument is that there is only a difference in degree and not in nature between the creation and application of law and that in this way the structural weakness of international law can be saved through the judiciary.[37]

The second part of Kelsen's argument was that the judgments of such a dynamic court had to be the starting point for the action of an international executive, such as the Security Council. Kelsen himself demonstrates that such is not what we have. Superficially, one may argue that the sovereignty of states is effectively limited by law because the UN Charter is a treaty and under this treaty states are bound by decisions of the Security Council. However, the Charter does not tie the Council in any way either to decisions of the Court or even to a reference to international law. The former may decide upon the use of force wherever it considers that a situation constitutes a threat to the peace under Article 39 of the Charter. It can also leave a decision of the Court unenforced. Nor is there anything to oblige the Council to consider any disputed question of fact in an impartial or quasi-judicial fashion. The Charter foresees what may be called a perfect independence of the Court and the Council, both principal organs of the UN.[38]

---

36. H. Kelsen, *Collective Security under International Law* (1954) 18.
37. C. Tournaye, *Kelsen et la securité collective* (1995) 43–4, citing Kelsen and referring to other literature.
38. Ibid., 63.

So, a State is prohibited by Article 2/4 of the Charter from having recourse to the use of force except when its territory is physically attacked. Thus, the State is deprived of any effective mechanism for the adjudication and enforcement of its legal rights wherever it considers that there has been a violation. The outcome is that the Charter represents a deterioration in the quality of international law in comparison to the classical law. It excludes the individualised sanction for a violation of law by a State acting on its own, but does not replace it with an effective collective sanction. This means that in terms of the minimum conditions for the existence of law one cannot expect that international law will function.[39]

Therefore, it is to be expected that, in practice, states will not refrain from enforcing their rights individually whenever they consider them violated. Given that there is no compulsory international adjudication, should we be able to say that minimum conditions for an international legal order can exist where states act *as if* they are organs of the international community when they defend their rights. Kelsen recognised that it was the minimum condition for the existence of a legal order that it could characterise acts of violence as illegal or as sanctions against illegal behaviour. International law does not have an objective instance (that is, independent of states themselves) to distinguish between delicts and sanctions. Therefore, Kelsen would like to say, we have to suppose that each State decides itself if it estimates itself injured and if it will ensure that the injuring State incurs sanctions. Yet recently a major logical defect of Kelsen's system has been highlighted.

Nothing has been said, in the setting out of the logical conditions for a legal order, about the reasons a State has to give for considering itself injured. The feeble level of explication required of an individual State means that it is impossible for an observing third State to distinguish the 'delinquent' from the 'sanctioner'. This is because it is not possible to follow a rule on one's own. The idea of a rule is that there is a common explication of the existence and content of the rule. Yet we do not have the adjudicative process that could guarantee this. Therefore, even from Kelsen's perspective, the minimum conditions for an international legal order do not exist.[40]

39. Ibid., 70, 77.
40. O. Pfersmann, 'De la justice constitutionnelle à la justice internationale: Hans Kelsen et la seconde guerre mondiale', *Revue française de droit constitutionnel* 16 (1993) 761 at 788–9.

State Sovereignty, Unilateral Interpretations of Law and the Use of Force with Vattel, the Paradigmatic Figure of Modern International Law

In one view Vattel was described as a man of 'keen and discriminating intellect, cheerful and tender, kind and generous of heart, who wisely lived a useful but all too short life amidst the pleasures of speculation and the friendly intercourse of his fellow men'.[41] The spirit of this perspective suggests that Vattel had a clear vision of how to take wars of ideological conviction out of the arena of law. He did not dispute the existence of objective standards rooted in natural law, and also enshrined in the human conscience by the Creator. It was this objective law that grounded the authority of States to wage just wars against their opponents and indeed to punish those who transgressed the objective law of nature as applied to nations. However, he hit upon an ingenious, utterly simple distinction, which was easily accessible to the Christian and perhaps especially Protestant conscience, which had shaped him and most of his readers. It was necessary to distinguish the 'internal law' from the 'external law'. The former signified that natural law fully bound States but only in their private conscience. They could not invoke it against one another. In external relations States were bound only by what they had freely agreed with one another, with the fall-back right to defend themselves where there had been a clear infringement of their own rights. Beyond that, it had to be accepted that there would be disagreement among states about what the objective law required, and, as all States were free and equal, no one State would have the authority to interpret this law against another. With a single stroke Vattel had disposed of the right of States to punish one another. Line by line he rejected the arguments of Grotius and others of the seventeenth century who had retained the right of States to wage just wars.

Vattel went even further. No State, among equals, would have a natural authority to care for the whole society of states. The primary duty of each State was to look to its own development and perfection. No other State could intervene coercively to guide it on its way. The principle of non-intervention in one another's affairs

41. E. de Vattel, *The Law of Nations*, Vol. 3, translation of the edition of 1758, Charles Fenwick with an Introduction by Albert de Lapradelle (1916) vi.

was primary. Vattel's legal philosophy was based upon an eighteenth-century Enlightenment view that one could remain agnostic about mixed regimes governing States, because each ruler at least notionally governed with the acquiescence of his people, precisely because he recognised his duty to govern in their best interests, as enlightened judgement dictated. Vattel's province in Switzerland, Neuchatel, was actually under the jurisdiction of Prussia.

I think there is so much to support this interpretation of Vattel in the *Preliminaries* and the *Introduction* to his work. In particular, paragraph 16 of these parts reads:

> Par.16 As a consequence of that liberty and independence, it exclusively belongs to each nation to form her own judgment of what her conscience prescribes to her, – of what she can or cannot do, – of what it is proper or improper for her to do: and of course it rests solely with her to examine and determine *whether she can perform any office for another nation without neglecting the duty which she owes to herself*. In all cases, therefore, in which a nation has the *right* of judging what her duty requires, no other nation can compel her to act in such or such particular manner: for any attempt at such compulsion would be an infringement on the liberty of nations. We have no right to use constraint against a free person, except in those cases where such person is *bound to perform* some particular thing for us, and for some particular reason which does not depend on his judgment, – in those cases, in short, where we have a *perfect* right against him.[42] (emphasis in the original)

Vattel proceeds to make what for me are unintelligible distinctions between what he calls internal and external law, perfect and imperfect right. It is clear that the former categories (internal, imperfect) and the latter (external, perfect) are respectively legally unenforceable and enforceable. However, I do not find in his text any systematic and categorical exposition of the aspects of international legal rules and principles to which these terms relate. One can guess that duties of humanity are not enforceable, but what of concepts of right arising out of treaty, or territorial security, where there are matters of judgement about the justice of the situation, interpretations of the extent of rights and so on? The matter is dealt with in paragraph 17 and we will have to come back to it when we look at aspects of the law of treaties and the law of security and self-defence. Paragraph 17 reads:

---

42. From *The Law of Nations* from the French of Emir de Vattel, edition of 1883 with notes by John Ingram. All the quotations in the texts following are from this source: <http://home.earthlink.net/~dybel/Documents/LawOfNations,Vattel.htm>.

> In order perfectly to understand this, it is necessary to observe, that the obligation, and the right which corresponds to or is derived from it, are distinguished into *external* and *internal.* The obligation is *internal*, as it binds the *conscience*, and is deduced from the rules of our duty: it is *external*, as it is considered relatively to other men, and produces some right between them. The internal obligation is always the same in its nature, though it varies in degree; but the external obligation is divided into *perfect* and *imperfect*; and the right that results from it is also *perfect* or *imperfect*. The *perfect right* is that which is accompanied by the *right of compelling* those who refuse to fulfil the correspondent obligation; the *imperfect* right is unaccompanied by that right of compulsion. The *perfect obligation* is that which gives to the opposite party the *right of compulsion*; the *imperfect* gives him only a right to *ask*.
>
> It is now easy to conceive why the right is always imperfect, when the correspondent obligation depends on the judgment of the party in whose breast it exists; for if, in such a case, we had a right to compel him, he would no longer enjoy the freedom of determination respecting the conduct he is to pursue in order to obey the dictates of his own conscience. Our obligation is always imperfect with respect to other people, while we possess the liberty of judging how we are to act: and we retain that liberty on all occasions where we ought to be free. (emphasis in the original)

However, it appears to me from paragraph 21 that Vattel is expounding a very broad concept of State sovereignty, which he does not understand as radical or threatening in a Hegelian sense, but rather as expressing the spirit of tolerance and compromise of which de Lapradelle speaks. So this paragraph 21 stresses the equality of states, thereby serving to exclude the authority of any one country to impose its values hegemonically on the international community.

> Par.21 Since nations are *free, independent*, and *equal* – and since each possesses *the right of judging*, according to the dictates of her conscience, what conduct she is to pursue in order to fulfil her duties the effect of the whole is, to produce, at least externally and in the eyes of mankind, a perfect equality of rights between nations in the administration of their affairs and the pursuit of their pretensions, without regard to the intrinsic justice of their conduct, of which others have no right to form a definitive judgment; so that whatever may be done by any one nation may be done by any other; and they ought, in human society, to be considered as possessing equal rights.
>
> Each nation in fact maintains that she has justice on her side in every dispute that happens to arise; and it does not belong to either of the parties interested, or to other nations, to pronounce a judgment on the

> contested question. The party who is in the wrong is guilty of a crime against her own *conscience*; but as there exists a possibility that she may perhaps have justice on her side, we cannot accuse her of violating the laws of society. (emphasis in the original)

It is easy to point to obvious weaknesses in Vattel's system. It supposed a community of enlightened agnostic states, each of which cultivated its own garden. It ignored the hegemonic, ideologically driven State, such as Napoleonic France, which may wish to dominate the whole European continent. Yet, remarkably, this vision of the fundamental structure of international legal order won overwhelming assent through the whole of the nineteenth and twentieth centuries, with the only caveat, after the calamities of the world wars in the twentieth century, that some institutional framework, some international organisation, was seen and continues to be seen as necessary to confront the rogue State, which perversely threatened this agnostic community. However, such an international body could only rest upon what Vattel had called the voluntary Law of Nations, which is their free consent expressed through formal treaty, precisely defining what is conceded by the states to the international organisation.

One could speculate that it is precisely this Vattelian framework that remains enshrined both in ethos and in detailed legal rules in the UN Charter. The groundwork of the Charter is in Articles 2/4 and 2/7 and Article 51. States must refrain in their international relations from the threat or use of force against the territory integrity or political independence of other states. Nothing in the present Charter shall authorise the UN to intervene in matters that are essentially within the domestic jurisdiction of any State or shall require the Members to submit such matters to settlement under the present Charter, apart from the right of the Security Council to take action under Chapter 7 of the Charter, which is itself limited to action with respect to threats to the peace, breaches of the peace, and acts of aggression. Finally, Article 51 reinforces the inherent right of states, pending action by the Security Council under Chapter 7, to exercise an inherent individual or collective right of self-defence *if an armed attack occurs*.

It is precisely this last article that covers the so-called problem of the failure of the Security Council to act. In that event the fall-back position is a return to the Vattelian Law of Nations position that a State has authority to act only in so far as it is itself directly affected, although several states may be directly affected by the same threat. As for the Security Council being blocked by disagreement, states had resolved by the Vattelian voluntary law that precisely where the Permanent Members of the Security Council or an overall majority cannot agree on how to act the UN as such has no authority to act. In such circumstances, it is inconceivable, within the agnostic Vattelian framework, which grounds modern positive international law, that any individual State should claim authority to act alone. One cannot use the argument that previous resolutions of the Security Council can be enforced by individual members – the so-called punishment of states that violate the objective standard of Security Council resolutions. These resolutions are the property of the Council itself. It is a matter for its judgement whether it is appropriate to go to war in particular circumstances, to ensure the observance of standards of conduct it considers appropriate. Outside of its, the Security Council's judgement, everything is subjective and no particular State has the authority to act against another equal member of the Society of States.

An alternative and less sanguine interpretation of Vattel's legacy is provided by James Brierly in the aftermath of the First World War, but he did not alter his view until his death and repeated it in all of the editions of his classic *The Law of Nations*. In this, for England, canonical introduction to international law, Brierly quotes at length the French international lawyer Albert De Lapradelle on the significance of Vattel. The Frenchman praises Vattel for having written in advance of the events that the book represents, the principles of 1776 and 1789, of the American and French Revolutions. Vattel is credited with projecting on to the plane of the law of nations the principles of legal individualism. Vattel has written the international law of political liberty.[43] Brierly comments astutely that the survival of the 'principles of legal individualism' has been a disaster for international law. The so-called natural independence of states cannot explain or justify their subjection to law and does not admit of a social bond between nations. Vattel has cut International Law from any sound principle of obligation, an injury that has never been repaired.[44]

Focus will be on Brierly's critique of Vattel on the use of force since it is most relevant. I will try to show later that it is very difficult to see how Vattel's taxonomy already referred to (in paragraph 17 of the *Preliminaries*) works itself out in this vital area. Brierly appears quite sure. Vattel makes each State the sole judge of its own actions, accountable for its observance of natural law only to its own conscience.[45] This reduces natural law to 'little more than an aspiration

43. Brierly, 6th edition (1963) 39–40.
44. Ibid., 40.
45. Ibid., 38.

after better relations between states'.[46] For instance, by necessary law (natural law) there are only three lawful causes of war: self-defence, redress of injury, and punishment of offences. By the voluntary law (effectively the positive law, based on consent) each side has, we must assume, a lawful cause for going to war 'for Princes may have had wise and just reasons for acting thus and that is sufficient at the tribunal of the voluntary law of nations'.[47] Brierly is telling us that the very categories of thought that the international law tradition, since Vattel, offers make it impossible to think of that law effectively restraining the recourse of States to violence.

This is not helped by the ambiguity that appears to surround Vattel's position. As Bartelson also stresses, the argument that humankind is divided into separate States does not overrule universal natural law, now reinstated in the rationalist context of Enlightenment philosophy.[48] Bartelson quotes Vattel that each nation

> may be regarded as a moral person, since it has an understanding, a will and a power peculiar to itself; and it is therefore obliged to live with other societies or States according to the laws of the natural society of the human race.

The difficulty remains that this universal morality is not immediately binding upon the external conduct of States. Again, he quotes Vattel, 'each has the right to decide in its conscience what it must do to fulfil its duties; the effect of this is to produce before the world at least, a perfect equality of rights among Nations'. This leaves the international law tradition with a contradiction. Without sovereignty, says Bartelson, after Vattel, the State cannot be understood as a moral person, but without a wider sense of universal values, this person cannot be sovereign.

This dilemma is what is meant by the question of whether international law is binding, whether treaties are legal instruments, and especially whether sovereignty can be legally limited. It is attempted to argue that Vattel's idea of sovereignty does not negate the very idea of international law. The profession never tires of repeating that States declare their adherence to international law. The difficulty is clearly that the doctrine of legal equality means that the interpretations of the law given by any and every State has equal value. Therefore, the

---

46. Ibid.
47. Ibid., 39.
48. Jens Bartelson, *A Geneology of Sovereignty* (1995) 194–5.

principle of auto-interpretation of the law is inevitable, which means a total relativity of interpretations. The very idea of legal obligation is negated precisely by the universal willingness of States to appeal to law to vindicate their positions. So the evidence of declared adherence to international law on the part of States is the problem that confronts us rather than the evidence that reassures us.

In my judgement, the roots of the strength of many critical legal studies attacks upon so-called mainstream international law are to be found in the conscious and quite deliberate heritage of Vattel. However, this need not have any policy-prescriptive conclusions. Ambiguity is then nothing more than an expression that nations, as individuals, have to live in a spirit of equality and compromise without any possible recourse to authority, whether ethical or institutional, to resolve their differences. However, Brierly casts a shadow over this optimism and I propose now to reflect, quite naively or directly, upon Vattel's own texts on treaty law and self-defence, to see whether one wishes to incline towards Brierly or back to De Lapradelle. These reflections stimulate in myself a very strange feeling of how Vattel saw international society. There always appears to be a spectre of menace, dark forces against which the community as a whole must unite itself. At the same time the subjective nature of threat and danger means that the dividing line between reasonable and unreasonable fear of danger is not always too clear.

Extensive Explorations of Vattel's Text: The Paradox of the Drift from the Natural Equality of Mutual Tolerance to the Violent Rivalries Rooted in Fear of the Unknowable Other

The natural equality of nations appears to mean clearly that some nations cannot set themselves up as models for others to follow. There is no place in Vattel's schemes for the morally ambitious goals of the USA and the EU to set their so-called democratic, liberal values (human rights, market economy and so on) up as objective standards for others to follow. In Book II, Chapter 1, paragraph 7, there is an unqualified rejection of the authoritarianism that Vattel saw as latent in the classical natural law thinking expounded by Grotius and probably the sixteenth-century Spaniards.

> Par.7 But, though a nation be obliged to promote, as far as lies in its power, the perfection of others, it is not entitled forcibly to obtrude these good offices on them. Such an attempt would be a violation of their natural liberty. In order to compel any one to receive a kindness, we must have an authority over him; but nations are absolutely free and independent

> (Prelim. § 4). Those ambitious Europeans who attacked the American nations, and subjected them to their greedy dominion, in order, as they pretended, to civilize them, and cause them to be instructed in the true religion, – those usurpers, I say, grounded themselves on a pretext equally unjust and ridiculous. It is strange to hear the learned and judicious Grotius assert that a sovereign may justly take up arms to chastise nations which are guilty of enormous transgressions of the law of nature, *which treat their parents with inhumanity like the Sogdians, which eat human flesh as the ancient Gauls, &c.*[7](91) What led him into this error, was, his attributing to every independent man, and of course to every sovereign, an odd kind of right to punish faults which involve an enormous violation of the laws of nature, though they do not affect either his rights or his safety. But we have shown (Book I. § 169) that men derive the right of punishment solely from their right to provide for their own safety; and consequently they cannot claim it except against those by whom they have been injured. Could it escape Grotius, that, notwithstanding all the precautions added by him in the following paragraphs, his opinion opens a door to all the ravages of enthusiasm and fanaticism, and furnishes ambition with numberless pretexts? Mohammed and his successors have desolated and subdued Asia, to avenge the indignity done to the unity of the Godhead; all whom they termed associators or idolaters fell victims to their devout fury. (emphasis in the original)

This analysis comfortably assumes that limits to the use of force will be drawn provided each is having to act only for his own security. The right to preserve ourselves from all injuries is a perfect one. This perfect right is a natural right, to preserve oneself from all injury, called the right to security (book II, chapter 4, paragraph 18). The supposition must be, for Vattel's system to have any normative force – which Brierly thinks is impossible – that concepts of threat and danger have some objective quality and are not mere irrational whims. Vattel says in paragraph 50 of the same chapter:

> Par. 50 It is safest to prevent the evil when it can be prevented. A nation has a right to resist an injurious attempt, and to make use of force and every honourable expedient against whosoever is actually engaged in opposition to her, and even to anticipate his machinations, observing, however, not to attack him upon vague and uncertain suspicions, lest she should incur the imputation of becoming herself an unjust aggressor.

There is so much apparent moral clarity in what Vattel writes that it is difficult to believe that this was mere padding to prepare for a resolute positivism that distinguished law from morality.

It appears safest to assume that Vattel assumes that existing nations should leave one another in peace, because there was no objective moral authority that could compel them to follow some concept of the public good, such as the Pope or the Emperor. Yet where some nations clearly violate the objective natural law standards to threaten international peace, other states can unite against them. In the same chapter (paragraphs 53 and 70) Vattel is clear that he is mounting an argument that has to be reconciled with the basic principles of his system. So he says:

> If there were a people who made open profession of trampling justice under foot, – who despised and violated the rights of others whenever they found an opportunity, – the interest of human society would authorize all the other nations to form a confederacy in order to humble and chastise the delinquents. We do not here forget the maxim established in our Preliminaries, that it does not belong to nations to usurp the power of being judges of each other. In particular cases, where there is room for the smallest doubt, it ought to be supposed that each of the parties may have some right: and the injustice of the party that has committed the injury may proceed from error, and not from a general contempt of justice. But if, by her constant maxims, and by the whole tenor of her conduct, a nation evidently proves herself to be actuated by that mischievous disposition, – if she regards no right as sacred, – the safety of the human race requires that she should be repressed. To form and support an unjust pretension, is not only doing an injury to the party whose interests are affected by that pretension; but, to despise justice in general, is doing an injury to all nations.

There is another central area concerning perfect rights, the duty to observe promises.

> There would no longer be any security, no longer any commerce between mankind, if they did not think themselves obliged to keep faith with each other, and to perform their promises. This obligation is, then, as necessary as it is natural and indubitable, between nations that live together in a State of nature, and acknowledge no superior upon earth, to maintain order and peace in their society. (chapter 12, paragraph 163)

While Vattel in this chapter appears to expound a liberal, commercial view of treaties as transactions – the parties cannot claim these turn out to be more burdensome than expected (paragraphs 157 and 158) – he goes much further in chapter 15, arguing that the keeping of promises is a sacred obligation, the breach of which is of concern to all nations and not just the one to which the promise is made (paragraph 218 and so on). The *ethos* at work is quite clear. Vattel says:

> Par.19. Between bodies politic, – between sovereigns who acknowledge no superior on earth, – treaties are the only means of adjusting their various pretensions, – of establishing fixed rules of conduct, – of ascertaining what they are entitled to expect, and what they have to depend on. But treaties are no better than empty words, if nations do not consider them as respectable engagements, – as rules which are to be inviolably observed by sovereigns, and held sacred throughout the whole earth.

At the same time, he does not wish to forget his liberal credentials and thinks one must be able to make a distinction between reasonable doubt about the extent of obligations and manifest bad faith. So, at paragraph 222, Vattel says,

> But we should be careful not to extend this maxim to the prejudice of that liberty and independence to which every nation has a claim. When a sovereign breaks his treaties, or refuses to fulfil them, this does not immediately imply that he considers them as empty names, and that he disregards the faith of treaties: he may have good reasons for thinking himself liberated from his engagements; and other sovereigns have not a right to judge him. It is the sovereign who violates his engagements on pretences that are evidently frivolous, or who does not even think it worth his while to allege any pretence whatever, to give a colourable gloss to his conduct, and cast a veil over his want of faith, – it is such a sovereign who deserves to be treated as an enemy to the human race.

We have twice now seen how Vattel thought that one could distinguish between reasonable and unreasonable behaviour with respect to a right to security and treaty rights. However, it is when Vattel comes to consider the settlement of disputes that it appears to me his whole system implodes and the contradictions between conscience and objective natural law gives way to a radical acceptance of subjectivity. In chapter 18 on methods of resolving disputes, Vattel says, in paragraph 333:

> In *doubtful causes* which do not involve essential points, if one of the parties will not accede either to a conference, an accommodation, a compromise, or an arbitration, the other has only the last resource for the defence of himself and his rights, – an appeal to the sword; and he has justice on his side in taking up arms against so intractable an adversary. (emphasis in the original)

It appears to me that he is saying that from each perspective, the other is intractable, where that 'other' will not accede to a peaceful means of resolving disputes, for example, arbitration. Yet subjectivity so prevails that it may appear that a State can resort to force even where the other side has not formally refused, for example, arbitration. The first nation may still have such necessary and prudent regard to its own security as to have recourse to arms without every conciliatory measure being already expressly rejected (paragraph 334).

> [I]t is sufficient that she have every reason to believe that the enemy would not enter into those measures with *sincerity*, – that they could not be brought to terminate in a happy result, – and that the intervening delay would only expose her to a greater danger of being overpowered. (paragraph 334)

The only sanction appears to be that the attacker must provide grounds for this distrust of the other by being able to justify his conduct *in the eyes of all mankind* (paragraph 334; emphasis is Vattel's).

It is clear that Vattel sees some limitation of the arbitrariness of the subjective behaviour of the sovereign in a kind of peer review of the opinion of nations, which will eventually be seen to round on a nation resorting to force on bare suspicions (paragraph 334). However, it appears to me that, in the following paragraph, Vattel has imploded any normative limitation on the conscience of nations in any and every context, including their determination of the extent of their perfect rights (presumably under treaties) and their natural security. This has the vital consequence that there is no way out of the uncertainty created by their natural conscience. There is no way to draw the boundary between the natural liberty of one nation and the natural liberty of another. The so-called voluntary law is no more secure than the natural law from which it has its origin. All normativity is dissolved into opinion, which is not salvaged by the fact that it should appear, from time to time, that one nation should become so threatening that most others come together to protect themselves. That same nation could just as well be the scapegoat that holds the rest of the community together by becoming its sacrificial victim, as described by René Girard in his numerous writings.[49]

49. For instance, R. Girard, *Violence and the Sacred*, trans. P. Gregory (1977) or *Things Which Have Been Hidden since the Beginning of the World*, trans. S. Bann and M. Matter (1987).

All of this appears clear to me in the vital paragraph 335 whereby Vattel uses his disquisition on peaceful settlement of disputes, as Brierly accuses him, to dissolve the whole of *The Law of Nations*. Despite the liberality of spirit that is attributed to Vattel, he begins this paragraph by assuming that morality is only the refuge of the weak and will last among the strong only so long as hypocrisy pleases. It will be the same with nations. In this way the natural conscience of nations eats into their perfect rights and their voluntary law.

> Par. 335 When, therefore, a nation pretends that it would be dangerous for her to attempt pacific measures, she can find abundance of pretexts to give a colour of justice to her precipitation in having recourse to arms. And as, in virtue of the natural liberty of nations, each one is free to judge in her own conscience how she ought to act, and has a right to make her own judgment the sole guide of her conduct with respect to her duties in every thing that is not determined by the perfect rights of another (Prelim. § 20), it belongs to each nation to judge whether her situation will admit of pacific measures, before she has recourse to arms. Now, as the voluntary law of nations ordains, that, for these reasons, we should esteem lawful whatever a nation thinks proper to do in virtue of her natural liberty (Prelim. § 21), by that same voluntary law, nations are bound to consider as lawful the conduct of that power who suddenly takes up arms in a doubtful cause, and attempts to force his enemy to come to terms, without having previously tried pacific measures. Louis XIV. was in the heart of the Netherlands before it was known in Spain that he laid claim to the sovereignty of a part of those rich provinces in right of the queen his wife. The king of Prussia, in 1741, published his manifesto in Silesia, at the head of sixty thousand men. Those princes might have wise and just reasons for acting thus: and this is sufficient at the tribunal of the voluntary law of nations. But a thing which that law tolerates through necessity, may be found very unjust in itself: and a prince who puts it in practice may render himself very guilty in the sight of his own conscience, and very unjust towards him whom he attacks, though he is not accountable for it to other nations, as he cannot be accused of violating the general rules which they are bound to observe towards each other. But if he abuses this liberty, he gives all nations cause to hate and suspect him; he authorizes them to confederate against him; and thus, while he thinks he is promoting his interests, he sometimes irretrievably ruins them.

It is hard to imagine a more morally tangled and confused conclusion to the natural liberty of conscience of nations. Why cannot Vattel find his way to accepting that any nation be said to have violated the voluntary, natural, or whatever *Law of Nations*, which, to use his language, tramples underfoot the natural security of all other nations and disregards the sanctity of treaties, as the foundation of all perfect rights, and finds itself, then, treated as the enemy of humankind, the focus of warlike actions by all of its neighbours? If Vattel does not take this course has he constructed any *Law of Nations* at all?

The beginning of book 3, which is devoted to the concept of War, appears to follow the same pattern as the earlier books. Paragraph 26 of chapter 3 appears to require a definite injury to a perfect right to give rise to a right of employing force or making war. Once again where nations start wars on mere pretexts they will become enemies of the human race and all nations will have a right to join in a confederacy to punish them (paragraph 34). If the case is doubtful there is the usual duty to take conciliatory measures, and equally the right to use force against the one who is not conciliatory (paragraph 38). Finally, Vattel's fundamental principle of respect for difference of opinion appears again:

> Par.40 It may however happen that both the contending parties are candid and sincere in their intentions; and, in a doubtful cause, it is still uncertain which side is in the right. Wherefore, since nations are equal and independent (Book II. § 36, and Prelim. §§ 18, 19), and cannot claim a right of judgment over each other, it follows, that in every case susceptible of doubt, the arms of the two parties at war are to be accounted equally lawful, at least as to external effects, and until the decision of the cause. But neither does that circumstance deprive other nations of the liberty of forming their own judgment on the case, in order to determine how they are to act, and to assist that party who shall appear to have right on his side; nor does that effect of the independence of nations operate in exculpation of the author of an unjust war, who certainly incurs a high degree of guilt. But if he acts in consequence of invincible ignorance or error, the injustice of his arms is not imputable to him.

Finally, I would like to note that it is in the same spirit of scepticism that Vattel approaches the vital question of whether neighbouring states may take measures against a State that is aggrandising itself (chapter 3, paragraph 42 et seq.). I think Vattel's very extensive discussion of this issue may reveal the truth of the point of Brierly that he has broken the bonds of society with his doctrine of a natural liberty of conscience and hence Vattel always has the tendency to believe that the distance that separates nations must mean that distrust and inclination to resort to pre-emption or preventive measures will be dictated by prudence. After Vattel's usual speculations about the right of neighbours to anticipate the dangers posed by a growing power that has a record of aggression (paragraphs 44 and 45), he nonetheless comes to the further startling conclusion about the inevitability of the eventual abuse of power by whomsoever acquires it. He takes the example of the expansion of the power of Ancient Rome, which indicates how endemic and perpetual are the features of human history that Vattel thinks he is describing:

> Par. 46 But, suppose that powerful State, by the justice and circumspection of her conduct, affords us no room to take exception to her proceedings, are we to view her progress with an eye of indifference? Are we to remain quiet spectators of the rapid increase of her power, and imprudently expose ourselves to such designs as it may inspire her with? – No, beyond all doubt. In a matter of so high importance, imprudent supineness would be unpardonable. The example of the Romans is a good lesson for all sovereigns. Had the potentates of those times concerted together to keep a watchful eye on the enterprises of Rome, and to check her encroachments, they would not have successively fallen into servitude.

While Vattel continues to recommend means other than the force of arms to resist the growth of one overwhelming power, it is clear that he does not exclude that force. Indeed, it is difficult to see what normative restraints Vattel imposes upon states at all. It is worth exploring further why it is that a message of tolerance and natural freedom of conscience leads directly to a portrayal of a world of mortal danger for all nations, where it is felt impossible that any normative restraints should be imposed upon their efforts to take anticipatory measures to protect themselves.

THE NATURE OF THE STATE AS A COMMUNITY AND VIOLENCE

Philosophy of the State as a Subject of International Law

Effectively, in the cases considered at the beginning of this chapter, the International Court of Justice has been acting from a State of nature, Hobbsean, doctrine. The State of nature, in which sovereign states still find themselves, is reinforced by predatory doctrines of pre-emption in the area of national security and of relentless expansion in the area of economic activity, itself continuously dominated by security interests.[50] This analysis may not be disputed by legal internationalists or

50. See further, chapter 4.

constitutionalists, but they continue to set themselves the task of harnessing the beast of the State, Aron's 'cold monsters', into a disciplined framework. There is no reason or wish to obstruct or denigrate these internationalist, constitutionalist efforts. However, their limitations need to be both understood and complemented by a new anthropology of international law. A question is whether there is an alternative anthropology of international law to the rapacious modernity offered by Tuck.[51]

The ideal State of international relations, with Hobbes surpassed, has already been expressed by Lebowicz. The inspiration of the *ius naturale* is that we return to recognise the other as similar, as reflections of the self, images of the self to be found in others because we have a common origin. It is the forces of exclusion, which found State particularism, the opposite of mutual comprehension. Yet the enemy is not on the outside but within the self, an evil that each has to rework. State law creates frontiers but without a human space between them. The conclusion of Ricoeur's philosophy of recognition will be the same. He says it was up to Leibniz to restore the other person to the idea of law, under the rubric that law's object is all that belongs to another person, that we can do for him, and that is within our power.[52] So, it is not simply contained in the idea of law that we should not injure another, that we attribute to each what belongs to him, and, finally, that we are pleased with the happiness of another. All of these mean also the joining of the self and the other in the very idea of law.[53]

However, the monumental nature of the task is made clearer for international relations – and hence also the implications for the use of force by states towards one another – by David Campbell's *Writing Security, United States Foreign Policy and the Politics of Identity*,[54] in which several key features of collective identity of the 'modernist' State are elaborated. One is to explain it as a vacuum that has to be filled through a negative construction of the 'other', which returns to give it material content. This process is a deeper level of the process of secularisation represented by Westphalia. Modern secularisation, the core of which is self-assertion or self-determination, in rejecting

51. R. Tuck, *The Rights of War and Peace, Political Thought and the International Order from Grotius to Kant* (2001).
52. Paul Ricoeur, *Parcours de la reconnaissance* (2004) 149–251.
53. Ibid., 254.
54. Revised edition (1998).

medieval or universal Christendom, presented the problem of securing identity 'in terms of how to handle contingency and difference in a world without God'.[55] Absent the metaphysical guarantee of the world by God, man is faced with danger, ambiguity, and uncertainty, all in a world now unfinished. Relating the argument directly to Westphalia, Campbell explains how the transfer of sovereignty from God to the State meant also 'the transfer of the category of the unconditional friend/enemy relation onto conflicts between the national states that were in the process of integrating themselves'.[56]

The so-called legal sovereignty of states and the rule of law limiting force in international society suffer the colossal symbolic burden in the post-Westphalian era that, in Campbell's words, 'discourses of danger are always central to discourses of the State and of "man".' The demands for external guarantees arise because modern culture has erased the ontological conditions for certainty. In place of spiritual certainty, the State tries to construct discourses of danger to give itself internal cohesion, thereby filling the ontological void. These replace the Christian language of finitude, contempt of the world, and eternal salvation with that of a State project of security. The State engages in an evangelism of fear to ward off internal and external threats.[57] Campbell concludes this part of his argument:

> [W]e can consider foreign policy as an integral part of the discourses of danger that serve to discipline the State. The State and the identity of 'man' located in the State, can therefore be regarded as the effects of discourses of danger that more often than not apply strategies of otherness. Foreign policy thus needs to be understood as giving rise to a boundary rather than acting as a bridge.[58]

A second part of Campbell's argument, intimately related to the first, is that ambiguity – read danger, uncertainty – is not disciplined by reference to a pre-given foundation. Campbell says: 'that "foundation" is constituted through the same process in which its name is invoked to discipline ambiguity'.[59] Just as the sources of the danger are not fixed, so the contours of the identity are constantly being rewritten, and it is only this process of repetitive inscribing that gives the permanence to

55. Ibid., 46.
56. Ibid., 47, quoting Hans Blumenberg, *The Legitimacy of the Modern Age* (1983) xxiv.
57. Ibid., 48–50.
58. Ibid., 51.
59. Ibid., 65.

what is by nature contingent and subject to flux.[60] The social totality is never really present, always containing traces of the outside within, and is never more than an effect of the practices by which total dangers are inscribed.[61] At the same time, sovereignty signifies 'a center of decision presiding over a self that is to be valued and demarcated from an external domain that cannot or will not be assimilated to the identity of the sovereign domain'.[62] The two themes developed by Campbell – the construction of the self through the exclusion of the other, and the repetitive character of the techniques used to construct the self – will appear to be determining, compulsively, causally, or however, in the interpretation of use-of-force norms.

James Der Derian's theory of classical diplomacy as a realistic expression of the alienation of the international space is also insightful in the present context in order to contextualise Campbell's argument in phenomenological terms. The difficulty appreciated so clearly by postmodernist theorists is that international disorder and anarchy – the problem for the very existence of international law – has been *constructed*, since the time of the Treaty of Westphalia, around the transfer or projection of what Der Derian has called self-alienation from within the State community, nation, or whatever, on to the international plane.[63] The very problem international law is compelled to face is how or why collective entities in international society construct themselves against one another. This is what post-modern international relations theory has so effectively explored. Enquiry into the nature of the *domestic/foreign* binary opposition is the starting point of *Postmodern Readings of World Politics*.[64] After mentioning Nietzsche and Foucault, Der Derian explains: 'Infused by their work, a genealogy of diplomacy is, in short, an interpretation of how the power of diplomacy, in the absence of sovereign power, constituted and was sustained by a discursive practice, the *diplomatic culture*.'[65] Der Derian devotes a whole chapter to the theme of

60. Ibid., 31.
61. Ibid., 62.
62. Ibid., 65.
63. See, generally, James Der Derian, *On Diplomacy: A Genealogy of Western Estrangement* (1987).
64. The sub-title of the volume edited by James Der Derian and Michael J. Shapiro, *International/Intertextual Relations* (1989). See especially the chapters by Richard and Ashley, 'Living on Borderlines: Man, Poststructuralism and War', and William E. Connolly, 'Identity and Difference in Global Politics'.
65. Der Derian, *On Diplomacy* 4; emphasis in the original.

alienation, taking as his starting point Nietzsche's axiom 'for us the law "each is furthest from himself" applies to all eternity – we are not "men of knowledge" with respect to ourselves'.[66]

Der Derian sets out a standard psychiatric definition of alienation as 'disturbance of the whole personality, e.g. failure of identity formation, adoption of false roles under external pressure, alienation from one's true self or from one's personal or cultural background'. At the same time he notes that the *Oxford English Dictionary* introduces the interpersonal dimension of alienation, as: 'To convert into an alien or stranger . . . to turn away in feelings or affection, to make averse or hostile, or unwelcome.'[67] Alienation is a word that designates separation, whether from the self or from the other, and a phenomenology of the alienation that undoubtedly exists among states is the true and ultimate starting point of a study of international legal personality. The question is whether there is a way to mediate this alienation. Der Derian argues that such has been the function of diplomacy, recognising and leaving unresolved the permanency of alienation as a diffuse human experience. Anti-diplomacy is described by Der Derian as any ideology, whether the French Revolution, fascism, or Bolshevism (or, for that matter, contemporary liberal market economy) that claims to be able to put in place a perfect philosophy that will remove rather than merely mediate the phenomenon of alienation, not recognising it as an ineradicable feature of the human condition.[68]

Philosophy of the Subject, from Hobbes, to Hegel to Ricoeur

We have mentioned Hobbes, Hegel, and Paul Ricoeur together. Ricoeur says that it is now well known that Hegel has taken Hobbes's challenge and responded with a theory of recognition, which attempts to overcome the amoral struggle of fear of death that underlies Hobbes's state of nature. As Ricoeur points out, the question is to know whether in this state of nature there is a moral element in the person or subject that can be isolated as the desire for recognition. It is with an original contribution to a theory of misrecognition that Ricoeur will revisit Hobbes, through Hegel.[69] Ricoeur notes the three primitive passions of competition, mistrust, and desire for glory, that

66. Quoted ibid., 8.
67. Ibid., both quotations at 13.
68. *On Diplomacy*. See chapters 7 and 8, on Anti-diplomacy and Neo-diplomacy.
69. Ricoeur, *Parcours de la reconnaissance* 241.

Hobbes highlights. Ricoeur remarks that while these passions may appear individualistic, they still depend for their force upon recognition by others. They are inherently social passions. It is the structure of the denial of recognition that one finds most closely in mistrust and most profoundly in vanity.[70] Hobbes is opposing himself to the natural law tradition (including Grotius) that considered law as a moral quality of the person, by virtue of which he could claim legitimately to have or do certain things.[71] With Hobbes one has entered the arena of contract, where there is no element of moral constraint, but instead an entirely voluntary and sovereign precaution, a calculation recommended under the pressure of fear.[72]

Ricoeur notes how there is no relation of one person to the other in Hobbes. Each renounces his right (of self-preservation) to the now sovereign State on condition that the other does. The State enjoys a unity itself, but is not in a legal relation to any of its subjects. The sovereign State is constructed out of a naturalist premise that men are equal enough to be able to kill one another, and that the social contract has a meta-ethical quality, providing security but without supposing any ethical element in the subjects of the State. The dispossession of self is not justified through an expectation from another. There is identification with self (that Locke recognised) but not with another who co-operates with oneself in a covenant.

It has already been remarked by O'Donovan how dangerous is contractarian theory, because its ahistorical nature is not grounded in any accumulation of historical community or identity. That has to be somehow created out of nothing and only adds to the insecurity of any community. Contractarian constitutionalism has a tendency to globalise itself into theories of world constitution, which merely accentuate the absence of relationship. From a phenomenological perspective, Der Derian also sees in this approach a failure to realise the importance of tact and distance in relationship, a desire to overcome anxiety (read insecurity), through the forced unity of a single humanity (80–2).

The dynamic of the movement from distrust to consideration and from injustice to respect, coming from the Aristotelian concept of justice as equality, opens itself for Hegel through an institutional structure of recognition, inseparable from a negative dynamic, where

---

70. Ibid., 242.
71. Ibid., 245.
72. Ibid., 246.

each stage is an overcoming of a specific threat, where the level of injustice and recognition follow one another, so that, in Ricoeur's words, indignation takes the place in the Hegelian political philosophy founded on the demand for recognition, that fear of violent death has with Hobbes.[73] For Ricoeur, thinking reconstructively, it is a matter of reorienting Machiavelli's and Hobbes's struggle for survival, based on fear, into a struggle for recognition based on respect. The relation to Fichte connects struggle and recognition in a link between self-assertion and inter-subjectivity.[74]

Full recognition means accepting the other as an absolute. In turn, a crime has the object to deny the specific reality of another who has one fixed in a subordinate relation of difference, while the vengeful response participates in this fixation as a form of slavery. To be fixed in difference is slavery, while to be free of it is to be the master.[75] However, recognition makes equal what the crime renders unequal. It proceeds from the overcoming of exclusion. For Hegel, the legal relation is precisely that the self ceases to be singular and is recognised as being valuable immediately in his being, necessarily recognised and recognising.[76]

For Ricoeur there is an answer to Hobbes insofar as one can find moral motives that can occupy at least some of the ground of the triad of rivalry, mistrust, and vanity, so as to find in conflictual interaction sources for parallel enlargement of individual capacities, understood as a human capacity to overcome self as identity (*ipseite*).[77] In a large argument, he makes a number of vital analytical distinctions. Discussing Axel Honneth's *Struggle for Recognition*, he says that recognition has two dimensions within the juridical sphere: the other person and the norm. As for the latter, recognition signifies, in the lexical sense, holding something to be valid; as for the former, the person, recognition has to identify each person as free and equal to all others. This is recognition of the self in terms of capacity, a gradual enlargement of the sphere of rights recognised for persons and a consequent enrichment of their capacities, all within the institutional structure of a struggle for recognition.[78] Ricoeur has to insist

73. Ibid., 255.
74. Ibid., 258.
75. Ibid., 260–3.
76. Ibid., 267–8.
77. Ibid., 274.
78. Ibid., 288–9.

that the notion of *identity* is given a differentiated moral and political significance that is not reducible to an argumentative practice demanded by an ethic of discussion.[79] The reason is that the concept of the person is not explained by norms or by discourse. Both presuppose the person, in relation to other persons.

At the same time there is, parallel to the idea of the person, the idea of responsibility, which expresses itself in indignation at the contrast between the equal formal distribution of rights and an unequal material distribution of goods, the humiliation felt where civil rights are denied, and the frustration felt at the absence of participation in the formation of the public will. Responsibility may pass through struggle, from humiliation and indignation on to a capacity to express oneself in a rational and autonomous manner on moral questions. Therefore, responsibility covers both the assertion of self and the recognition of the equal right of the other to contribute to the advance of rights and the law.[80]

The process of critique reveals a new dimension of the person, that of understanding another world other than one's own, comparable to learning another language or understanding one's own language as one among others. Translation and the capacity for compromise, as a mutual recognition of situations of conflict, are always liable to be denounced as appeasement, particularly in the Hobbesean context where the person is not considered to have any moral dimension. However, for Ricoeur a capacity for compromise is part of the capacity of the person to recognise himself as a figure of passage from one regime to another, without accusations of relativist disillusionment or superficiality.[81]

The crucial and original question, which Ricoeur poses as against Hegel, Honneth, and Kojève, is directed to the idea of struggle itself. This is born of the desire to respond to the state of nature of Hobbes, itself already opposed to the thesis of the natural law school that human beings have a common sociable nature. It is opposition to classical natural law that grounds a determination to exclude every motive that is originally moral, in the way of coming out of the state of war of all against all. In Hobbes's world one does not even recognise the other as a partner in passions of glory, mistrust, and competition. Hegel's response is the element of the negative, the struggle,

79. Ibid., 298.
80. Ibid., 292–3.
81. Ibid., 307.

which puts the stress on the forms of the denial of recognition but keeps as a mystery until the end the question of the being-recognised to which the whole process tends.

Hegel has no final goal, identifying the nature of the person. If the final result of a successful struggle is to be *self-confidence, respect*, and *self-esteem*, the question remains, when will a subject consider himself to be truly recognised? Ricoeur's question is whether the demands for affective, juridical, and social recognition (the Hegel–Honneth triad) become a 'bad infinitive', an indefinite demand. The question concerns not simply the negative sentiments of the lack of recognition, but also the new capacities that are conquered, and thus delivered over to an insatiable quest. Does the struggle for recognition not give rise to a new 'bad conscience' driven by an incurable sentiment of victimisation and an unattainable collection of ideal wishes? The question is how to develop concepts of truce, without oversimplifying the ideas of struggle and of conflict, and without treating their moral dimension as illusory.[82]

Ricoeur provides the framework in which one can understand the ethnic-nationalist and Marxist responses to the bourgeois capitalist, Hobbesean State, while at the same time endorsing the realisation that both offer chaotic responses so far as they rest at the purely formal level. The principles of friendly relations among states, the rights of self-determination of peoples and of economic development, have no clear point of objective realisation and indeed promise endless struggle, which may as well be destructive. The forces at work are much more materially dense than the ethic of discourse that does not comprehend any theory of personality. They clearly escape a formal theory of legal development, which rests upon the will of the State as the law-giver, or even the trilogy of democracy, the rule of law, and human rights.

Legal positivism, which has contractarianism at its origin, reflects upon *what has been produced by the will and never on the embedded context of the will.* In her study of Ricoeur, Molly Mann places Ricoeur in the context of what she calls the myth of constitutive autonomy in Kant and Rawls. The idea that the individual is completely autonomous before entering into the social contract assumes that individual associations with one another remain uncertain and revocable. She writes that in tracing out the philosophical history of the principle of autonomy, Ricoeur works to undermine the fiction of

82. Ibid., 315–18.

the self-foundation of the contractual, specifically Hobbesean State and of the Kantian will by arguing that morality must necessarily return to the dialogic and social dimension marked by ethics.[83]

Ricoeur argues that the fictions of contract and autonomy are intended to compensate for forgetting the foundation of deontology in the desire to live well with norms and the ethics of discursive argument. Instead, these cannot be confined to themselves apart from the issue of personality. Ricoeur means, as Mann says, that there is no way an ahistorical contract can be binding on an historical community, if we do not have recourse to the solicitous mediation of others that is continually fostered in the institutions of society.[84] The process of acculturation is both historical and ethical. Mann quotes also Dallmayr's comment on Ricoeur, that 'being human is not something "given" (by nature or reason), but rather a practical task requiring steady cultivation in social contexts'.[85]

So the dynamic of international legal argument and the normative development of international law is to be found in the embedded historical contexts of the individuals and communities they are both supposed to ground. On their own, the legal arguments and norms cannot even be understood and must appear as an endlessly inconclusive circular and self-defeating game.

The introduction of the contextual dimension not merely grounds intelligibility in a hermeneutic understanding of intentionality. It also grounds normative reasoning on the principle that law as justice can only be found where one recognises that contractualist theory cannot 'substitute a procedural approach for every attempt to ground justice on some prior convictions concerning the good for all, the common good of the *politeia*, the good of the republic or the *Commonwealth*'.[86]

This radical thesis can be immediately illustrated by returning to the theme of fear and the drive to pre-emptive attack, which, as Tuck has highlighted, grounds Hobbes's theory of the state of nature and of international relations. The monological, self-constituting nature of the social contract of Hobbes is possible and necessary only if

---

83. Molly Mann, 'Ricoeur's Dialectic of Solicitous Giving and Receiving: Instruction, Recognition and Justice', 20–1: Paper Presented at the Colloquium, 'Thinking the Present', University of California at Berkeley, May 2005 <http://www.criticalsense.berkeley.edu/mann.pdf>.
84. Ibid.
85. In *Paul Ricoeur and Contemporary Moral Thought*, John Wall (ed.) (1992); Fred Dallmayr, 'Ethics and Public Life', in ibid., 221.
86. Mann, *Ricoeur's Dialectic* 23, quoting Riceour, *The Just* (2000) 37.

we remove ourselves from that cultural history that expresses our will to live together.[87] Ricoeur responds with the question, to both Rawls' constitutive autonomy and Kant's autonomy of practical reason, concerning the problem of motivation and instruction. Any arguments of justice or distribution have to be tied to the essential convictions of society.[88] A collective recognition practice, capable of achieving a collective reconciliation, requires 'a wise deliberation, in the tradition of Hegel, for whom the recognition and reconciliation of difference is the central task of the modern state'. Mann ends on the note that these social bonds 'form a dialectical circuit that is at once the foundation and the project of civilisation'.[89]

THE STATE CONCEIVED AS A CORPORATE ENTITY OR THE STATE AS AN ANARCHIC EPISTEMIC COMMUNITY: SOME CONTEMPORARY PRACTICE

Introduction: A Phenomenology of the Use of Force as a Matter of Distorted Intersubjective Relations among States

Notwithstanding Jouannet, the French tradition of the State, Jennings, Watts, and Kelsen – not to mention Vattel, the view preferred here is that developed in the previous chapter on international legal personality. The State as an international entity, that is, in its relation with other states, is an autonomous epistemic community, to be understood in the sense of Scandinavian realism, as a complex of peoples, groups, individuals, a medley of attitudes, in some measure held together by common habits, prejudices, and ideals. However, postmodern theorists such as Campbell and Der Derian have alerted us to how unstable these configurations of ideals and prejudices are, and the reasons thereof – an assessment with which Kelsen would have agreed.

Perhaps the most concrete way of illustrating the role of interacting recognition practices for international law and relations is to tackle directly the problem of cultural incommensurability, the supposed absence of a common measure between cultures, which, according to Paul Keal, in his study,[90] has been a crucial element in the development of relations between European and non-European peoples.

87. Ibid., also Ricoeur, ibid., 56.
88. Ibid., 25.
89. Ibid., 26.
90. Paul Keal, *European Conquest and the Rights of Indigenous Peoples* (2003) 56 ff.

From Keal's perspective, Europeans generally made no attempt, or else failed to understand, non-Europeans in their own terms. However, this apparently political issue can reach a philosophical level, when it is formulated, as Keal does, following Anthony Pagden's account,[91] as a matter of an attempt to understand the practices of others by translating a variety of experiences from an alien world into the practices of their own.[92] The idea of incommensurability has been developed most sharply in relation to the so-called issue of *Orientalism*.

The issue, where it is related to the Ottoman Turks, to the so-called Eastern Question is immensely involved. Perhaps the most authoritative English language international law/international relations study of European–non-European relations in historical perspective is Gerrit Gong's *The Standard of 'Civilisation' in International Society*, a doctorate undertaken at Oxford University under the supervision of Hedley Bull. Gong becomes unwittingly embroiled in controversy by beginning his consideration of relations with the Ottomans with a quotation from the Middle East specialist Bernard Lewis. According to Lewis, Ottoman military might and traditional learning underscored the Ottoman sense of the 'immeasurable and immutable superiority of their own way of life' and caused them 'to despise the barbarous Western infidel from the attitude of correct doctrine reinforced by military power'.[93] Gong takes this quotation as authority for his own immediate remark that it was this sense of Ottoman superiority that made the 'infidel Turks' (that he puts in quotation marks, perhaps ironically) a threat to Christian and European civilisation.

Yet, as is well known, Lewis is a cardinal target for Edward Said's critique of *Orientalism*. In his *Orientalism: A Reader*, Macfie identifies how Said treats such a style of argument as an essentalising of a so-called Ottoman mind, an Arab mind, an oriental psyche, and so forth.[94] Said argues that this is not merely an imaginative phenomenon but also 'part of an integrated discourse, an accepted grid for filtering the orient into the Western consciousness and an integral part of European *material* civilisation and culture – that is to say, an instrument of British, French and later American imperialism'.[95] In

91. Anthony Pagden, *European Encounters with the New World* (1994).
92. Quoted by Keal, *European Conquest* 62 from Pagden, *European Encounters* 36.
93. Gong, quoting Lewis, in *The Standard of 'Civilisation' in International Society* (1984) 108.
94. A. L. Macfie, *Orientalism: A Reader* (2000) 4.
95. Ibid.

turn, Lewis is taken to object that Said is responsible for an ignorance of historical fact, capricious choice of countries, persons, and so on. He is himself firmly wedded to a traditional (realist) approach to the writing of history, while Said bases his approach on the work of what are usually regarded as postmodernist scholars, including Jacques Derrida (deconstruction), Antonio Gramsci (cultural hegemony), and Michel Foucault (discourse, power/knowledge).[96] Inevitably, it is bound to be virtually impossible to agree upon epistemological terms of debate between these two positions.

One may be sympathetic to a modified form of the 'Orientalist debate' taken from Sadik Jalal Al-'Azm, 'Orientalism and Orientalism in Reverse', introduced by Macfie.[97] This author identifies that the cardinal assumption of all Orientalism is 'the insistence on the essentialist separation of the world into two halves: an Orient and an Occident, each with its inherently different nature and traits . . . Orient and Occident fundamental ontological categories'.[98] He picks up on Said's critique of Lewis, explaining Muslim political phenomena in Western categories as being as accurate as a description of a cricket match by a baseball correspondent. Al 'Azm comments:

> In other words, the vast and readily discernible differences between Islamic societies and cultures on the one hand, and European ones on the other, are neither a matter of complex processes in the historical evolution of humanity nor a matter of empirical facts to be acknowledged and dealt with accordingly. They are, in addition to all that, a matter of emanations from a certain enduring Oriental (or Islamic) cultural, psychic or racial essence, as the case may be, bearing identifiable fundamental unchanging attributes. This ahistorical, anti-human and even anti-historical 'Orientalist' doctrine, I shall call *Ontological Orientalism.*[99]

Methodologically, this approach requires that one consider Ottoman-Turkish and so-called European relations historically in terms of possibly recurring patterns of behaviour, attitudes, and even concrete problems that, for all their tendency, are not immutable ontologically and therefore capable of modification, forcibly through events and also consciously, through negotiation.

At the same time, a possibly modified postmodernist approach will recognise that there are collective, if not immutable, actors, whose

96. Ibid., 3 and 5.
97. Ibid., item 24, 217–38.
98. Ibid., 225.
99. Ibid., 230.

mutual relations are in large, but never quantifiably definable, measure a matter of reciprocally modified perceptions of the self and the other. Collective identities may dissolve almost completely. Bearing in mind this possibility can only help to understand the nature and limits of the apparent consistency of collectively formed identities. However, such developments of total dissolution in international history are infrequent and anyway always a matter of what Fernand Braudel calls the *long duration*. In the meantime, the standard of value with which one has to work is the quality of mutual interpretation. Al 'Azm notes how Said recognises that it is impossible for any culture, be it Eastern or Western, 'to grasp much about the reality of another, alien culture without resort to categorisation etc., with the necessarily accompanying distortions'. Domestication of alien cultures in terms of one's own is inevitable.[100]

One needs to be realistic about the varieties of possibility of distortion that occur. Since Hegel's *Phenomenology* we have the paradigm of *the master–slave struggle*. Alex Honneth has elaborated at length on this as Ricoeur has noted. The question is whether conflictual, mutual (mis)interpretations can have developmental and positively transforming consequences. In my view, the most historically sound working assumption or starting point for European–Ottoman–Turkish relations is that they have been mutually defining since the beginning of at least the thirteenth century and especially in the relatively short key period since the failure of the second siege of Vienna at the end of the seventeenth century.

How to characterise these relations in all their complexity is best illustrated by George Steiner in *After Babel: Aspects of Language and Translation*.[101] This is not to favour the subjective and postmodern over hard material facts, but merely to recognise the primacy of consciously held ideas, especially about desirable social organisation, in any deliberate negotiating process. Steiner's close readings of varieties of translations allows one to be much more specific about the stages of negotiation among cultures, and the evaluative significance of each stage, in a context that

> concentrates to a philosophically dramatic degree the human bias towards seeing the world as symbolic, as constituted of relations in which 'this' can stand for 'that', and must in fact be able to do so if there are to be any meanings and structures.[102]

---

100. Ibid., 221.
101. Second edition (1992).
102. Ibid., 312–435, chapter 5, 'The Hermeneutic Motion'.

Steiner outlines four stages of the hermeneutic motion. In his own words, he says that the first motion is a donation of trust, which remains ontologically spontaneous and anticipates proof, often by a long and arduous gap. The translator gambles on the coherence and on the symbolic plenitude of the world. After trust comes aggression, a move of incursion, which is extractive. The postulate is that all cognition is aggressive, an inroad on the world.[103] While this process comprehends by encirclement and ingestion, it is still to be distinguished from the third movement that is actual incorporation, in the strong sense of the word, that the import is domesticated into the native semantic field.[104]

This is where the trouble starts, to put it banally. Steiner notes that 'the act of importation can potentially dislocate or relocate the whole of the native structure. The Heideggarian

> 'we are what we understand to be' entails that our own being is modified by each occurrence of comprehensive appropriation . . . Where the native matrix is disoriented or immature, the importation will not enrich . . . It will generate not an integral response but a wash of mimicry.[105]

This can lead to a negative reaction, where 'the native organism will react, endeavouring to neutralize or expel the foreign body'. This is an explanation of the romantic movement, especially of nationalism. Acts of translation may incorporate alternative energies, or we may be mastered and made lame by what we have imported.[106]

So the hermeneutic motion requires a fourth stage, where it mediates into exchange and a restoration of parity. Steiner insists that 'the enactment of reciprocity in order to restore balance is the crux of the *metier* and morals of translation. But it is very difficult to put abstractly.'[107] Steiner follows Hegel and Heidegger, 'that being must engage other being in order to achieve self-definition. Existence in history, the claim to recognizable identity (style) are based on relations to other articulate constructs.'[108] Steiner concludes his definition of the task of the translator with the words:

---

103. Ibid., 213–313.
104. Ibid., 314.
105. Ibid., 315.
106. Ibid., 315.
107. Ibid., 316.
108. Ibid., 317.

> He is *faithful* to his text . . . only when he endeavours to restore the balance of forces, of integral presence, which his appropriative comprehension has disrupted. Fidelity is ethical, but also, in the full sense, economic. By virtue of tact, and tact intensified is moral vision, the translator-interpreter creates a condition of significant exchange. The arrows of meaning, of cultural, psychological benefaction, move both ways.[109]

Misunderstanding is not coercion, even if it is the context in which coercive relations usually develop. However, it is a central argument of this book that no positive law norms are necessary to 'outlaw' the use of force. Coercive relations are phenomenologically pathological and can be guaranteed to spiral out of control and to reproduce themselves endlessly. The signature moments of contemporary history are the 11 September 2001 massacre of the Twin Towers and the US–UK Invasion of Iraq in March 2003. The worthwhile task of the international lawyer is to recognise and understand the presence of violent conduct, its ramifications and how to counter it. For such purposes the following analysis of the Iraq invasion is helpful.

A phenomenological grasp of the consequences of unilateral enforcement of supposedly universal liberal values of democracy and the rule of law stresses the inevitably solipsistic aspect of such behaviour. In his study of the US invasion of Iraq, Manuchehr Sanadjian offers to explain that the massively self-destructive pillage of all public institutions following the US-led invasion was the symbolic Iraqi way of rejecting liberation as a gift from outside. During Saddam Hussein's dictatorship Iraqis negotiated a space for themselves professionally through their engagement in such national institutions as schools, hospitals, museums, libraries, power stations, and so on, which they gratuitously destroyed afterwards. This was their way of damning the status of liberated conferred upon them by their occupiers.[110] In his phenomenological analysis, the author shows how such a unilateral juridical exercise of power can only become the right of the ruler to rule.

> By making the mediating institutions dysfunctional the Iraqis closed a major area for the total exchange between themselves and the Americans and the British . . . The distance from which the American and British forces watched the extravagant destruction of public functions was a reflection of their disengagement with the Iraqi people.[111]

---

109. Ibid., 318; emphasis in the original.
110. Manuchehr Sanadjian, 'Fetishised Liberty, the Fear of the Other and the Global Juridical Rule in Iraq', *Social Identities* 10 (2004) 665 at 666.
111. Ibid., 666.

The use of extreme violence by the Americans and the British de-subjectivised the Iraqis as national agents, turning the relationship between the invaders and the occupied into one of asymmetrical power imbalance to which Iraqis responded with a non-discursive, disaffiliating use of force.[112] Not merely the self-destructive disposal of public property showed the Iraqi disengagement, but also 'the predominantly private reception of the remains of the victims of the former regime's violence obstructed the representation of these remains as the evidence of the crime committed by the State'.[113] The introduction of a devastating military power in the relations between nations, by making power irreversible, that is, recognising no right to oppose it, meant that there could be no distinction between power and right. It would only be the creation of a political space that

> would have civilised the fear of the other by fostering a shared sense of community in which divisions and conflicts were confronted and recognised through efforts to eliminate them via recourse to the notion of the right of (wo)men to be equal.[114]

The same phenomenological description determines the quality of military occupation and explains the violations of prisoners' rights. In Sanadjian's words, the 'disturbing liberty with which the detainees had become the object of their interrogators' sadistic gaze reflects the absence of politics outside of which the fear of the other will remain as uncivilised'.[115] The military occupation creates a gap from the Iraqi people too large for politics to bridge. What one sees, instead, is a neocolonial ethnicisation – Iraqianisation – of the Western occupation.[116] Indeed, predicting the narrowness of the list of charges that would be brought against Saddam Hussain when he was eventually brought to trial, Sanadjian describes the situation phenomenologically:

> The inability to verify – to objectify – the crimes committed by the former ruler was the symptom of the lack of political community that is sustained by a set of shared values on how to address the divisions and conflicts among the members of the community through recourse to a universal notion of rights.[117]

112. Ibid., 668.
113. Ibid., 670.
114. Ibid., 671.
115. Ibid., 673.
116. Ibid., 673–4.
117. Ibid., 675.

Strikingly, the massive anti-war protest marches in mid-February 2003 were also a collective enunciation of dis-identified subjects. Without recourse to the narrative of a universal victim to encompass them all, these protestors

> rejected their position as the beneficiary in the policy of military intervention, whether to protect them from Iraqi threat or to uphold standards of humanitarian behaviour. This anti-political rejection was as closely associated with the patterns of militarisation as the fetishized liberty that had become the object of a forced, hierarchical gift.[118]

However, this separation from the political space is not as severe as the nihilistic drive to mutual annihilation, 'designed to make the self immortal through physical destruction of the other'.[119]

The form of the unilateralism needs to be further demarked as an essential part of understanding the so-called legal conviction of the Americans and the British. These remain oblivious of their transgression, because of their self-identification as agents of good. The fusion between expansion of a power base and universalisation of ethical values also brings with it an expanding economy of global violence in which power is inevitably freeing itself from institutional constraints, meaning – concretely – that the Iraqis can see that their borders become redundant against an imperial power that recognises no limits, and indeed their borders become projections of global disorder and paranoia.[120] This is a further consequence of the militaristic abolition of distance between political communities. In this context of militarised destruction of distance, the role of democracy, rule of law, and human rights is completely problematic. Iraqis who become cosmopolitan are taking refuge from a humiliating experience of being a national. They deny any national agency by belonging to a more universal religious and ethnic community beyond national borders. Marxist theory, following Gramsci, realises that to become internationalist, without being mediated through a national agency, is thereby to become chauvinist.[121] The specifically chauvinist character of this internationalism is that it excludes the other from a universal representation, which can only be national when it is heterogeneous. This is inevitable because they come into play on the Iraqi scene only after the population of Iraq has become

118. Ibid., 677–8.
119. Ibid., 679.
120. Ibid., 678–9.
121. Ibid., 681.

disposable.[122] Its political space has been militarised. However, this is not only happening in Iraq. It is a global feature of contemporary capitalism that the State perpetuates its status as the giver of the gift of liberty, which is sustained as a fetish, through a hegemonic order

> in which the State subsumes the multiple, often incompatible interests operating in society . . . to buttress up a new global form of sovereignty in a 'shrinking world' in which the sovereignty of the state has become increasingly untenable.[123]

One comes back again, full circle, to the nature of unilateralism. The guardians of power have been relieved of reliance on the opinion of the many as the power base in their own constituencies. Bush and Blair have a compelling truth that is platonically indifferent to the national constituency in the face, instead, of a paranoid global space. As Sanadjian concludes this stage of his argument:

> [A] paranoid space characterised by unstable boundary between subject and object militates against the formation of politics as a domain of contested representations, where distance is maintained through representatives and the represented. The erosion of this distance is conducive to prophetic calls to restore the order by a variety of Truth-tellers.[124]

The combination of the neo-conservatives in the US and the cosmopolitans in Iraq

> purportedly seeks an order in which the individual is granted the status of citizenship beyond the limits imposed by the state . . . What their cosmopolitanism harbours is chauvinism, that is to say a homogeneous universality from which even the internal other is excluded.[125]

Further indication of how a phenomenology of inter-community relations would work as an agenda for research and reflection on states and the use of force, is provided, in general terms in the work of Barry Buzan. More detailed case studies will follow this section. His approach only makes sense in the context of a material definition of the personality of the State as a historical cultural community, the descriptive analysis of which has also to be evaluative.

122. Ibid., 682.
123. Ibid., 682.
124. Ibid., 683.
125. Ibid., 684.

His categorisations are in terms of mature and immature political societies, embedded in State structures. The definition and application of international legal rules can be understood, across the board in terms of a phenomenology, to a greater or lesser extent, of maturity and immaturity.[126]

At the same time his definition of (im)maturity extends to relations among States, for instance India and Pakistan, or the US and the Soviet Union during the Cold War. Clusters of relationships cover a mixture of (im)mature relations. This concrete concept of alienation is less abstract than Der Derian's. How far two states define themselves against each other depends on the circumstances. The State practice needs to be illustrated more fully and shown to be related to clusters of recognisable international legal rules. At the same time, such a descriptive, analytical framework of essentially socio-cultural relations needs to be complemented by a normative phenomenology of desirable degrees of density of relations among States. Such an ontology of the desirable limits of community among States[127] provides the final picture of how far it is possible to develop and apply legal rules among States.

Buzan identifies precisely the problem of defining ideas of 'threat' and 'security' in a manner that is decisive for international law. The international law concept of threat of force or use of force is purely directed against the physical territory and 'physical' institutions of the State, in particular its government officials. This is to ignore the vital element of the character of the State, itself dependent upon distinctions between the idea of the State, the institutions of the State, and its physical base.[128] Whether a State such as the US feels 'threatened', for example, by the Soviet Union, in the time of the Cold War (1982) will depend crucially upon the part played by anti-communism in the construction of the idea of the US. This type of inherent instability continues to be built into many of the world's 'trouble spots', particularly Israel/Palestine and India/Pakistan. It is difficult to see how 'threats' to security can be eliminated in these areas without a fundamental change in the idea, and, at the same time, the institutions and physical base of these states. The viability of legal rules based on reciprocity, such as mutual recognition, of equality, and non-intervention is put into question in these cases.

---

126. Barry Buzan, *People, States and Fear* (1982).
127. Following Helmut Plessner's *The Limits of Community, A Critique of Social Radicalism* trans and introduction, Andrew Wallace (1999).
128. Buzan, *Peoples, States and Fear* esp. chapters 2 and 4.

Equally decisive are internal weaknesses in the idea of the State as such. When the population has no common interests, purposes, and ideas the society or population of the State will be liable to internal divisions that will automatically lead other States to treat the physical base of that State as a legal vacuum, making it prey to various levels of intervention. A mature anarchy in the relations of States supposes that the States are themselves mature as distinct from immature. By 'mature', Buzan means 'well ordered and stable within themselves'.[129] Only mature states can support strong common norms for the system as a whole. The idea of international law expresses this mature anarchy, mutual recognition of sovereign equality, the right of national self-determination, the sanctity of territorial boundaries, the resolution to settle disputes without recourse to force, and, most importantly, refraining from interfering in the domestic affairs of other equal States. Any State that does not reach the necessary level of maturity automatically falls out of this net of reciprocity, and the vacuum of physical space that it represents is not filled by international law. So the international lawyer has to make his way through a web of ideas, expressing political culture, more or less unevenly within and between states, and it is this alone that supports a law based upon reciprocity.

The philosophy of international law, in respect of reflection on the State practice of the use of force, has to begin with the personalities of existing States, in their concrete, feverish condition, the product of their histories with themselves and with one another, and in the context of their fragile and ever-changing political cultures.

The Conflict between the Liberal Democracies and (Primarily) Arab Islamic 'Fundamentalist' Jihad

It is argued here that international legal order can no longer be usefully conceived as an abstract social contract, viz. the definition of the law as the rules consented to by states, themselves abstract entities whose existence is certified by the mere fact that they are identifiable as addressees of the already mentioned norms. This way of thinking has to be seen for what it is – a way of thinking, a product of Kant- and Rawls-like abstracting of the individual from any social or historical context and attributing to him an unlimited autonomy to formulate contract-like rules on any subject. It is an optional way of looking at international society chosen by a specific historical

129. Ibid., 96–8.

group of self-styled, Western-educated international lawyers who please themselves to 'look at things in such a way'. It is impossible to ask whether their perspective has any 'reality' as answers will only be circular.

Once one can rethink the grounds of international legal personality, the possibilities of an ethically grounded phenomenological observation can easily arise. As argued in the chapter on international legal personality, a social-realist perspective will go beyond the definition of the State in analytical terms (*elements of government, territory, population*), and offer a minimum of political sociology with respect to the collective, territorial-based elements that still dominate international society. It is not a matter of essentialising ideal entities, but simply a matter of realising certain relative constancies in this society. Indeed, it is precisely the instability of these identities, their dynamic to expand and contract, interacting more usually negatively than positively with others, that creates the whole drama within which international law operates. Ontological insecurities of states and nations determine the parameters of disputes about such issues as recognition of territorial title, rights of peoples claimed to secession, minority rights, attempts to suppress 'terrorism', and so on.[130] In this context each group, and indeed each individual, sees itself as a subject and the others as objects, while also being objectified by how others see us and how we see ourselves as trained by those in authority to see ourselves.

One should have to abandon the abstractions of statehood for the political sociology of democratic nations, as a framework of epistemological reference. O'Donovan has made clear that the imprisonment of particularly the Anglo-Saxon/American world in a political philosophy of contractarianism has led to a compulsive compensation for an absence of an ontological grounding for collective identity, in an ambition, or 'mission' to impose its 'substitute' identity (communities *committed* to 'values' of freedom, rule of law and so on) on other countries.

So, for instance, the US is a historically situated, territorially based people (subject), not a population (object) with inherited traditions, prejudices, strivings, and aspirations, which all contribute to the style and content of its behaviour. The positive dimension of

130. A. Carty, 'Scandinavian Realism and Phenomenological Approaches to Statehood and General Custom in International Law', *EJIL* 14 (2003) 817, at 820.

phenomenology is that one does not react to such an entity in terms of a reductionist ideology critique, which treats it as an object, but instead aims to provide a pathway to de-objectification, through an understanding of the self – here a collective self – embedded also in relations with one another. This may open up the possibility, in relations characterised by grave inequalities and coercive power, of disentangling the contradicting intentionalities of the collective entities in relations with one another.

Once this context is accepted, it is possible to give concrete shape to a discourse ethic in international legal relations, and who better to undertake this than Jürgen Habermas himself. He has put the question of whether one can any longer think of the development of an international legal constitution in the light of the conduct of the US since 9/11 and does this particularly in terms of the unilateralist behaviour of the country and the contradictions that this represents in terms of its traditions. He is realistic about what has to change if one is to take up again a path of constitutionalisation. The whole argument is an exercise in contemporary history, while being as well a normative critique from his idealist perspective of uncoerced communication. In his study *Hat die Konstitutionalisiering des Völkerrechts noch eine Chance?* Habermas addresses directly the challenge of the Iraq invasion of March 2003. One superpower that thinks itself strong enough to enforce its will sets itself above the basic international law norm on the prohibition of force, while, at the same time, the United Nations does not break up. This, for Habermas, is an ambiguous situation[131]. What is especially interesting in this context is the manner in which Habermas sees the crisis of international law as both a negative dialectic of the relations of the US with the rest of the world and as negative contradictions within American collective identity. This concretises his critique of the violent character of the US's approach to international law. Habermas notes dramatically the diplomatic silence over the future of international law – a rhetorical weakening of the legal concept of armed attack, the threat of the Carl Schmitt-style division of the world into *Grossraumordnungen* of various powers.[132]

While one may dream of a change of policy with a change of government, in fact what the practice suggests is a power that uses its military, technological, and economic superiority to create a geostrategically suitable world order in accordance with its religiously

131. In Jürgen Habermas, *Der gespaltene Westen* (2004) 113 at 146.
132. Ibid.

shaped concepts of good and evil. Habermas contrasts Kant's concept of impartially promulgated and applied norms that could have the effect of rationalising political power, with the hegemonic unilateralism that takes decisions, not following established procedure, but through insisting on its own values. This latter is not an ethical alternative to international law but a typical imperial variant of international law.[133] Whether international law is understood as a State-centred system that expresses the multi-lateral relations of states or the hegemonic law of an imperial power that incorporates it into its national law, these understandings of the relation of law and power do not remain untouched by the normative self-understanding of the State actors. For this reason, the relationship does not have a purely descriptive character. Following the Kantian model of the significance of a democratic constitution and the capacity to behave with a long-term view of its interests, such a State should respond in future to the growing power of other Great Powers not with preemptive strikes, but with a timely re-establishment of a political constitution of the State community.[134]

However, for the moment, that is clearly not the character of the US. President Bush, with a good conscience, enforces a new liberal world order, because he recognises thereby, as a world standard, the spreading of American values. Replacing the law of the international community with the American ethos means that from then on what is called international law is imperial law.[135] At the same time, given the huge power asymmetries at present, whatever political decisions a single superpower makes are going to appear ambivalent. The conceptions of national interest and of global interest are bound to become mixed.[136] The September 2002 national security doctrine and the January 2003 State of the Union address denouncing the UN prohibition of force ('The course of this nation does not depend upon the decision of others') show a profound contempt for one of the most important achievements of humankind, a clear intention to replace the civilising power of universalist legal proceedings with the determination to use military force to give an American ethos a claim to universality.[137]

This latter fact has to mean that there is no prospect that international and intercultural dialogue can serve to correct any US

133. Ibid., 147.
134. Ibid., 148.
135. Ibid., 180.
136. Ibid., 180–1.
137. Ibid., 181–2.

misapprehensions or self-delusions. Habermas stresses the cognitive disasters that must accompany US partisan unilateralism. No matter how carefully it may proceed, the well-meaning hegemon, taking decisions about self-defence, humanitarian intervention, or the setting up of a tribunal, when it comes to weighing up all the relevant aspects of a decision to take, can never be sure whether it distinguishes its own national interest from the general interest. The inability is a question of the logic of practical discourse and not of goodwill. Each proposition coming from one side as to what is rational for all sides can only be put to the test when it is left open to a discursive procedure of opinion and will-formation. Egalitarian decisions depend upon ongoing argumentation, where they are inclusive and require the participants to take over mutually one another's perspectives. This is the cognitive sense of impartial decision-making. From this perspective, a unilateral proceeding, calling upon supposedly universal values of one's own political culture, is clearly ethically deficient. This is not helped if the superpower is a democracy, because its own citizens suffer the same cognitive limitations as their government. These citizens cannot pre-empt the interpretations that the citizens of other political communities put on universal values and principles from their own local perspective and their own cultural context.[138]

Nonetheless, these citizens, in the company of at least the other Anglo-Saxon polities (especially Australia and Great Britain), will continue to do precisely what Habermas would forbid. This is why it is necessary to probe more deeply into the cultural traditions, unconscious memory, and unconscious reflexes of the Anglo-Saxons so as to unravel their legal thought processes and bring them to the light of day. The context has already been set most profoundly by Campbell but now it is essential to proceed to a more in-depth study of collective psychology in the context of the 'war against terrorism', of which international legal discourse is a part. The exercise will have three parts. The first is to consider deep structural features of American culture from a theological and historical perspective. The second is to consider the legal discourse of the G. W. Bush eras. The third is to update it briefly with aspects of the Obama Presidency.

Deep structural aspects of American thinking are provided by Robert Jewett and John Shelton Lawrence, *Captain America and the Crusade against Evil.*[139] and John Lewis Gaddis, *Surprise, Security and*

---

138. Ibid., 183–4.
139. In *The Dilemma of Zealous Nationalism* (2003).

the American Experience.[140] Both studies consider international law important and both claim that the fundamental cultural forces shaping American identity are equally shaping its dominant approaches to international law. A greater part of Campbell's own study also takes up the detail of American history to illustrate the same points with respect to America from the colonial period up to the early 1990s.[141] However, his story stops here and the advantage of the following studies is that they focus directly on the detail of the Bush Administration since 2001, while also providing a historical sweep.

The argument seeks to give more concrete shape to the distortions of the post-Westphalian order. If international law is taken to be either an objective order standing above states, according each their place, or a median reference point that states use to balance their relations with one another, in either case the compulsion to define the self against the other will express itself, also, through *the inclusion of international law within the identity of the self, so that it merely serves as a boundary for the self and as a weapon against the other.*

The special value of Jewett and Lawrence is that as a theologian and a philosopher they appeal directly to the specific intellectual context of the Bush presidency, its character as a so-called 'faith presidency'. The difficult part of their argument for a lawyer to follow is that they think, given the importance of the Protestant religions to dominant strands of American identity, the correction of mistaken theology is essential to the restoration of the place of international law in American cultural identity. However, it is no part of their argument that a 'true' international law has to find once again religious roots.

It is one of the strongest commonplaces of Western international law that, since Grotius and the Peace of Westphalia, international law is a secular branch of knowledge separate from the Christian Churches and able to unite peoples regardless of religious background. Jewett and Lawrence do not directly contest this. They are concerned to show how particularly Protestant misinterpretations of the Old Testament of the Christian Bible lead to a short-circuiting of the idea of legal process and hence – and this is the centre of their argument – of America's adherence to the international legal process. The authors still conceive international law in secular terms – above all, as a framework for the impartial adjudication of right, especially with respect to their factual foundations, on a basis of

---

140. (2004).
141. Especially chapters 5 and 6.

equality. However, the authors draw upon Daniel Moynihan's *On the Law of Nations*[142] for detail of the erosion of the US's commitment to international law, as a result of the stalemate of the Cold War (*Captain America and the Crusade against Evil* (CACAE), 319). In other words, they consider the crisis of American adherence to international law to go back much further than the crisis of 9/11. They go to press in October 2002 and offer a grim history of US foreign policy.

Before exploring the detail of the authors' explanation of what they call the Deuteronomic subversion of international law, I propose to offer a justification of the focus on theology by pointing to a key study of Bush's religious beliefs that appeared just before the 2004 presidential elections. In *The New York Times Magazine*, an extensive article by Ron Suskind, entitled 'Without a Doubt',[143] is taken as demonstrating plainly the central role of religion in Bush's entourage. The question is what kind of religion. Suskind describes the 'faith-based presidency' as 'a with-us-or-against-us model'. Suskind records a meeting for the introduction of Jim Towey as head of the President's faith-based and community initiative on 1 February 2002. Bush saw Jim Wallis, editor of the *Sojourners*, and came over to speak to him. Wallis commented on Bush's January 2002 State of the Union address (that included the *axis of evil* argument), where Bush had said that unless we devote all of our energy, and so on, to the war against terror we are going to lose. Wallis added that if we don't devote our energy to the war on poverty, we will lose both the war on poverty *and* the war on terrorism. Bush, who said he had just been given Wallis's book *Faith Works* by his massage therapist, said that was why America needed the leadership of its clergy. Wallis responded, 'No, we need your leadership on this question . . . Unless we drain the swamp of injustice in which the mosquitoes of terrorism breed, we'll never defeat the threat of terrorism.' Wallis recalls that Bush looked at him quizzically and they never spoke again after that.[144]

Suskind has highlighted the 'there is no need of facts' element to the Bush presidency's decision-making as absolutely crucial. Many congressmen and cabinet ministers have found that when they pressed

---

142. (1990).

143. *The New York Times*, 17 October 2004. I am grateful to my Westminster and American law colleague Andrea Jarman for bringing this article to my attention.

144. Jewett and Lawrence explain Wallis's own theological views about responses to 9/11 at CACAE, 3.

for explanations of the President's policies, which seemed to collide with accepted facts, the President would say 'that he relied on his *gut* or his *instinct* to guide the ship of state, and then he *prayed over it*' (emphasis in the original). Suskind explains more precisely what this means. He was once called in by a White House aide to hear critical feedback about an article he had written in *Esquire* about a former White House communications director, Karen Hughes. The following, in Suskind's view, goes to the heart of the Bush presidency:

> The aide said that guys like me were 'in what we call the reality-based community' which he defined as people who 'believe that solutions emerge from your judicious study of discernible reality.' I nodded and murmured something about enlightenment principles and empiricism. He cut me off. 'That's not the way the world really works anymore,' he continued. 'We're an empire now, and when we act, we create our own reality. And while you're studying that reality – judiciously, as you will – we'll act again, creating other new realities, which you can study too, and that's how things will sort out. We're history's actors and you, all of you, will be left to just study what we do.

Suskind ends by calling again upon Wallis. Faith can cut in so many ways. If you are penitent and not triumphal it can move us to penitence and accountability. But when it is designated to certify our righteousness, it is dangerous, pushing self-criticism aside. There is no reflection.

Jewett and Lawrence do still argue within a religious tradition, calling for a correction of it to achieve a restoration of the rule of law in international society. So it may be helpful to afford an, as it were, outsider's introduction to the contextual significance of their argument. They will claim that the 'faith-based' presidency, with the full connivance of the wider American public, absorbs the Judeo-Christian tradition into American identity in a blasphemous manner, rooted in what the authors call the Deuteronomic principle, arrogating to themselves the righteous identity of an infinite God rather than appreciating that a transcendent and accusing God independently challenges their own utterly finite, and repeatedly erroneous, moral choices. The essence of those choices is idolisation of self, banishing fear and danger on to a demonised other. Simple regard to and perception of independent fact, the transcendence of the world beyond the self, are the first conditions of due process and the rule of law. They are eclipsed by what Jewett and Lawrence call a pop fascism, which absorbs all the elements of law into American identity. The central mistake concerns what the authors call the Deuteronomic dogma.

Jewett and Lawrence ask that one try to interpret, for instance, the exultant American attitude after driving al-Qaeda and the Taliban from the cities of Afghanistan in the winter of 2001.

> To account for this phenomenon, we must trace the impact of the biblical models of the triumphant God and his victorious people as understood in the moral framework of right producing victory and wrong producing defeat. We need to explore the zealous interpretations of defeat and examine the psychic impact of unresolved defeat. (CACAE, 274–5)

The failure to understand the Vietnam defeat is central to understanding the present American crisis. The Nixon–Kissinger ambition to withdraw without appearing to be defeated was based upon the idolatrous Deuteronomic principle that victory for one side and defeat for the other clearly reveal God's justice and power. This

> places the honor of self or nation in the position of ultimate significance. Whenever this occurs a terrible distortion in perception follows. Having lost its due sense of finite worth, a nation embarks on campaigns to sustain its presumed infinite superiority, using means that are the very antithesis of the virtues it seeks to defend . . . It calls for a defense in every theater of competition. The sense of proportion disappears as the nation squanders its energies against specters on every hand. Every battlefield, no matter how dubious, is pronounced holy. (CACAE, 280)

The basic approach to the so-called 'war against terrorism' is marked by enthrallment to the Deuteronomic principle. The current interpretations of the crisis, which place blame firmly outside ourselves and repeat the naïve resolve never to make a mistake again like Vietnam, 'simply confirm in us the conviction that we are the innocent and the guilty should be bombed' (CACAE, 289). To admit defeat, to 'disenthrall ourselves', is the task before America's would-be Protestant leaders. The authors say,

> our culture's blindness to tragedy has been the superficial grasp of the theology of the cross by our dominant Protestant tradition . . . What American religious leaders need today is Paul's theology of the cross, with its grasp of human weakness. (CACAE, 290)

The conclusion of this general part of the authors' analysis is that

> to admit defeat should be to acknowledge the transcendent justice of God. To admit defeat should mean to have discovered that the justice

> we sought to accomplish in Vietnam after 1954 and the current effort to rid the world of terrorism cannot be claimed as identical with divine justice – indeed, may have been repudiated by it. (CACAE, 290)

The heart of Jewett and Lawrence's argument, to give it the necessary political weight and significance, is linking a distorted theology to popular culture, Captain America, the Lone Ranger, Superman, Rambo, and so on. This has to be done to demonstrate in terms of cultural sociology the dominance of the Deuteronomic principle. So the authors point to the way the major German magazine *DER SPIEGEL* presented Bush and his team as pop culture military heroes in February 2002. The President was flattered and the US Ambassador to Germany asked for 33 poster-size copies of the cover of the magazine (CACAE, 40–3). It is necessary to single out the exact forms in which legal processes are short-circuited as a matter of popular imagination. Hence the authors speak of pop fascism. The impatience with the UN and the Security Council have deep roots. The four tenets of American pop fascism are:

> 1. that superpower held in the hands of one person can achieve more than the workings of democratic institutions;
> 2. that democratic systems of law and order, of constitutional restraint, are fatally flawed when confronted with genuine evil;
> 3. that the community will never suffer from the depredations of such a super leader, whose servant-hood is allegedly selfless;
> 4. that the world as a whole requires the services of American superheroism that destroys evildoers through selfless crusades. (CACAE, 42–3)

The iconic character of John Brown and *The Battle Hymn of the Republic* illustrate this. Jewett and Lawrence claim it comes directly from chapter 20 of the Book of Revelation, where the saints rule the earth after the destruction of the beast (CACAE, 63). The message of John Brown, as developed by H. D. Thoreau, was not to recognise unjust laws and that, in any case, he could not be tried by his peers because these did not exist. Instead, in Brown's own words, 'the crimes of this guilty land will never be purged away, but with blood' (CACAE, 172–3). The impatience with restraint shows itself after 9/11 with the warning of Senator John McCain that the terrorists must be disabused that America has not the stomach to wage a ruthless war, risking unintended damage to humanitarian and political interests (CACAE, 175).

Despite the argument that populist religion has widespread pull in American society, the authors are fully aware of the disciplinary dimension of identity formation. The struggle to exclude and demonise the other requires suppressions of the self, and a repressive construction of the self, if the latter is not to disintegrate into a seamless mass of boundaryless self and other. It is not only no accident but a permanent feature of the holy American wars that they are fought with a systematic deception not only of international opinion but also of American domestic opinion. This is not openly to facilitate manipulation of domestic opinion in a democracy, but also to preserve the image of crystalline purity of the super-hero warrior America.

There is no need of facts because, say the authors, 'the man who is privy to God's will cannot any longer brook argument, and when one declines the arbitrament of reason, even because one seems to have all reason and virtue on one's side, one is making ready for the arbitrament of blood' (CACAE, 187). At the same time wariness of overt anger and extremism means that the violence perpetrated has to remain largely hidden, even from oneself. The door is opened to impassive killings, for pure motives and without the need to regard consequences. The same artful zeal, in the hands of a Nixon–Kissinger-style team, can only be impervious to regret, since it is driven by desire for power, rather than any transcendent norm of justice. Not restrained by public disapproval they can arrange the deaths of hundreds of thousands:

> Their protestations about innocent motives are sufficient to defend the most blatant misuse of power. Such individuals will despise constitutional precedents and make political use of the very religious leaders and traditions that could stand in judgment of them, as the equally artful Bill Clinton showed. The only things they fear are the cracks in the zealous façade. That they will consider journalists and congressional investigators as mortal enemies is logical. (CACAE, 188)

Jewett and Lawrence see a clear alternative in international law. The famous inscription from Isaiah at the United Nations envisages the nations bringing their disputes to it voluntarily, looking for impartiality. The idea of law is no respecter of persons (CACAE, 318). It clearly need not have a particular religious denominational foundation. However, the solution, which the authors propose, to restore the place of law in America's international relations, is probably foreclosed by the modernity that Campbell has described through the work of Blumenberg on the significance of Westphalia as a secularisation process. The reason is that, without a theological, ontological foundation, humans *can only slip into the compulsive stereotyping of self and others to ground themselves in opposition to others.*[145]

The problem, as Jewett and Lawrence see it, is the American mistake of stereotyping. This is a religious and not an intellectual problem. The stereotypes are of good and evil,

> beliefs that provide a clear and apparently defensible sense of the identity of and solution to evil and an equally clear and gratifying sense of national self-righteousness. To give them up is to acknowledge problematic aspects of one's national or peer-group history. (CACAE, 237)

It is impossible to do justice to the richness of the authors' argument for law as the true foundation for world order. It involves a multi-faceted journey through American obsessions with crusades, evil, conspiracies, redemptory violence, triumphalist resurrections, and, most of all, certainty about matters that, as Paul says, can only be seen through a glass darkly. However, perhaps the key element of their perspective is that Jesus was always anxious to ensure that his gatherings were not of like-minded persons. He always chose people who had acted out stereotyped roles that made co-existence impossible: tax collectors, prostitutes, despised outcasts, Roman collaborators (CACAE, 242). To complement this perspective, one needs to develop *institutions of co-existence*, structures of customs and law that allow competing groups to interact peaceably, by treating ideological opponents as equals (CACAE, 243). *Zealous nationalism* will oppose this as it seeks to redeem the world by destroying enemies. However, the authors oppose to it *prophetic realism*, which 'avoids taking the stances of complete innocence and selflessness. It seeks to redeem the world for coexistence by impartial justice that claims no favoured status for individual nations' (CACAE, 8).

So the idea of law itself must rest on a deeper metaphysic. The prophetic vision views humans as involved in a tangled web of their own sin, social alienation, in which the best they can hope to achieve is a modicum of justice by the grace of God (CACAE, 198). As for the events of history, victories, and defeats of nations, whether

145. This is also the regular theme of Rene Girard's work on the importance of scapegoating for the constitution of collective identity. The only solution he, Girard, is prepared to acknowledge is the Christian doctrine of the passion and death of Christ.

they 'may reveal the justice and power of God is a matter that may be glimpsed at times, but only *in a glass darkly*, with the eyes of faith' (CACAE, 280; emphasis in the original).

So far some illustration – of Campbell's argument – has been provided through the pre-emptive appropriation of the idea of international law into American identity so that it performs an essential part in defining the boundaries of American identity and thereby constitutes a threat to the integrity of its various 'others'. A second essential part of Campbell's argument is that the ontological lack in the identity that has to affirm itself in opposition also has to reaffirm the process of *self-constitution in opposition, through repetitive re-enactment of its foundations*. Gaddis provides just this interpretation of history, again within a critical perspective. He sees explicitly the implications for changing views of international law.

Gaddis warns against the potential self-destructiveness of a process that he describes in the secular Greek term hubris, rather than the Judeo-Christian terms of demonic or blasphemous spiritual pride. It is a form of madness to equate one's own security with that of the whole planet. Yet it has been the case in decisive moments of American history, since the very beginning of the Republic, to pre-empt danger through an expansion that is, in the final analysis, unilateral and hegemonic. The central part of Gaddis's argument is that, in moments of crisis, America will inevitably, given the pull of an already constituted identity, repeat its most practiced responses automatically. The post-9/11 era is such a moment. Gaddis himself concludes on a critical note that the only way out of the madness of hubris is to come to see oneself as others see one. Yet that necessitates a very dynamic and pressing insistence on consensus by its erstwhile allies. Meanwhile a new doctrine of pre-emption will render the UN Charter redundant.

I come to Gaddis largely because of his celebrity as a major historian of America and the Cold War, particularly, more recently, as the author of the post-Cold War reflections, *We Now Know: Rethinking Cold War History*.[146] These works translated him to a professorship of History and Political Science at Yale University. Gaddis argues that from the time of the 1812 War with Britain, which involved the traumatic surprise of the British burning of Washington in 1814, America's response to threats to its security has been that safety comes from enlarging rather than from contracting its sphere

146. Council of Foreign Relations (1997).

of responsibilities (*Surprise, Security and the American Experience* (SSAE), 12–13). Gaddis says:

> Most nations seek safety in the way most animals do; by withdrawing behind defences, or making themselves inconspicuous . . . Americans, in contrast, have generally responded to threats – and particularly surprise attacks – by taking the offensive, by becoming more conspicuous, by confronting, neutralizing, and if possible overwhelming the sources of danger rather than fleeing from them. Expansion, we have assumed, is the path to security. (SSAE, 13)

Early nineteenth-century applications of the doctrine were, first, John Quincy Adams' note to Spain that it must either garrison Florida with sufficient forces to prevent further incursions, or it must 'cede to the United States a province . . . which is in fact a derelict, open to the occupancy of every enemy, civilized or savage, of the United States' (SSAE, 17). The same philosophy applied throughout the whole nineteenth century to expansion into the Amer-Indian West, to the Mexican hinterland, and finally interventions in Central America.

A second feature of American policy, after expansionism, was unilateralism, that the US could not rely upon the goodwill of others to secure its safety, and that real independence required a disconnection from all European interests and politics. For instance, the Monroe Doctrine was based upon the premise that Great Britain would enforce it, if necessary, but the US would not agree to the common statement between the US and Great Britain to exclude other European powers from the Americas, which Britain had proposed (SSAE, 24). Instead, even at this time the US expected to obtain what it wanted – hegemony on the American continent – without having its hands tied by an alliance with Great Britain.

The final feature of US policy highlighted by Gaddis was hegemony, that from the start the US should not co-exist on the North American continent (again J. Q. Adams) on equal terms with any other power (SSAE, 26). This policy gradually became one of making certain that no other great power gained sovereignty within geographical proximity of the US. It was a key reason for resistance to Confederate secession. Gaddis concludes that despite the difference between a continental and a global scale, the American commitment to maintaining a preponderance of power – as distinct from a balance of power – was much the same in the 1990s as in the days of Adams. The policy was always stated to avoid hypocrisy, as Bush said in June 2002 at West Point: 'America has, and intends to keep, military strengths beyond challenge' (SSAE, 30).

The underlying theory is that this tradition is so embedded in American historical consciousness that in case of default Americans will fall back on the trio of expansion, unilateralism, and hegemony. If there is a disconnection between security and how it has been achieved, it is better to accept the moral ambiguity, for instance that one does not really want to return what has been taken (such as Mexican territory), preferring to live by means that are at the same time difficult to endorse (SSAE, 33).

This part of Gaddis's argument is most cogently stated. The rest is not as clear. His problem in pointing to an American experience is that Roosevelt chose a different response to the Pearl Harbour surprise attack, one that was multi-lateral, based on sovereign equality and consent of allies, and that repeatedly rejected the possibility of pre-emption. There were to be four Great Powers in the UN, and a quiet American predominance would be based on consent. Pre-emption as a device was no longer necessary because the threat from the Axis, and then the Soviets, was actual, not potential (SSAE, 51–8). It is not clear why, in Gaddis's argument, the US did not take the chance to pre-empt Soviet power in Europe, nor why it preferred to build a wall that pitted the West, not the US alone, against communism. There was no felt need to rethink this in the 1990s because the US faced no obvious adversaries (SSAE, 66).

However, it is clear that even before 9/11 US leadership thinking was reverting to older patterns. Gaddis quotes the US Commission on National Security/21st Century warning in March 2001, 'The combination of unconventional weapons proliferation with the persistence of international terrorism will end the relative invulnerability of the US homeland to catastrophic attack' (SSAE, 73–4). After 9/11 the Bush Doctrine became a programme to identify and eliminate terrorists wherever they are, together with the regimes that sustain them. The return of pre-emption reflects the return of frontier danger, but today's dangers are not on a frontier, and targets can be everywhere. The National Security Doctrine (NSD) (September 2002) provides a legal form for its argument: international law recognises 'that nations need not suffer an attack before they can lawfully take action to defend themselves against forces that present an imminent danger of attack'. There is a preference for pre-empting multi-laterally, but, if necessary, 'we will not hesitate to act alone'. This type of pre-emption requires hegemony, so that there is 'the capacity to act wherever one needs to without significant resistance from rival states' (SSAE, 86–7).

At the same time Bush in his West Point speech and in the NSD assumes that American hegemony is broadly acceptable because the hegemon is relatively benign and it is linked with certain values, such as abhorrence of targeting innocent civilians for murder, and that associates unchallengeable strength with universal principles (SSAE, 88–9). However, there are problems of the relationship of pre-emption, hegemony, and consent (SSAE, 95). These crystallised over Iraq. The determination of the US was to shake up the status quo in the Middle East that had become dangerous to US security (SSAE, 99). Yet it unsettled allies as well, and in eighteen months the US exchanged a reputation as the great stabiliser for a reputation as the principal destabiliser (SSAE, 101). Here Gaddis makes a distinction between Adams and Bush. The former thought that the US should not go abroad in search of monsters to destroy, lest it become the dictatress of the world. It should confine itself to allowing no great power to gain sovereignty in its proximity (SSAE, 28–9). However, Gaddis comments, for the present:

> a nation that began with the belief that it could not be safe as long as pirates, marauders and the agents of predatory empires remained active along its borders has now taken the position that it cannot be safe as long as terrorists and tyrants remain active anywhere in the world. (SSAE, 110)

Gaddis himself regards this as arrogant, an equation of one nation's security as coterminous with that of everyone else (SSAE, 110). Instead, the US should return to the system of quasi-federalism represented by Cold War alliances, balancing the leadership needed in seeking a common good against the flexibility required to satisfy individual interests. This is a reference to the consensual coalition maintained throughout the Cold War to contain international communism (SSAE, 112–13). Hegemony requires consent, which also translates the idea that Americans need to fear what the ancients called the sin of pride. They need to see themselves as others see them, for consent to hegemony rests on others having the conviction that the alternative to American hegemony is worse (SSAE, 117).

What the cultural studies approach offers is the possibility of understanding nuances in the uses of international law language that could very well appear collective, multi-lateral, and rule of law-oriented, but actually involve elisions of meaning and barely concealed, as it were, Plan B agendas, which offer unilateral strengthening of a supposedly failed multi-lateral resolve and a determination to enforce a single view of international legal obligation. That is to say, having already appropriated international law into American identity, American elite reactions to alternative interpretations of the law will be inclined to assume that those making the interpretations are putting themselves outside the law and beyond the boundaries of the US.

At the same time, the heart of the cultural argument concerns perception rather than concepts. Is there a danger? Why will not others face it? Why should one nonetheless act alone? Bitter arguments boil down to apparently irresolvable differences as to facts. Yet concerns about the scarceness of facts are recurrent. These concerns may point to defective qualities of judgement and perception. They may also point to a lack of a mature, reflective willingness to submit to a framework for impartial judgement.

So the cultural context argument supposes that one will be able to identify in certain American international law arguments characteristics typical of the Bush Presidency. It is not intended to suggest that the legal arguments are unprofessional in the sense of being opportunistic or instrumentalist. They are most probably as sincerely held as the views of the administration. Rather, the argument is that international lawyers are so embedded in the dominant American culture that they provide an unreflective and therefore faithfully representative reproduction of the dominant culture in international law terms.

It is a very slippery matter to argue that the US is hostile to a concept of international law as such, or to a concept of collective security. As has been seen from the interpretations of Jewett, Lawrence, and Gaddis, the strongest Bush presidency supporters could argue that American and world security go together, and that the primary aim of American policy is to tighten and make more effective multilateral institutional frameworks for ensuring collective security.

In his very measured (that is, unzealous) critique of the role of his country and of many of its international law writers and legal advisors, *The United States and the Rule of Law in International Affairs*, John Murphy argues that 'one may safely conclude that the current US administration is no fan of the collective security approach enshrined in the UN Charter'. He contrasts Oscar Schachter's definition of an indivisible peace, which all states have an interest in maintaining, with John Bolton's apparent view that the US should essentially confine interest in the threat or use of force to circumstances arguably justifiable as an exercise of individual or collective self-defence. For instance, this would cover an attack against the US itself, a close ally, or a massive threat to the US through the use of terrorism, for example, Iraq.[147]

However, it is precisely the willingness of the US to take an apparently much more altruistic, but nonetheless disturbing, view of its mission, that Gaddis, Jewett, and Lawrence have noticed. Gaddis relates that the justification for pre-emptive strike in Cuba in 1898 culminated in Roosevelt's 'international police power' role for the US in 1904: 'Chronic wrongdoing, or an impotence which results in a general loosening of the ties of civilized society, may . . . ultimately require intervention by some civilized nation' (SSAE, 21). It is rather this zealous approach that appears in the ascendancy and that puts pressure on the rest of the international community to facilitate a multi-lateral approach, under menace of unilateralist behaviour by America *if the rest of the world fails in its duties*. Jewett and Lawrence see in this type of reasoning an unconscious equation of American and universal interest, rooted in a zealous self-righteousness, which, by definition, is unreflective. The logic of the anti-communist crusade was a mirage of the US as a selfless Christian nation (in the eyes of John Foster Dulles) struggling against a conspiracy of evil (CACAE, esp. 90). In a section titled 'Arrogant missteps of global idealism', the authors point to the tendency, reappearing in the Kennedy Administration's religiosity, to treat God as man's 'omnipotent servant', with 'faith as a sure-fire device to get what we want' (CACAE, 96). This led to the Kennedy myth of calibrated brinkmanship, 'the belief that if you stand tough you win' (CACAE, 100). Jewett and Lawrence trace Britain's place in this crusade back to Churchill. He had warned that to check the expansion of the communist bloc 'the English-speaking peoples – a sort of latter-day *master race* – must sooner or later form a union' (CACAE, 80; emphasis in the original).

The difficulty with this brand of collective security again comes with the US's response to 'the failure of resolve' of others to confront 'immanent threats'. Take again Murphy's measured critique of his country and some colleagues concerning Kosovo. Murphy goes against the general current of scholarship and opinion that intervention by NATO was justifiable, morally if not legally, as a form of humanitarian intervention in the face of an impending humanitarian disaster. In an extensive treatment, he points to the fact that NATO imposed as a last-minute condition for the Rambouillet negotiations – when it looked as if they were succeeding – a NATO force with free access to

147. (2004) 192.

Serbia, and independence for Kosovo after three years. NATO violated the Charter when it did not return to the Security Council after talks broke down.[148] As for the humanitarian argument, a ground military intervention may have been appropriate, but the exclusive reliance on bombing both exacerbated the situation hugely in Kosovo and led to a great loss of civilian life in Serbia.[149] Yet it is possible to take a different perceptive on these events in the eyes of the 'zealots' of the new Bush approach to a 'collective security of the willing'. Such a precedent as the Kosovo NATO intervention points both to the way that the Security Council should go in the future and how the Coalition of the Willing should go if the Security Council fails in its resolve.

In the July 2003 issue of the *American Journal of International Law*, among a wide range of contributing authors, there are a number who, in my judgement, show an unambiguous black-and-white perception of the nature of *evil* (terrorist threats and rogue states) that turn issues into resolve and willingness to use force in the face of indisputable danger. Everywhere precedents exist of coalitions of the willing. Kosovo is one such precedent.

This is how Jane Stromseth presents what still appears essentially a constructive proposal for a resurrected collective security within the United Nations. In 'Law and Force after Iraq: A Transitional Moment',[150] she notes that all major protagonists in the Security Council seek to explain their actions within its framework and the Security Council itself has shown an evolution of the idea of 'threats to the peace' to included humanitarian emergencies, protection of democracies, and so on (633). Stromseth accepts that the new American NSD, as a response to 9/11, has raised concerns about the reassuring nature of US power in many parts of the world (636). Yet through the later 1990s and in the immediate build-up to the 2003 war, the Security Council *lacked the collective spine on Iraq* (636; emphasis in the original). She opposes France's wish to use the Security Council to counteract American power, while the final fact nonetheless remains 'if France and others are not willing to support coercive diplomacy backed by a credible – and authorized – threat of force, then the United States will cease to turn to the Council' (637). The fundamental issue and the recommended institutional response are defined in carefully chosen, but ultimately zealous, terms:

148. *The United States* 155.
149. Ibid., 160–1.
150. *AJIL* 97(3) (July 2003) 628–42.

> [W]hat is especially needed today is a careful re-examination of the concept of imminence as well as of 'necessity' and 'proportionality' – in short the scope of the right of self-defense – in response to the urgent and unconventional threats posed by terrorist networks bent on acquiring weapons of mass destruction. (638)

Immediately, it is clear that regional self-defence organisations would be a good place to start (638). There is the Australia, New Zealand and United States Security Treaty (ANZUS), for Australia has experienced directly the harm of terrorist attacks (638 – supposedly Bali). The next step could be to work with Britain and others on a similar initiative within NATO. The OAS could be next (638).

None of this need appear a challenge to the doctrine of collective security, that is unless one wonders about the 'fall-back' position if, in the view of America, collective collaboration fails.

At one level, Stromseth is clearly advocating multi-lateralism, but for Jewett and Lawrence that was usually unbalanced in favour of American-dominated intentions, even during the Cold War. Stromseth argues: 'America's friends and allies will be critically important in long-term counter-terrorist efforts' (639). But what if America's friends fail her? In the 1990s there was an increasing disconnection between Security Council mandates and the means to enforce them, for some of which Stromseth blames the US. However, in other cases, 'coalitions of the willing enforced Security Council demands when the Council was not prepared to expressly authorize force – as in the 1991 efforts to protect Iraqi Kurds, the 1999 intervention in Kosovo, *and the 2003 Iraq war*' (628; emphasis in the original). Stromseth shows no awareness that the Kosovo action was problematic in the sense highlighted by Murphy and numerous other very prominent Americans he cites, such as Richard Bilder and Zbigniew Brzezinski.[151] One has to be completely clear that, for Stromseth, Kosovo and Iraq are all about *collective spine in the face of an evident danger that requires an automatic response.* Whether there are independently agreed criteria to determine whether international legal standards had been violated and what may then be a legally permissible response are not matters Stromseth considers.

The priority for *resolve* over careful deliberation is clear in Stromseth's recommendations for Security Council revitalisation. In her view others are making pleas for equity in representation, while what

151. *The United States* and so on, 155 and 161.

is really needed is a category of long-term non-permanent member that clearly articulates the contribution it is prepared to make – in terms of finances, material, or forces, to maintain peacekeeping and other enforcement purposes, including such UN purposes as the protection of human rights (641).

Another attempt to bring together Bush's new war strategy and collective security is Richard Gardner's *Neither Bush nor the 'Jurisprudes'*.[152] Here, once again, it is necessary to read between the lines of Gardner's argument to recognise the underlying cultural patterns it represents. The Bush doctrine of pre-emptive self-defence, as a doctrine of general application, is so ominous as to merit universal condemnation. As Gardner says, effectively, it would give *ex post facto* justification to Japan's attack on Pearl Harbour (588). The proper way to approach the Iraq problem was by reference to previous UN Security Council resolutions about material breach, although when the US finally realised this, public opinion at home and abroad had come to see the Iraq War as the first application of a new doctrine of preventive war (588–9).

Gardner's concept of collective security once again means that States should aim to implement their view of the meaning of Security Council resolutions, along with such other States as are willing to meet their obligations. The decisions of NATO (invoking Article 5 of the NATO in the context of terrorist attack) and the United Nations 'provide a sufficient legal basis for military actions the *United States needs* to take to destroy terrorist groups operating in countries that do not carry out their obligations to suppress them' (589; emphasis in the original).

Once again, there is a totally uncritical treatment of the so-called Kosovo precedent, as a way of representing regional back-up for the universal organisation. Gardner says that the successful military campaign undertaken by NATO to put an end to ethnic cleansing in Kosovo

> protested against by some UN members but not disowned by the Security Council, provides another example of a reinterpretation in practice of Article 2/4, this time to permit humanitarian intervention to stop genocide or a similar massive violation of human rights where the intervention has the sanction of a regional organization. (589)

152. *AJIL* 97(3) (July 2003) 585–90.

Gardner's arguments need to be read very carefully. The importance of his conclusions is in the last sentence. The Bush Administration is right to ask for international law to be re-examined in the face of the new dangers of *catastrophic terrorism* but wrong in its proposed solution. Instead, a modest reinterpretation of the UN Charter is enough. In particular, out of four interpretations, the one most in keeping with the Kosovo and Iraq 'precedents' is the first.

> Armed force may now be used by a UN member even without Security Council approval to destroy terrorist groups operating on the territory of other members when those other members fail to discharge their international law obligations to suppress them.

In terms of the analysis of Jewett and Lawrence, who question the emotional and psychological stability of their *fellow Americans* (Jewett and Lawrence's emphasis) when they perceive danger, Gardner's reinterpretation is once again a form of *carte blanche*. It will provide a cover for President Obama's much expanded practice of targeted killing through drones (see later in the chapter). It is no wonder that Gardner concludes his modest proposal to find his way between Bush and the 'Jurisprudes' with the words: 'The United States needs to claim no more from international law than this. The rest of the world should concede no less' (590). No sentence could show more clearly what Gardner means by collective security. There is an objective necessity that America will recognise, and one can only hope that one's allies will as well.

Similar comments may be made about the arguments of Ruth Wedgwood, in *The Fall of Saddam Hussein: Security Council Mandates and Preemptive Self-Defense*.[153] She sets as her task 'whether to accept the procedural blockage of the Council, or to seek an alternative route to legitimacy and the recognition of legality' (577). Of course, procedural blockage, much like Blair's 'unreasonable veto', means opposition to the wishes of the US and its allies. West African regional organisation practice in relation to Liberia and Sierra Leone, as well as NATO's intervention over Kosovo, would suggest that regional organisations may be able to take enforcement action without prior Security Council approval. Wedgwood recognises that there are difficulties in predicting customary law change, but the

153. *AJIL* 97 No. 3 (2003) 576–85.

characterisation of evil personalities is not long in coming and shows clearly the US 'cops and robbers' view of the world:

> But surely one central ingredient is the moral necessity of action – the credible invocation of shared community purposes. Indeed, Justice Holmes' 'bad man' theory of law may have an unexpected application – whenever a particularly disruptive personality causes more than one genocidal conflict, alternative methods of countering his renewed threats are likely to be tolerated. This theory of exception plausibly fits the example of Slobodan Milosevic and Charles Taylor, as well as Saddam Hussein. It is a further step to suppose that any *non-regional* 'coalition of the willing' can substitute for Council action . . . In the light of the UN Charter's human rights commitments, the new Community of Democracies may be entitled to more substantial weight than any geographical artifact. (578; emphasis in the original)

This long quotation illustrates a total dissolution of the formal aspect of law into a series of material, somehow, authoritative judgements about evil to be punished, which takes on a definitely new character now that the Cold War is passed, in terms of the post-9/11 threat of terrorist attack in the form of WMD. The 'bad man' takes on a cosmological dimension. Wedgwood distinguishes deterrence and containment as the core doctrines of the Cold War. The brave new world is where there are no credible disincentives to non-State terrorists who have access to WMD. Indeed, a 'rogue state that is utterly heedless of its people . . . may not care about the potential collateral damage from a responsive military strike' (582). The question is whether a State can use pre-emptive force in unique cases

> when intelligence is reliable and timing is sensitive, and a state is sponsoring or hosting a network acquiring weapons of mass destruction . . . [T]he abstract answer to many strategists is yes – a given regime might have a record of conduct so irresponsible and links to terrorist groups so troubling that the acquisition of WMD capability amounts to an unreasonable danger that cannot be abided . . . In a teleological understanding of the Charter, strengthened by commitments to human rights and democracy, defensive force may be necessary to counter the unpredictable violence of states and non-state actors. This should inform the reading of Article 51 as much as the scope of Chapter VII. (584)

Once again the whole remit of a formal approach to law vanishes. Instead, one has the unilateral demonisation of the opponent with whom one is in no human relationship whatsoever. Indeed, it is precisely the teleological interpretation of a very general reference to international law, the so-called principles of democracy and human rights embedded in the UN Charter, which allows the 'Community of Democracies' to draw an absolute boundary between themselves and the 'other', the rogue states and the 'terror network with unworldly motivations' (583). The two elements of Campbell's characterisation of the working of identity are most clearly present here.

First, there is the projection of responsibility and evil entirely outside of oneself on to the other. International law merely functions as an additional, boundary-drawing instrument to achieve this goal. Of course, the Community of Democracies and the rogue states and non-State terrorist networks are an, as it were, standard postmodern example of a binary opposition. The self and the other are not separate. They are a single entity. The second dimension of Campbell's analysis, here vitally illuminated by Gaddis, is the repetitive application of this defensive identity mechanism, through the specific instrument of the pre-emptive attack on terrorists and rogue states, following the end of the Cold War and the disappearance of the 'communist menace'. Gaddis himself thinks the Cold War was remarkable for American abstention from the doctrine of pre-emptive attack, but he does say that it will appear where America feels most acutely threatened. Campbell shows how the disposition of the Post-Westphalia State to feel threatened is always there. Furthermore, the pseudo-religiosity portrayed by Jewett and Laurence is also a symptom of this ontological void. In the next chapter a neo-Marxist description of the American Security State, with its military-industrial-media based structure, will be added.

Finally, John Yoo, in *International Law and the War in Iraq*,[154] operating within the same parameters as Wedgwood (that is, non-State terrorist networks and rogue states) elaborates considerably on Wedgwood's analysis of how defensive measures to counter the unpredictable violence of States and non-State actors should inform a reading of Article 51, and so on. The three criteria for the use of pre-emptive force that Yoo elaborates all depend upon judgements about levels of danger and material perceptions of the other. The first question is whether a nation has WMD and the inclination to use them. Apart from the Iraq case, in future the decision will depend upon intelligence about rogue nations' WMD programmes and their ability to assemble a weapon (575). The second question nations will

154. *AJIL* 97 (2003) 563–76.

have to take into account is what Yoo calls 'the available window of opportunity'. The problem is, of course, the suicide bomber, immune to traditional methods of deterrence, besides being difficult to trace in innocent populations. The 'window of opportunity' may exist for the 'United States and its allies' before a rogue nation transfers weapons to a terrorist organisation. If it had to wait for the transfer to occur, it would be more difficult for 'the United States, for example' (now apparently without its allies), to act, given the sporadic nature of terrorist attacks (575). The third question, or consideration, is the degree of harm from a WMD attack, given that 'the combination of the vast potential for destructive capacity of WMD and the modest means required for their delivery make them more of a threat than the military forces of many countries' (575).

The final stage of Yoo's argument has the merit that it is reduces to nonsense a whole tradition of secular authority in international relations that Campbell highlights as beginning with Hobbes and the Westphalia settlement: the apparent construction of order based upon the opposition of the domestic and the foreign and the paradox of a State system, which rests upon the mutually exclusive suppositions that each is a self for itself and an other for all the others. Yoo finds himself, along with the whole of the international law profession, trapped in what is not a logic of his own making. Starting from the reasonable supposition that the degree of harm from an WMD attack would be catastrophic, he appears to commit himself to the view that danger is unlimited in degree, all-pervasive in extent, and requiring ceaseless pre-emptive attacks. In other words, we are in an impossible position, at the bankrupted end of an international law tradition:

> Thus, even if the probability that a rogue nation would attack the United States directly with WMD were not certain, the exceptionally high degree of harm that would result, combined with a limited window of opportunity and the likelihood that if the United States did not act, the threat would increase, could lead a nation to conclude that military action is necessary in self-defense. Indeed, as President Bush recently cautioned: 'If we wait for threats fully to materialize, we will have waited too long.' (576)

It is essential to update this American international law story to include the years from 2008 and the Obama Presidency. The newest version of the American mission argument, shared across the spectrum of the US presidential campaign in 2008, from advisers such as Robert Kagan for the Republicans (cf. Kagan 2008) to Ivo Daalder for the Democrats (cf. Daalder 2006), is that America must lead a Coalition of the Democracies to provide governance to the world, including, where necessary, in the eyes of the democracies, pre-emptive use of force and humanitarian intervention – all in the face of the rising autocracies, of which Russia and China are the most worrying.

Barack Obama in his *Foreign Affairs* article 'Renewing American Leadership' is broadly comfortable with this rhetoric. There is the usual identification with an America that 'stood for and fought for the freedoms sought by billions of people beyond our borders'. There is the same tendency to identify supposedly universal ideology with narrower American interests in such expressions as 'this century's threats . . . come from rogue states allied to terrorists and rising powers that could challenge both America and the international foundation of liberal democracy'.[155] This is not to deny that Obama is able to appreciate the need for co-operation with Russia and China on many matters, particularly nuclear weapons proliferation. John McCain is more unqualified in his support for a Coalition of the Democracies, with a less nuanced picture of the dangers of Russia and China.

The idea of a Coalition of the Democracies may appear less arrogant than the neo-conservative unilateralism of the Bush Presidency, but it is still based upon a pre-eminence of one country. When the liberal polity tries to universalise itself, it is confronted by spectres that it creates for itself. The first is the spectre of the autocratic regimes of Russia and China. The distinction between the foreign and domestic is denied as the democracies determine to project themselves globally. As Kagan puts it in the extraordinarily crude and monolithic terms:

> The autocrats' interest in self-preservation affects their foreign policy, as well. In the age of monarchy, foreign policy served the interests of the monarch. In the age of religious conflict it served the interests of the church. In the modern era, democracies have pursued foreign policies to make the world safe for democracy. Today the autocrats pursue foreign policies aimed at making the world safe, if not for all autocracies, at least for their own.[156]

155. B. Obama, 'Renewing American Leadership', *Foreign Affairs*, July/August 2007 <http://www.foreignaffairs.org/20070701faessay86401/barack-obama/renewing-american-leadership.html>, accessed 27 September 2008. I. Daalder (ed.), *Beyond Pre-emption* (2006).
156. R. Kagan, *The Return of History and the End of Dreams* (2008).

A similar call to arms comes from French 'intellectuals' in a manifesto serving as a rallying call for the war in Afghanistan and wherever next. The title reads: *Manifesto 'The United Nations versus Human Rights'* (Badinter et al. 2008). The polemic of the 'intellectuals' plays fully into the hands of Carl Schmitt, for whom all politics is a definition of the enemy, whom one is ready to kill. A sample of their rhetoric reads:

> If according to the UN blasphemy is to be assimilated to racism, if the right to criticise religion is to be outlawed, if religious law is to be inscribed into international norms, this would be a regression filled with disastrous consequences and a radical perversion of all *our tradition of struggle against racism, which has been able to, and can only be able to develop with the most absolute liberty of conscience.*[157]

In other words, there can be no compromise with the 'enemies of freedom'.

When the case for a Coalition of the Democracies is set out in a more rigorously academic way than is the case with Robert Kagan's polemic, it becomes clearer that it does represent a picture that is intended to be bipartisan as between Republicans and Democrats. There is a much earlier presentation of the idea in *Forging a World of Liberty under Law*, by Ikenberry and Slaughter in their 2006 Princeton Project on National Security. This is a nuanced and extensive document. However, its aim is still simply to build what it calls a liberal order, where Americans recognise that they are far better off

> if American power is exercised within an institutional framework of co-operation, where others have a voice – *although not a veto* – and nations endeavour to work in concert towards common ends. *Such a world is one in which other nations bandwagon with the United States rather than balance against us, and where they seek to facilitate American goals, not to inhibit them.*[158]

---

157. E. Badinter et al., Manifesto 'The United Nations versus Human Rights', 2008 <www.licra.org/news/pdf/get_file.php?file_name=the_united_nations_versus_human_rights__english_version_.pdf>, accessed 27 September 2008; emphasis in the original.
158. G. J. Ikenberry and A. M. Slaughter, *Forging a World of Liberty under Law*, 2006 <http://www.princeton.edu/~ppns/report/FinalReport.pdf>, accessed 27 September 2008.

The authors go on to explain that both liberty and law must be backed by force. It is necessary to maintain the military predominance of the liberal democracies and the United States must encourage the development of military capabilities of like-minded democracies in a way that is compatible with US security interests: 'The predominance of liberal democracies is necessary to prevent a return to great power security competition between the US and our allies, on the one side, and an autocracy or a combination of autocracies on the other.[159]

A difficulty with this type of analysis is that it does not appear to be self-reflective about the possibility that its ideology is generated by American interests related to declining American power. Of course, Americans are not alone in this type of analysis. Recently, Timothy Garton Ash has written an essay entitled 'We Friends of Liberal International Order Face a New Global Disorder' (2008). The author points to the huge shift in economic power towards Asia and Russia, now accentuated at the time of writing (September 2008) by the virtual collapse of American banking and a ruinous Iraq war that leaves China in a position of increasing financial dominance in the world. Ash even sees the Olympic Display as a threat. The authoritarian Chinese regime could mount 'the latest audio-visual hi-tech . . . placed at the service of a hyper-disciplined collectivist fantasy, made possible by financial resources no democracy would have dared to devote'.[160] After speaking of fascism and communism as forms of illiberal modernity that have been defeated, Ash goes on to say that 'in China we glimpse the prospect of a modernity which is both non-Western and illiberal'.[161] For this reason, he distinguishes himself from those Europeans who are sceptical 'of the notion canvassed by policy intellectuals supporting both John McCain and Barack Obama, of a "concert of the democracies'.[162] Still Ash avoids fundamentalist dichotomies of West and non-Western in looking for liberal values. He also appreciates, although he does not elaborate on the fact, that the West also has interests as well as values. Nonetheless, the title of the essay remains grim and exclusivist. What Ash fails to appreciate is that the international relations tradition of the West has always been problematic and incomplete.

159. Ibid., 29.
160. T. G. Ash, 'We Friends of Liberal International Order Face a New Global Disorder', *The Guardian*, 11 September 2008 <http://www.guardian.co.uk/commentisfree/2008/sep/11/1>, accessed 27 September 2008.
161. Ibid.
162. Ibid.

Modernity in the West constructed around Machiavelli's and Hobbes' theories, that is to say, around theories of the strong State and of national security, left the international space and indeed the so-called non-West in a vacuum outside any universal moral order. In other words, what is Western is not and never has been the universal. At present, a contradiction arises in the logic of Anglo-American liberal international law and morality, between its conviction as to the value of freedom and its belief that it has both the authority and capacity to judge how others exercise their freedom. For instance, Shashi Tharoor, a former UN under-secretary general, writes the following concerning the idea floated by advisers of McCain and Obama – Robert Kagan and Ivo Daalder, among others – for a *League of the Democracies* that would go around the United Nations and undertake global governance, in opposition to the supposedly new authoritarian powers Russia and China:

> The legitimacy of the democracies comes from the consent of the governed; when they act outside their own countries no such legitimacy applies. The reason that decisions of the UN enjoy legitimacy across the world lies not in the democratic virtue of their members, but in its universality.[163]

While Tharoor does go on to admit the United Nations needs radical reform, this is not to say the need for agreed authority can be bypassed. As the post-war unipolar moment 'slowly but surely makes way for a world of multiple power centres and a rising new superpower, there has never been a greater need for a system of universally applicable rules and laws that will hold all countries together in a shared international community'.[164] So, he recommends not systematically dividing the world into autocracies and democracies. He says, of the so-called authoritarian states, if 'instead of encouraging their gradual democratisation, wouldn't we be reinforcing their sense of rejection by the rest?'[165]

In a most convincing and exhaustive interpretation by Jean François Susbielle (2008), the whole project of a Coalition of the Democracies as it floats into the general American political atmosphere, is an attempt to

163. S. Tharoor, 'This Mini-league of Nations Would Cause Only Division', *The Guardian*, 27 May 2008 <http://www.guardian.co.uk/commentisfree/2008/may/27/unitednations.usa>, accessed 27 September 2008.
164. Ibid.
165. Ibid.

block and eventually cripple the one serious rival of the United States, which is China. The United States are actively encouraging India and Japan to regard China as their enemy and encouraging Europe to regard Russia as their enemy. This is despite the fact that Japan and China are natural trading partners and the economies of Russia and Europe complement each other perfectly.[166] Neither of these pairs of countries/regions have any interest in allowing political or ideological values to get in the way of peaceful economic exchange and growth. However, these developments exclude more and more the United States from the Euro-Asian landmass both economically and, eventually, politically, and so the United States have every interest in keeping them divided from each other. It is not possible in this context to follow up exhaustively the arguments of Susbielle's book. However, specific reference may be made to the polarisation of US–European and Russian relations.

At the time of the 2008 US Presidential election the Georgia crisis was in full swing and Secretary of State Rice situates Russia in a context of the struggle of democracies against authoritarian regimes. In her strongest attack since Russian forces routed Georgia's military in a five-day war, Rice said President Dmitri Medvedev and his Prime Minister, Vladimir Putin, had launched Russia on a path to pariah status.[167] Rice continues her argument by turning to the question of NATO enlargement in the context of Georgia: 'Since the end of the Cold War, we and our allies have worked to transform NATO . . . into a means for nurturing the growth of a Europe whole, free and at peace.'[168] And she insisted that Russia would not be allowed to dictate who joined the NATO alliance:

---

166. J. F. Susbielle, *Les Royaumes Combattants* (2008).
167. There does appear to be a clear divergence of the European Union from the United States. Russia has agreed to 200 EU monitors to be placed in a ring around the South Ossetia border within Georgian territory. According to Traynor, '[T]he Sarkozy peace plan has attracted muted criticism from Washington and NATO officials for being too lenient on the Russians. EU officials dismissed the jibes. "Without the EU, you don't get the Russians out [of Georgia]. There is no alternative. The Americans cannot be part of the solution here", said an EU official. I. Traynor, 'Aggressor Russia Facing Pariah Status, US warns', *The Guardian*, 19 September 2008 <www.guardian.co.uk/world/2008/sep/19/russia.usa>, accessed 27 September 2008.
168. BBC (2008), 'Rice Criticises "Isolated" Russia', 18 September 2008 <http://news.bbc.co.uk/2/hi/americas/7623555.stm>, accessed 27 September 2008.

> We will not allow Russia to wield a veto over the future of our Euro-Atlantic community – neither what states we offer membership, nor the choice of those states to accept it . . . We have made this particularly clear to our friends in Ukraine.[169]

Finally, Rice gives the Russians a lecture on how to govern themselves, very much in the spirit of the *Coalition of the Democracies*. The Secretary of State was also critical of the domestic situation inside Russia: 'What has become clear is that the legitimate goal of rebuilding Russia has taken a dark turn – with the rollback of personal freedoms, the arbitrary enforcement of the law [and] the pervasive corruption at various levels of Russian society.'[170]

Russia, in turn, had been recently trying to persuade the Europeans that America was actively engaged in encouraging the Georgians to use force against South Ossetia, that it has been arming the country for several years and that US military advisers were on the ground throughout. The Russians remained inside Georgian territory after the expulsion of Georgian forces from South Ossetia for as long as was necessary to destroy all the military equipment supplied by the United States. Prime Minister Putin directly accused the United States of trying to frighten Europe into taking anti-Russian positions. He described Georgia's attack on the breakaway region on 7 August 2008 as unexpected and unprovoked. He accused the United States of training the Georgian army before its attack on the South Ossetian capital, Tskhinvaliu: 'They sent instructors who helped to mobilise the Georgian forces. Of course we had to respond.'[171] He accused both US Presidential candidates of 'playing the Russian card' of 'anti-Russian phobia'.[172] Instead of expanding NATO to include the Ukraine, Putin proposed that it was time to create a security architecture for Europe in which Moscow had no imperial aims.

Again, it appears that the Russian commentator Fyodor Lukyanov has encapsulated, at a more abstract and theoretical level, exactly the essence of the idea of the Coalition of the Democracies in his call for the United States to abandon their hyper-hegemonic idealism and return to a more modest Great Power *realpolitik*:

---

169. Ibid.
170. Ibid.
171. Cited in J. Steele, 'Bush Failed to Halt Georgia War, Says Putin', *The Guardian*, 12 September 2008 <http://www.guardian.co.uk/world/2008/sep/12/putin.georgia>, accessed 27 September 2008.
172. Ibid.

> Discussions in the West pivot on one idea – how to ensure western leadership in the new conditions. A global 'concert of powers', which would provide for the equal participation of all influential actors in the formulation of new rules of the game, is not even discussed. The best they are offered is to discuss terms on which they would recognise the West's supremacy and benefit from that . . . The return of the US from the hyper-power category into the ranks of great powers, which have a very great, yet not dominant influence on international relations, would be a step towards the restoration of balance in the world. This would require from Washington the formulation of its own national interests and the development of a system of priorities. However, attempts to retain hegemony at any cost, amidst institutional chaos, imbalance of power and the growing ambitions of other countries, would bring about new and increasingly dangerous conflicts.[173]

The Obama 'war on terror' has a considerable input from lawyers, to restrain the use of force, particularly drones, within the limits of international law and the US Constitution. This remarkable development is described by Charles Savage in *Power Wars, Inside Obama's Post-9/11 Presidency.*[174] Obama's aim has been to have transparency in the decision-making process concerned with the 'war on Terror' and, probably for this reason, this Washington correspondent of *The New York Times* has published minutes of the meetings of about thirty-six lawyers, who probably qualify as 'free professionals and intellectuals' in the Habermas sense of eighteenth- and nineteenth-century liberal middle class, since they are already high-ranking academics and practicing lawyers when they come, at their discretion, into government service and usually remain no more than a couple of years, with frequent abrupt resignations over legal policy differences.

As Savage explains in an introductory chapter, Part I.2 *Acting like Bush,* Obama has approached the Bush era not in terms of foreign policy strategy differences, but in terms of purely legal formalism. Decisions should be openly taken, after full inter-agency exchange of views, in accordance with clear legal criteria and after the fullest possible investigation of the facts. At the domestic level, this means seeking, where legally required, Congressional authorisation. At the international level, care is taken to define the conflict as a war and

173. F. Lukyanov, 'History Never Went Away', *The Guardian*, 19 September 2008 <http://www.guardian.co.uk/commentisfree/2008/sep/19/russia.nato>, accessed 27 September 2008.

174. (2015).

not simply a matter of pursuit of criminal activity, where domestic criminal procedures and civil or human rights have to be observed. One will return to the detail of the distinctions the Obama lawyers make, shortly, but here it may be noted that Savage sees the resolution of controversy about this distinction to be found in the nature of customary international law. It evolves with the customary practice of states and if the US fails to persuade the rest of the world to accept its innovation as a new form in the light of changing circumstances, then the criticism of Obama's lawyers as trading loyalty to Law for influence over the Executive may be remembered. If a consensus emerges for the Obama lawyers' view then that may appear to be the standard way of making sense of twenty-first century terrorism and technology.[175] It may be added, that if Savage's type of investigation could be widely replicated in the world, a new form of international customary law, at least in a formal sense, could reproduce the style of legal debate envisaged by the founders of the Institute of International Law in 1873.

The revelations about the role of lawyers in Obama's administration are extraordinary. In the concluding chapter, Part IV.12 *The Tug of War*, Savage considers the debate between Bruce Ackermann and Trevor Morrison about Executive Branch Lawyering. The former thinks this activity actually accentuates lawlessness as it is a 'bipartisan project of executive aggrandizement'. Ackerman argues, 'Law is a disciplined conversation between lawyers and judges. But without any judges, law is a conversation between lawyers and other lawyers – and they are all on the same side, building upon one another.' Morrison, a former Obama White House lawyer, argues against Ackermann, that large parts of law do not come before judges. It is permissible for the President to pursue policies he thinks constitutionally defensible, even if they are not consistent with his best view of the law. This is especially 'where conventional sources of legal meaning suggest a number of plausible answers to a particular question but do not readily identify any one answer as clearly best, and where the area is one in which the practice of the executive branch may give some content to the law over time'. Savage prefers Morrison's view.[176]

In addition, Savage recounts the distinction between Jeh Johnson, as the Department of Defence General Council and Harry Koh, as the

175. Ibid., 248.
176. Ibid., 681.

State Department Legal Chief. The former, a professional litigator, sees himself as representing his client, adapting to the client's mind-set, and rigorously putting together facts to achieve what the client wants, so long as the conclusion is reasonable. For Koh, the academic, the emphasis should be a lawful US foreign policy, through the lens of human rights law.[177] Savage does not actually point to decisive differences of legal policy between the two, as will be seen, and the general character of the Obama administration is marked, in Savage's view, from the testimony, as lawyer-like overall in the search for precedent and in the articulation of policy in terms of frameworks.[178]

The heart of the 'war on terror' is in Part II.6 *Targeted Killing*. This concerns mainly the use of drones in the Middle East, above all in Yemen, Pakistan, Libya, Syria, and Iraq against Al-Qaeda and ISIS operatives who are 'waging war' against the US and/or its allies. As Savage describes numerous interviews, working memos, and published papers, the vast range of Obama's lawyers debated rigorously around at least five issues: the immanence of the threat – whether it was on the point of being made, or whether a target was known to be continually planning attacks; whether one could target an individual or simply a group known to be hostile, such as Al Qaeda and under what circumstances could another group be 'looped into' such a clearly defined terrorist group; whether an area of a country was sufficiently policed so as to make physical apprehension of the suspect or target required by the rule of law and human rights, or whether the area was so dangerous, such a so-called 'Badlands' that only drones could be used against the 'target', to avoid 'too great a risk' to American combat forces; whether the Middle Eastern country was unable or unwilling to take measures itself to deal with the Al Qaeda or other operatives – although frequently the international law issue was subsumed under the idea of covert US operations, with the acquiescence of the local government, on condition that it should claim the actions as its own; and whether it was significant that the operative was an American citizen.

It does appear from Savage's account that all of these distinctions were rigorously and continually debated, that they led to some strong disagreements, and that a number of members of the legal team left for a variety of reasons, including personality clashes. It would normally go without saying that a major part of the lawyerly

177. Ibid., 72–3
178. Ibid., 65–6.

task would be to assess whether the evidence of the imminent threat posed by an individual or group was sufficiently cogent to satisfy a lawyer that the threat was actually imminent. On many occasions the Obama administration did not proceed to action, according to Savage's record. There are numerous cases of large numbers of civilian casualties, which are very well known, but in principle, the rule about avoidance of any serious measure of collateral damage, that is, civilian casualties, was given extremely serious weight.

If the international law issue is whether the US, or another Western country, may use lethal force within the territory of another country, with or without that country's assent, to confront the tactical and strategic threat that Al Qaeda and like groups, and ISIS represent, then the most an international lawyer can hope for is what Obama has provided –teams of critical international lawyers, who, in open debate, are likely to air all the issues and, as they are doing so transparently, there is the possibility of international response. Procedurally, formally this appears as much as one can expect. It is worth remembering that Jouannet says one cannot blame Vattel for what she calls the decentralisation of international institutional authority. Savage notes how Koh, the human rights lawyer, moved openly into the centre of the international legal policy camp of Johnston and earned fierce criticism from New York University law students for doing so. Even if it true, as Ackerman warns, that the lawyers have never come to a conclusion that they thought contradicted US national interest, this does not have to mean, Gaddis notwithstanding, that the equation of international law with US national interest would be necessarily an act of hubris – *given the formal parameters of Obama's understanding of legal analysis*.

Savage points to a presentation by John Brennan, while he was White House counter-terrorism adviser, to a Harvard conference in which he spoke at length about executive- branch lawyering on national security issues inside the Obama administration. He provides a picture that is, formally, similar to Haaland's:

> The interagency lawyers will get together to look at what is being proposed and then have a discussion, that is very rich, about whether or not what is being proposed is consistent with the law and consistent with best practice, or are we actually sort of now going into new areas and new directions . . . What we have now within U.S. Government, at the insistence of the president and others, is that type of discourse among lawyers. We want to make sure that we hear all the different views and perspectives. That provides us [with] a good sense of what those legal parameters are within which we can work.

> I have never found a case that our legal authorities, or legal interpretations that came out from that lawyers group, prevented us from doing something that we thought was in the best interest of the United States to do . . . Can there be shifts [in the law?] Yes. And those shifts are affected whether we're attacked, you know, on 9/11, or in other types of threats and challenges to our system . . . That is why a Harold Koh and a Jeh Johnson, when they get together and they talk about these things – they really want to wrestle it to the ground. Is there a right answer? Truth is elusive – as is 'right'.[179]

Habermas's critique of American democratic culture's validating itself beyond its borders – and also the just mentioned critique of Tharoor – comes, nonetheless, into the picture at the strategic level of American foreign policy in *material terms*. Savage is vaguely aware of this and it causes him to make some qualifications to his overall argument about the effectiveness of lawyering in Obama's use of force in the 'war on terror'. Obama and Brennan correctly assessed that Al Qaeda and others were essentially in the business of attacking the US and so there was no question but that the US was at war with them.[180] However, this was intensifying and coming to embrace more and more of the Middle East. Also the scale of the military operations is increasing. It is time to address specifically against whom the 'war on terror' is being waged. Internal lawyerly dialogue is better than 'cowboy-style' shooting from the hip. However, it is also time to address the contexts, above all relational and historical, which are engaging the US and other Western, that is, European states, in the war with large areas and populations of the Middle East. The unknowability and the increasingly threatening nature of the 'Other' is bound to affect even the most conscientious lawyer's attempts to put contours around his targets. To put it at its most simple, what is the quarrel that the US and the West generally has in the Middle East? Does the Middle East really 'hate our values, our tolerance, our way of life'?

For the most of Savage's story the 'Badlands' – a formal expression to cover parts of a country in which police and other security forces cannot operate effectively – only included rural Yemen, tribal Pakistan, Somalia, and the chaotic regimes of Syria and Libya. In these contexts, Brennan insists that it should not be necessary to

179. Ibid., 278–9.
180. Ibid., 246.

do a separate or distinct self-defence analysis each time a possible target came up for consideration, or where other governments were unable or unwilling to act.[181] Yet Savage recognises that by 2010–12 many hundreds were being killed, whose names were not known, and about which only fragmentary information existed in Yemen and Pakistan. The US was actually secretive about the standard of cogency of threat being applied, and, whatever the intention of the lawyers' groups, the risk to civilians was proving high.[182]

By 2015, with the overrunning of the capital of Yemen, Sana, Savage noted that Obama's directives on targeting in Yemen appeared to permit attacks on clusters of presumed militants even when there was not a high-value terrorist individual who could be presumed to be continually planning attacks on the US. Obama was widening the scope of drone attacks in the light of the increasing momentum of Islamic militants. Obama was giving way to the intelligence community's demand to 'widen the aperture' in the face of the danger that al-Qaeda was supposed to pose in the whole Arabian Peninsula. Yet with the bombing of a Libyan compound by US F-15 jets Obama was targeting a country that 'had collapsed into a hotbed of al-Qaeda and Islamic State militants'. Obama was opening new fronts for targeted killing away from traditional battlefields. So the apparently carefully elaborated legal policy with respect to targeted killing has lost all pretence of legal restraints in the context of the widening conflict in the Arabian Peninsula and the Middle East generally. Obama was opening new fronts for targeted killing away from traditional battlefields. [183]

Savage ends on the note that a number of attempts of US citizens to bring court cases within the US about deaths of relatives in these attacks, who were alleged not to be 'terrorists', were resisted in 2014 by the Justice Department on the grounds that it would interfere with executive branch decisions to protect national security in wartime. Justice Rosemary Collyer agreed and refused even an evidentiary hearing. She said that the Executive had to be trusted. Otherwise, even the chance of a later lawsuit would make officials hesitate to act decisively in the future in defence of US interests.[184]

---

181. Ibid., 248.
182. Ibid., 255–7.
183. Ibid., 289.
184. Ibid., 290.

CONCLUSION

The aim of this chapter has been to reimagine the proper subject of an international law reflection on the use of force. It is not the case that one can usefully imagine an independent normative order standing above States that can be impartially applied to them. Kelsen has definitively shown that, in this sense, there is no international legal order. This is not to say that some States may not scrupulously observe legal rules, or that academics cannot observe that individual states have broken such rules as Articles 2/4 and 51 of the UN Charter. The difficulty is that the particular historical context of conflicts at present may have changed dramatically and what is at issue is to understand the dynamics of what are in fact very individualised 'bad relationships', as opposed to the mere objective and separable 'Badlands', to use the metaphor of Obama's vast lawyer team.

The essential importance of Vattel is to see him as the first true post-modernist. With all concepts radically subjectivised, there is no alternative but to try to understand how each individual collectivity – Vattel calls them Nations, but now most usually States – understands the threats that it faces. However, that in itself is not enough, for the reasons that Habermas gives. Even a society as transparent as Obama's lawyer team is still talking to itself, as Ackermann has crispy observed. It is in the very nature of a non-hierarchical international society of interlocking relationships that it will always be necessary to try to unravel particular 'bad relationships' in all their long drawn out historical complexity. Each relationship will be distinctive and it does not matter whether and how much one can generalise from one relationship to another.

There is little or no prospect of understanding if one does not delve into the depths of the particular relationship. For this reason, the so-called *inter-temporal rule* is misguided. There is simply no point in a horizontally understood international society for one side in a quarrel to tell the other that nothing that it did to the other before a certain time – at least in the latter's perception – is now legally relevant because 'it was usual for one to so behave at the time'. That is precisely the issue in contention. Most of the concrete, illustrative, aspect of this chapter concerns the so-called 'war on terror' that directly affects the Middle East. It may be fashionable among Western international lawyers to declare that the use of force in international law and the right of conquest were not made illegal until sometime between 1928 and 1945, and that it would be impossible to violate the principle of self-determination – as a legal principle – any time before the 1980s. This profoundly marks the categorisation of Arab – nowadays Islamic – political violence as 'extremist' and 'terrorist'. It is on the basis that the status quo in the Middle East since the 1920s and at the latest 1949 was legally unassailable.[185]

It may be objected that terrorism involves the indiscriminate – indeed the deliberate – targeting of innocent civilians, but this has been fundamental to Western strategies of warfare since the Second World War and is enshrined in the doctrine of nuclear deterrence, which was further legitimised by the World Court in the *Legality of Threat and Use of Nuclear Weapons Case* discussed in this chapter. Not simply political amnesia but also institutional inertia makes it clear that where a State's existence is threatened – that is, it thinks its existence is threatened – then, to borrow the language of the US White House used in various contexts, including the 'war on terrorism', – 'all options are on the table'. In any case, the European Convention on the Suppression of Terrorism 1977 does not distinguish between political violence against 'military objectives' and innocent, civilian targets. It characterises the act of violence itself as terrorist, including any firearm or explosive, with the option for States to add any act of violence against the life, physical integrity, or liberty of (any) person.[186]

Obviously, the interpretation of the background to the escalation of violence between so-called Islamic extremists and fundamentalists and Western, and indeed, global upholders of the 'rule of Law', is bound to be not only controversial, but also, quite simply, subjective. Philosophy of international law is not a 'method' of coming up with 'legal solutions' through interpretations of existing norms. Nor is it offering ready-made ethical platitudes about 'listening to one another' and 'understanding one another'. Since States usually owe their origin to violence rather than successful legal argument before a supreme legal tribunal , there is always going to be a problem of any communications with others, where they regard this as a threat to their security. These beasts are not at all open to a Habermasian dialogue conducted with Vattelian civility. For one thing they do not understand themselves. Individual consciousness is radically limited both by history and by contemporary social and family pressures of integration. This limits profoundly individual judgement and responsibility. It limits the exercise of 'right reason' in ways that one can hardly begin to measure.

---

185. These issues are discussed in Anthony Carty, Review Article, 'Israel's Legal Right to Exist and the Principle of the Self-determination of the Palestinian People?' *Modern Law Review* 76(1) (2013) 158–77.

186. <https://www.imolin.org/doc/amlid/Belgium_Convention_27_January_1977_English.pdf>.

To return to possible 'dialogic partners' for the West in its 'war on terrorism', the history of the Middle East is well known and surprisingly uncontested. The American historian David Fromkin explains graphically how Syria and Iraq were constructed by France and Britain after their defeat of the Ottoman Empire, in violation of wartime promises to particular Arab leaders and in disregard of the wishes of the population. The Western forcing of the Jewish State of Israel on the Middle East is only one part of the picture, and, in economic and military strategic terms, not a vital part.[187] The contemporary international lawyer will say that the inter-temporal rule applies and any attempt to change the status quo is terrorism. Another American scholar Daniel Byman appears to assume that neither Islamic State nor al-Qaeda have this principle of the inter-temporal rule as part of their legal conviction. Of course, they are not subjects of the international legal order and so their legal conviction or absence of it does not matter to the international lawyers, as Nicholas Luhmann would so comfortingly explain if he was still with us. Byman, who is not an international lawyer, helpfully explains that al-Qaeda wants the West and especially the US out of the Middle East. Islamic State is primarily interested in 'purifying' Syria and Iraq, in sublime ignorance of the inter-temporal rule, but full of their own sense of time and history.[188]

Of course, none of this is to downplay the Arab world's authoritarian and militaristic traditions. Nor is it to attribute to the West full or even partial responsibility for the feudal, conservative religiously grounded monarchies of the region.[189] However, not a day passes but mention can be found of the sheer size of American, British, and other European arms shipments to these countries[190] at present, particularly in the context of the Saudi intervention in the Yemen since

187. David Fromkin, *A Peace to End All Peace* ([1989] 2001), chapters 48–51 and 57, but also all of the references in the index to the Sykes–Picot–Sazanov Agreement of 1916.
188. Daniel Byman, *Al Qaeda, The Islamic State, and the Global Jihadist Movement: What Everyone Needs to Know* (2015).
189. Consider, for instance, Jean-Pierre Filiu, *From Deep State to Islamic State: The Arab Counter-Revolution and Its Jihadi Legacy* (2015).
190. Mohamed Bazzi, 'Obama May Be Preaching "Tough Love" to Saudi Arabia – but Arms Sales Tell another Story', *The Guardian*, 22 April 2016 <http://www.theguardian.com/commentisfree/2016/apr/22/us-saudi-arabia-weapons-arms-deals-foreign-policy>; 'The Yemen and the Scandal of UK Arms Sales to Saudi Arabia', *The Guardian*, 17 September 2015 <http://www.theguardian.com/world/2015/sep/17/yemen-and-the-scandal-of-uk-arms-sales-to-saudi-arabia>

early 2015, in response to the same developments as were mentioned at the end of the discussion of Obama's vast international lawyer team. The increasingly wide terms of reference given to US drone targeting in Yemen is, therefore, only a miniscule part of the Yemen tragedy, as well as the tragedy of the whole Middle East.

None of this is to deny personal responsibility to individuals. Indeed, individuals play a central role in the development of international events and, without a direct dialectical engagement with them, one is simply whistling in the wind. For instance, Gerry Kearns draws our attention to the role that Bernard Lewis has played in the thinking of the G. W. Bush Administration's Middle East policy, and, in particular, in the mind of Dick Cheney. As Kearns says, Lewis explains Arab identities solely in terms of religion and in a feeling of humiliation at having been overtaken by inferior civilisations, such as the West – violence then as a civilisational jealousy.[191] This means, for US elites, that Islamic societies are somehow inherently hostile towards the West, an essentialised conflict in which politics and history play no part.[192] It is precisely such individual mind-sets among Western elites that set the frame for responsible engagement by critical international lawyers.

The consequences of the use of force are clearly abhorrent and always have to be undone through a collective, mutual, and dialectical resolution of their consequences. The shaping of historical identities can be distorted in their creation (that is, through violence, both physical and psychological) but they have to be part of the frame if one is to engage in a critical phenomenology of individual and collective consciousness and unconsciousness. All of these are only the first steps to personal responsibility and to the ultimate goal of 'right reason', always itself an individual journey.

Place has to be given to the relationship between ethics and ontology. This is what lies at the foundation of the conflict between the humanists and the scholastics recounted by Tuck. Hans Morgenthau had a more profound understanding of the limits of Reason in face of the power of Fate. The scholastic ontology of Reason supposes an ultimately benign concept of Reason, which hopes that Reality is ultimately governable by the Good, but Morgenthau focuses his critique on the rationalist, secular reason of Europe since the seventeenth century, which he

---

191. G. Kearns, *Geopolitics and Empire: The Legacy of Halford Mackinder* (2009) 238.
192. Ibid., 239.

castigates as ontologically superficial. For critics such as Morgenthau, international law is a liberal construct, which applies to international relations, the logic of domestic relations among individuals. States are treated as individuals and their relations with one another have to be marked by a mutual respect of freedom and equality. This equality has implicit in it that the international community is plural and that relations are marked by a secular, rational logic of equality. This thinking is a response to the apparent actual plurality of international relations from a European perspective.[193]

There is much that post-modernism has written on the manner in which the so-called Enlightenment excludes the 'barbarous Other' in its definition of rationality and civility, for which Vattel is most reputed. Fitzpatrick has set this out in his study 'The Desperate Vacuum: Imperialism and Law in the Experience of Enlightenment'.[194] Fitzpatrick's arguments are perhaps a variant of Tuck's, that Enlightenment's liberal, rationalism cannot project the universal, but has to define itself against the 'Other'. For this reason, Kearns bases his whole argument for the basis of geopolitics in the racist foundations of Anglo-American liberal internationalism. Geopolitics had to govern beyond the boundaries of the democratic world.[195] The universalist project contains an anti-universalist contradiction. The affirmation of the universal has to include the exclusion of what is not recognised as worthy to be part of the universal. Tuck, perhaps in contrast, recognises that a new humanist vision of Roman-inspired greatness was more crudely conflictual and did not have to conceal its brutality beneath an ideology.

Morgenthau's account of the rule of law ideology as applied to international society is inevitably somewhat diffuse. Since the seventeenth century the West has become dominated by rationalism, the belief that the intellect triumphed over biology and emotion, to discern logical principles or causal laws that explained the operation of the world. Grotius and Leibniz are the founders of this movement. The belief that humans use unequal resources to strive to dominate one another is replaced by the belief that certain social systems, for example, feudalism and aristocracy, *cause* war, while others such

---

193. Hans J. Morgenthau, *Scientific Man vs. Power Politics* (1946).
194. Peter Fitzpatrick, 'The Desperate Vacuum', in *Post-modern Law*, A. Carty (ed.) (1990) 90–106.
195. Kearns, *Geopolitics and Empire*. It is the general argument of his book.

as liberalism appreciate the soundness of rational exploitation of resources, free exchange and communication, and the regulation of disputes through compromise – based upon free communication – and through impartial adjudication.[196]

It remains to elaborate how these starting principles apply to international relations and what Morgenthau calls 'the Science of Peace'.[197] Domestic regimes based upon democracy, free consent of the ruled to their rulers, and free exchange of labour, goods, and capital signify a public space free of violence and in which disputes can be resolved through negotiation or arbitration. The projection of this domestic image on international society signifies that nations are as individuals, autonomous, entitled to freedom from interference, and with no obvious reason to want to dominate and absorb one another. Rivalries need not be destructive, beyond the spirit of robust competition and striving for maximum individual autonomy.

Out of these general principles come more precisely recognisable legal principles such as non-intervention, non-recognition of territorial change produced by force, the prohibition of the use of force (the right to war), the advantages of confederal arrangements, including international organisations, especially for economic matters, and the use of international adjudication to resolve any clashes of these general principles, which treat all nations and individuals as identical. Above all, these principles are a projection of domestic liberal polity on to the international plane. This means that it is only democratic regimes, with boundaries to their States, which broadly reflect the consent of the ruled, that can hope to afford a peaceful international regime. There may be disputes on small matters, such as territorial boundaries, but these are legal matters that can be adjudicated according to recognised principles, virtually of private law, such as evidence of continuous undisputed occupation, consent of the inhabitants, and so on.

This is all in sharp contrast to Morgenthau's vision of an anarchy of many States, fatally unequal in size, hugely diverse in religious, cultural, ethic, geographical, and other characteristics – especially unequal distribution of resources – that face one another in an environment of constant change and instability. Morgenthau is not here arguing a realist thesis that such liberal principles do not govern

---

196. Morgenthau, *Scientific Man vs Power Politics* esp. chapter 2, 'The Age of Science and the Social World', and chapter 3, 'The Repudiation of Politics'.
197. Ibid., chapter 4.

world society. Quite the contrary, liberal powers such as the USA, Britain, and other European powers enjoy military ascendency in the world and are capable repeatedly of enforcing such principles and making them an effective reality. Instead, he is objecting that such principles of liberal internationalism ought not to be enforced because they involve a fundamental metaphysical misunderstanding of the nature of social reality, and thereby increase the havoc and chaos of international society.

The fundamental reason is precisely that the international rule of law distorts social reality.[198] This is in a number of precise respects. Given that the liberal model of world society is too simplistic, it is inevitable that the characterisation of clashes among States in legal terms will have the effect that:

> The legal decision, by its very nature, is concerned with an isolated case. The facts of life to be dealt with by the legal decision are artificially separated from the facts which precede, accompany, and follow them and are thus transformed into a 'case' of which the law disposes 'on the merits'.
>
> A political situation presenting itself for a decision according to international law is always one particular phase of a much larger situation, rooted in the historic past and ramifying far beyond the issue under legal consideration.[199]

Morgenthau goes on to consider what if Sweden had allowed Britain and France to come to the rescue of Finland when it was the subject of Russian aggression, by granting them free passage through its territory? The wish made sense in liberal international law terms. But would it have made sense for Britain and France to have found themselves at war with both Russia and Germany at the end of 1939?[200]

The social reality of international society is of power seeking. For Morgenthau this dangerous world calls for what he calls political evaluation:

> The test to which political decisions in the international sphere must be subject refers, therefore, to the measure in which those decisions affect the distribution of power . . . The question which Richelieu, Hamilton . . . or Disraeli would ask before they acted . . . was: Does this decision increase or decrease the power of this and other nations?[201]

198. Morgenthau, *Scientific Man vs Power Politics* 108–21.
199. Ibid., 118.
200. Ibid., 119.
201. Ibid., 101.

However, it is important to understand what precisely Morgenthau means by 'political evaluation'. Considering international law issues and the principles that should or could have been brought to bear, for example, on the Sudetenland question in 1938 (principle of self-determination, speculation about Hitler's war intentions and so forth, and the value of a treaty Hitler would sign), Morgenthau argues that 'the choice is not between legality and illegality but between political wisdom and political stupidity'.[202] Morgenthau quotes the speeches of Edmund Burke at the time that the American colonies were struggling for independence. Lawyers and sheriffs cannot but follow the law, but '*legislators . . . have no other rules to go by, but the great principles of reason and equity, and the general sense of mankind*'.[203] Even in domestic society, peace and order depend not upon the victory of the law with the aid of the sheriff and of the police '*but upon that approximation to justice which true statecraft discovers in, and imposes upon, the clash of hostile interests*'. This requires not '*the legal acumen of the judge but . . . the political wisdom of the legislator and of the chief executive*'.[204]

Morgenthau is not attempting to save a wider concept of Law than the one with which he is familiar, the liberal rule of law. However, if one revisits the concept of natural law, not in its rationalist form expounded in the eighteenth century by Vattel, but in its classical medieval form, as still partially grasped by Grotius, then it becomes clear that Morgenthau is searching for an idea of law that has been lost. He is not calling for opportunistic calculations that individual politicians may resort to for their own polity, but a vision of balance and moderation, which can bring harmony, always only for a time in constantly changing circumstances, to the conflicts among all the polities that affect his own. Law is therefore a just measure and proportion of relations among things, then in the seventeenth century as now in the twenty-first century.

FURTHER READING

Campbell, David, *Writing Security: United States Foreign Policy and the Politics of Identity* (1998).

Der Derian, James, *On Diplomacy: A Geneology of Western Estrangement* (1987).

---

202. Ibid., 120.
203. Ibid.; emphasis in the original.
204. Ibid., 121; emphasis in the original.

Der Derian, James, *Virtuous War: Mapping the Military-Industrial-Media-Entertainment Network*, 2nd edition (2009).
Habermas, Jürgen, *The Divided West* (2006).
Jouannet, Emmanuelle, *Vattel and the Emergence of Classical International Law*, trans Gina Bellande and Robert Howse (2017).
Kelsen, Hans, *Collective Security under International Law* (1954, reprinted 2011).
Morgenthau, Hans, *Scientific Man Versus Power Politics?* (1946).
Nijman, Janne E., 'Paul Riceour and International Law: Beyond "The End of the Subject"', *Leiden Journal of International Law* 20 (2007) 25–64.
Ricoeur, Paul, *The Course of Recognition*, trans. David Pellauer (2007).
Savage, Charles, *Power Wars: Inside Obama's Post 9/11 Presidency* (2015).
Richard Tuck, *The Right of War and Peace: Political Thought and International Order from Grotius to Kant* (1999).
von Bernstoff, Jochen, *The Public International Law Theory of Hans Kelsen: Believing in Universal Law* (2014).

4

International Economic/Financial Law – A Critique

INTRODUCTION: FROM VATTEL TO MANDEVILLE TO DE SADE TO FOUCAULT

There is, supposedly, a formal human right of peoples to economic and social self-determination enshrined in the two UN Human Rights Covenants. This would be compatible with how Vattel himself understood the laws of nations. It enshrined the right of every nation to decide itself how best to conduct its internal economic life and supposed a duty of all other nations to respect this right. There could be no objective international economic order to which all nations should have to subscribe. Such would be comparable to a resurrection of the fanaticism of the Wars of Religion preceding the eighteenth-century Enlightenment. The element of conscience and subjective assessment should also enter into economic and financial affairs.

However, this is a far cry from the actually very highly charged atmosphere of economic ideology in the world today, especially in the West. The onward march of monetarism and neoliberal economics makes it appear that every micro-decision taken by a national authority is a profit-and-loss accounting exercise, whether it is the running of a hospital, a university, a company, or a nation state. The latter is supposedly powerless to regulate a molecular capital monetary flow that appears to permeate every nook and cranny of social being.[1] Economic nationalism and social democracy both have to give way to the inexorable drive of market opportunity. The rhetoric is that the market-State provides the open forum for opportunity, in contrast to the nation state that attempted to impose legal

1. The term *molecular* is taken from D. Harvey, *The New Imperialism* (2003) 29–32.
2. P. Bobbitt, *The Shield of Achilles: War and Peace and the Course of History* (2002) xxxii.

regulations on behalf of particular moral commitments.[2] The reality appears to be that the relentless drive of the all-consuming market sweeps away all social democratic attempts to direct investment or stem speculative currency transactions that play havoc with democratic controls of the economy. These arguments have to maintain that capital has no significant territorial location and no particular social concentration.

In the Introductory chapter we have followed through the analysis that Koskenniemi specifically affords of the nature of Vattel's so-called *Voluntary Law of Nations,* and its association with Mandeville's theory of the erotic play of interests, and following on this, Dufour's reflections upon de Sade's more intense accounts of human exchanges. All of this insists upon strong elements of personal choice and responsibility in the otherwise apparently abstract march of historical structures and supposedly iron laws of economics imposing themselves on modern societies as passive recipients. The disempowerment of modern societies is, to a significant degree, a disempowerment of choice.

It is quite possible that international lawyers have also simply absorbed what has already been called the atmosphere of post-structuralist gloom. In *Cultural Pessimism: Narratives of Decline in the Post-modern World*, Oliver Bennett places economic developments since the early 1970s in a wider context of Western cultural decay. He traces the immediate cause of contemporary economic anomie to the break from fixed to floating currency exchanges in 1973. This marked the end of the balance between organised labour, large corporate capital, and the nation state.[3] The post-1973 shift to speculative financial markets (in the region of $1.5 trillion in 1997) means these come to more than fifty times the level of daily world trade. The role of futures and derivatives – a global bond market of approximately $200 billion a day compared to about $25 billion trade in equities – marks the independent force of global finance with its own laws. The same measureless expansion in the role of the trade of multi-national enterprises (MNE) reaches in 1998 about $16.3 trillion a year, growing at 8 per cent, with intra-MNE trade at about 50 per cent of all international trade. Transport costs are negligible in comparison to savings in raw materials and labour costs, brought about by mobility.[4]

---

3. O. Bennett, *Cultural Pessimism, Narratives of Decline in the Post-Modern World* (2001) 146.
4. Ibid., 153–4.

What is crucial is the socio-political impact of these developments. The commitments of shareholders to companies can be cut by a phone call, leading to slash-and-burn restructuring strategies. Factor-price equalisation means that workers' salaries can be kept at a lowest global common denominator, and for 70 per cent of American employees, salaries are stagnant or declining. It is impossible to tax corporate profits that can so easily move to cheaper locations. As a percentage of US revenue they are down from 39 per cent in 1939 to 12 per cent in the 1990s, resulting in huge public borrowing commitments and budget deficits. The greater inequality of the new capitalism means a propensity to uncontrollable structural change, merging, and down-sizing, with a consequent breakdown of all connective ties of family, friendships, and communities. This is the economic background to crime, divorce, and other social breakdown – an untrammelled individualism in transactional societies – where long-term co-operative relationships are replaced by short-term market transactions, governed by expediency and self-interest.

These market values spread into medicine, education, and so on, and signify the end of common interest.[5] Some predict an immanent disintegration of the global capitalist system, with a new capitalism locked into a negative dialectic with tribalist identity politics, where a mounting scarcity of resources and conflicts of interests are matched by a decreasing capability for co-operation.[6]

Bennett places these economic developments alongside developments in politics, sciences, and the arts, pointing to a general culture indicating marks of clinical depression. Global capitalism leads individuals into feeling trapped, with no control over their lives. Rampant individualism is accentuated by maladaptive social comparisons, pressurising with overwhelming idealised standards, in an environment of unprecedented levels of competitive assessment in education and employment – a modern plague of the law of self-esteem. This is all within a framework of consumerism focused on increased personal insufficiency – that operates with an increased differentiation of products whose built-in deterioration engenders perpetual dissatisfaction in the consumer.[7]

Parallel developments in the political aspect have been, since the nuclear standoff of the Cold War, a threat of nuclear extinction, which

5. Ibid., 160–1.
6. Ibid., 170–2.
7. Ibid., 162, 190.

causes a moral sickness, a disassociation from feeling that is necessary to exist in a society threatened by annihilation. The widespread numbing of moral sense encourages a Dionysian immersion in sensation, leading to ever-increasing levels of schizophrenia and anomie. Chaos paradigms of world society multiply, as there is breakdown of the governing authority of states, and a transfer of power to sectarian groupings, criminal organisations, and private security agencies. The most obvious source of immediate political danger comes from the increasing sectors of third-world societies dropping out of the world economy, providing a source of growing resentment, which easily leads to terrorism, given the access to arms, explosives, and other means of aggression.[8]

The prevalence of terrorism, for Bennett, is best understood in the wider climate of total political disintegration, marked by epidemics of torture, genocide, and politicide, which McBride, speaking for Amnesty International in the 1960s, said marked a massive breakdown of public morality and of civilisation itself. By the 1980s more than a third of the world's governments used torture and Amnesty could note that public campaigning made no difference. There was no public outrage. The figures of genocides and politicides (government-sponsored murders) range from nine million to twenty million, respectively. The crucial dimension is comparison fatigue and the failure of any 'political' process of response.[9]

The criticism that Marxists make of post-structuralist elaborations of this picture is the depoliticising impact that they provide. They offer an alternative ideology that does lead to the multiple resistances of which Koskenniemi speaks, when he says:[10]

> The time of conspiracies theories is over. There is neither an overall 'plan' nor overarching wisdom located in the United States, or elsewhere . . . But instead of making room for only a few non-governmental decision-makers I am tempted by the larger vision of Hardt and Negri that the world is in transit towards what they, borrowing from Michel Foucault, call a biopolitical Empire, an Empire that has no capital, that is ruled from no one spot but that is equally binding on Washington and Karachi, and all of us. In this image there are no interests that arise from states – only interest positions that are dictated

8. Ibid., 61–5.
9. Ibid., 65–75.
10. In his contribution to M. Byers and G. Nolte, *The United States Hegemony and the Foundations of International Law* (2003) 98.

> by an impersonal, globally effective economic and cultural logic. This is a structural Empire which is no less powerful as a result of not being ruled by formal decision-making from anywhere.

Foucault's anti-Marxist decentralised contestation of power resists what it sees as any attempt to replace one set of social relations with another – that would only be a new apparatus of power-knowledge. Rather than being unitary, power is a multiplicity of relations infiltrating the whole of the social body, with no causal priority to the economic. This process does not simply repress and circumscribe people, but constitutes them. Power evokes resistance, albeit as fragmentary and decentralised as the power relations it contests.[11]

However, the constitutive character of knowledge has been identified as a key epistemological foundation of cultural pessimism. Bennett points to the argument that knowledge as a way of life is impossible: either we are on the outside – in which case its essence eludes us – or we are on the inside and too close.[12] For Foucault, also, power is always already there; one is never outside or on the margins. Resistance is possible but it is nothing more than the oppositional other of the prevailing apparatus of power – knowledge, minor, local knowledges in opposition to the scientific hierarchisation of knowledges. In such an ontological void – to refer back to Campbell – there is no point of transcendence that could allow a total critique of this reality. Post-modernism claims to have demolished 'grand narratives'. However, the effect of exclusion of any 'total perspective' is that one remains trapped within and remains entangled in incestuous quarrels. This can appear as a theoretical foundation for pluralism – opposition to a so-called will to totalise that is a refusal to accept the possibility of difference and discontinuity. Instead, it should be recognised that there are irreducibly different perspectives, each in its way critical of existing social reality. This approach reflects the rise of a medley of social movements – feminists, ecologists, black nationalists, and so on. They all insist upon change without a totality, piecemeal. Yet the Foucault perspective, in a Marxist view, is itself a total vision that evacuates any political content from the concept of resistance, objecting to any political action except waging war on the totality.[13]

---

11. A. Callinicos, *Against Postmodernism* (1989) 82.
12. Bennett, *Cultural Pessimism* 16.
13. Callinicos, *Against Postmodernism* 84–6.

THE FAILURE TO CONCEPTUALISE A PUBLIC INTERNATIONAL ECONOMIC AND FINANCIAL ORDER: THE NIHILISM OF THE WORLD ECONOMY

There is no longer even the pretence of a global project to integrate the formerly colonial world into a common world order. From the 1950s to the 1970s there was a project of development, Truman's 'Fair Deal', although there was no real transfer of resources to the so-called developing countries. It appeared as if there was an American and even European post-colonial alternative to the subordinated and openly exploitative treatment of the non-Western world during the previous four centuries. Agriculture should have been the basis of transfer of resources to a growing industrial base within developing countries, encouraging the strengthening of nation-State-based economies. This process was to be supported by foreign investment and soft development finance, through the World Bank (WB) and International Monetary Fund (IMF), which allowed a place for monetary policy to reduce unemployment and inflationary pressure. Nonetheless, there was no Western acceptance of cross-society political alliances within developing countries. These were seen as 'extremist' and destabilising in the context of the Cold War. They could only survive with Soviet support. They were caught up in the ideological conflict of the Cold War and subject to periodic Western military interventions, such as in Guatemala, the Dominican Republic, Chile, Vietnam, Angola, and many other instances. Consequently, there were the severest international political constraints standing in the way of assuring the widening of the purchasing power and consumer demand of non-Western societies.[14]

Even the neo-Keynesian development project was abandoned in the 1980s and replaced by a once again openly predatory transfer of capital resources from the developing countries to the West. This has covered suppression of natural resource prices, protection and subsidisation of the exports of Western agriculture and simply the buying up and destruction of local industrial capacity, in the context of devaluation of assets and debt rescheduling. Market and opportunity mean simply removing any redistributive element from politics. Such redistributive politics are branded as 'extremist' or 'illusory'.

The crucial weapon/instrument in the implementation of these policies has been the US's control of the world currency, the dollar. Once again it is a direct link between the political impossibility of

---

14. Arrighi and Silver, *Chaos* 205–11 see infra, footnote 73.

monetary reform and the continued pillage of the Third World – so vindicating Stiglitz's sceptical prognosis. As Will Hutton graphically explains, it was raw power that enabled the US to insist upon the dollar as the international unit of account in 1944. However, at the time, government policy was still Keynesian: to achieve income equality, employment, and economic stability. There was to be no devaluation of the dollar against gold, with full convertibility. Yet in the early 1970s the US imposed a world financial system in which the dollar would be the principal currency against which the others would float, but it accepted no obligations in managing its own currency. While the dollar fell, it had no rival currency and so the US was able to appropriate 80 per cent of the industrialised West's current surplus for its own strategic and military purposes. Without interest rate ceilings or reserve requirements, American banks lending out of London could come to dominate global banking.[15]

The creation of a new world currency, managed by a world central bank – that Stiglitz suggested may be made out of expanded Special Drawing Rights managed by an IMF whose voting system was reformed – was out of the question for simple reasons of national interest. Reagan abandoned tax on dividends paid to foreign holders of American financial assets. By the end of the 1980s virtually every country had been forced to remove outward capital controls and, by 1999, virtually 80 per cent of the world's current account surplus had been won for the US. The structures for US deficit financing of its consumer boom and armaments programme were in place. These developments 'have been the results of a series of consistent policy choices over thirty years reflecting essential US reflex dispositions towards unilateralism'.[16]

Such a stranglehold on credit has offered huge possibilities of enrichment. The increase in interest rates for the dollar in the 1980s not only ensured the inflow of capital to deficit-finance the arms race; it forced most Latin American economies with huge dollar debts into recession, to devaluation of their currencies, and to debt-equity swaps that facilitated a general US buy-up of productive assets.[17] The same pattern was repeated with the Asian financial crisis of 1997, when the US picked up large sectors of Korean industry at knockdown prices,

15. W. Hutton, *The World We Are In* (2001) 234–9.
16. Ibid., 240–2, esp. 242. Also Harvey, *The New Imperialism* 127–32, 'The Powers of Mediating Institutions'.
17. Ibid., 243–5.

so that US dollar loans could be repaid. The dollar is used for 77 per cent of international loans and 83 per cent of foreign exchange transactions, as much as in 1945. Hutton warns that this has not been irrational economic dogma: 'It was the dogma of the expanding superstate. The international financial system has been shaped to extend US financial and political power, not to promote the world public good.'[18] Hutton succinctly describes the global political deficit of the international financial system in social democratic terms. There is no equality of opportunity, nor an equitable sharing of risk. Nor is there a social contract for the redistribution of income with investment in social, physical, and human capital.[19]

A social democratic order is the alternative to civil war whether at a national or an international level.[20] Increasing numbers of the states of the non-Western world are now torn by unresolved socio-economic conflict. This expresses itself in essentially class-based ethnic division, reversion from secular nationalist ideology to religious fundamentalism, terrorism, and massive waves of cross-border migration. The privatised Western concept of a legal order offers a mono-cultural explanation of this State disorder in terms of inefficient, corrupt, and authoritarian State structures in *foreign* countries, with the subtext that it is not the function of the State to resolve internal social tensions through the redistribution of economic resources. The most significant dimension of the Western transformation of the international legal order from the 1960s through the 1980s to the present is to change the focus from the social dimension of international development to the political-military dimension of combating terrorist threats of violence and international crime.

A central focus of Western international law scholarship is now on making human rights law effective, eventually through humanitarian intervention and the forceful spread of the right to democracy. There is an increasing development of so-called rapid-reaction military forces that should be able to intervene in countries torn by civil war and plagued by 'vicious dictatorships', and so on. This use of force is ostensibly to defend human rights, but in practice it means responding to the consequences of international political and economic chaos exclusively through the use of violence. It is hardly

18. Ibid., 247–51, esp. 251. Also Harvey, *The New Imperialism* 137–82, 'Accumulation by Dispossession'.
19. Ibid., 247.
20. This is the central argument of Alain Joxe, *Empire of Disorder* (2002).

surprising that so-called humanitarian intervention as a principal measure to resolve internal conflict or to spread democracy becomes entangled with informal Western State intervention through the use of mercenaries. The line between formal and informal intervention (State and private) becomes fuzzy as the line between a 'regular' and 'black' (mafia, terrorist, drug, or other crime-driven) economy in Western economic relations with non-Western states.[21] This fuzziness is again an inevitable consequence of the absence of an international public morality.

Non-Western states now find themselves increasingly compelled to assent, through treaties of co-operation, to measures to counter international criminal activity, whether in the export of drugs, dirty money, or population flows. These agreements will frequently include forms of military assistance in terms of Western bases and equipment. The primary and readily applied sanction for non-co-operation is economic boycott and embargo. The ultimate sanction for non-co-operation remains military/humanitarian intervention. However, the distinction between economic and military sanction is not fundamental. The coercive character of this imposed legal acquiescence by non-Western countries comes from its overall objective. It ignores the overall basic function of civil-political society that is to replace civil war (and even criminal violence) with freely agreed measures for overcoming social inequalities and achieving class peace. Instead, the measures of economic and military sanction are defensive, a re-establishment of control over non-Western State territory in the interests of Western security.

This breakdown in any role of civil-political society is at least profoundly reinforced by the economic and social theory of methodological individualism, which is the essential cultural ideological arm of an Anglo-American world economic dominance. It makes a clearly universal claim that leads the members of this same culture to suppose that the removal of any State structure will cause everywhere the reconstitution of civil society. In his topology of legal cultures Green situates the US (and effectively the neoliberalism of the UK as well) within a metaphysics of a warrior's perspective. As trials of strength become the means by which an individual can prove his worth, one can triumph only by having more power than another. The State provides a legal framework, as an 'impartial spectator' (see Adam Smith,

21. Mary Kaldor, *New and Old Wars. Organised Violence in a Global Era* (1999).

but also the critique of Dufour in the introduction) ensuring an 'even playing field' (an Anglo-Saxon sporting metaphor) by excluding certain forms of 'foul play' from 'the game', such as the use of violence or fraud. Apart from that the ethical climate is Hobbesean.[22]

In her global topology of State–business relations the Australia-based specialist in comparative politics, Linda Weiss, picks up the same themes as Green in her reflections on English-language literature about specifically Taiwan, Korea, and Japan and their government–business relations. This literature considers that either government dominates or business dominates. The State either succeeds in *imposing* a course of action or meets *resistance* in one form or another. She questions whether the changes in these countries in the 1980s and 1990s constitute inter-systemic change (that is, from a State-guided to a market-led pattern). Instead, she points to intra-systemic change (involving increasing complexity of tasks and modes of fulfilling them). Her general conclusion from her empirical research is that in the 1990s in East Asia 'the State has promoted, strengthened and maintained a social infrastructure (a dense organisational structure of industrial networks, cartels, trade associations, and vertical and horizontal councils) to pursue those very leadership strategies on behalf of a given sector'. She concludes that it means nothing to ask who is following whom, and that 'there is much about the East Asian political economies which confounds and eludes conventional Anglo-Saxon categories'.[23]

It is this Anglo-American cultural judgement that underlies the whole rationale of the World Trade Organization (WTO), World Bank, and IMF. The aim is to assure the retreat of the State in the allocation of resources and the advance of the market. Government oppresses, whether efficiently or inefficiently (that is, in its own terms). Authoritarian behaviour, by foreigners, both creates uncertainty and induces a State of infancy. It is assumed that individuals act to increase their own wealth, but only provided that they are

---

22. M. K. Green, 'Cultural Themes in European Philosophy, Law and Economics', *History of European Ideas* 19 (1994) 805, at 805–6. Green refers to a study of articles in the *Harvard Business Review* from 1940 to 1970, which concludes that the ethical climate of American business is Hobbesean in the sense that the culture is full of conflict and change as individuals attempt to build a place for themselves in a hostile world.
23. Linda Weiss, *The Myth of the Powerless State, Governing in a Global Era* (1998) 69–72.

certain about the consequences of their actions. If the State is acting according to an uncontrolled discretion, this serves to increase uncertainty, and therefore this uncertainty will lead to hesitation, even to indecision and apathy, that is, to economic stagnation. In practice, Dunkley argues that while it is difficult to distinguish between the effects of globalisation and anti-welfarist ideological trends, it is likely that the downward pressure on taxation and welfare will continue worldwide, with cost considerations becoming more important.[24] What this really means is the destruction of the very idea of the right of economic self-determination of peoples. International economic relations after 1945 were to be regulated upon the belief that economic sovereignty and nationalism must be restrained through international organisation, so as to ensure that cross-border transactions are not restricted by discriminatory and predatory practices. However, at the same time it was assumed that national economic sovereignty could be legitimately used for the social democratic purpose of ensuring a minimal of social welfare in national societies. Since the mid-1970s international economic relations have entered a new phase of finance capital-based movement or speculation, which is outside any regulatory control.

Arguably modern economics, viz. capitalism, created and needs the nation State as a framework for development. The unified market, the control of a currency, and a stable fiscal regime are essential for capital accumulation. The question is how to cope with the plurality of such entities. Free trade has the primary objective of assuring, in the first instance, the co-existence of nation States as opposed to struggles for existence among them, which could lead to mutual destruction. The principle of comparative advantage, as an ideal, means that each nation has such a thing, and, therefore, exchange among the nations will assure trade without friction, and ensure international peace.

At the same time this happy logic has internal contradictions. The logic of capitalism is perpetual expansion and there is no reason, in economic terms, why one or a small number of States should not successfully absorb all of the others, or at least set completely unequal terms of exchange. Resistance to this 'natural tendency' need not confine itself to economic instruments or means. The flourishing of the General Agreement on Tariffs and Trade (GATT)/WTO and regional trade areas (RTAs) since 1945 have been directed against

---

24. G. Dunkley, *The Free Trade Adventure* (2000) 162.

the nationalism that was seen as the cause of the pre-1945 conflicts. The question is how to interpret this development.

The view accepted here is that there was a single, overwhelming, strategic victor in the Second World War: the United States.[25] Even if the Soviet Union played the major part in the defeat of Nazi Germany it was not skilful enough to realise the fruits of its victory. In stages, and without it being a question of implementing a completely preconceived plan, the US has managed to unite the West, including Japan, in an informal political, economic union, first against the Soviet Union and then against those states south of the 'colour-line' in a management of the world economy in which the explicit legal rules of the Bretton Woods system were always only a part. In this construction, the demonisation of nationalism as particularist, divisive, and, finally, self-destructive, is essential. There is no place in the rhetoric of human rights, the rule of law, and democracy, coming out of international institutions and RTAs such as the EU, for national State autonomy. The latter is not seen as an economically meaningful concept precisely because the aim of 'deep integration' is the elimination of all barriers, at least among the 'Group of Seven (Eight?)'. The WTO expresses only a part of this integrative project. The project has entailed the elimination of European colonial empires, the cause of one if not two world wars. It has made 'nationalist' conflict among Western powers appear ridiculous.

Yet it is precisely this disappearance of traditional conflict that needs to be examined closely. It is partially a function of the exhaustion of all of these powers except the US after 1945, so that only the latter has been able to act with the coherent sense of its national interest, which others had separately exercised with apparently disastrous results. However, it is misleading to speak exclusively of a completely separate US national policy. There has arisen a Western/Northern economic identity, which former members of the Soviet bloc wish to join. In other words, this identity is white. Yet its intercontinental character makes it difficult to continue to use comfortably the label *national*, albeit that one can continue to think of the political organisation of a territorial space to ensure the development of economic activity, a space that may not be global. Indeed, it is argued here that if this space is not truly global, the continued use of the term *national* in its pejorative sense, is justified. 'The West'/North is a concept of national identity.

25. This follows Robert Biel, *The New Imperialism, Crisis and Contradiction in North/South Relations* (2000) 1–130.

What does West/North exclude? The so-called third world remains a primary provider of raw materials and low-technology, intensive manufactured products, as well as a source of cheap labour for continued 'Fordist' manufacturing production. Apart from this division between North and South, the traditional arguments for international trade are largely formal. Exchanges in manufactures and services are merely reproductions of the same (for example, cars or computers) wherever in the West. They could be produced 'at home' in a national market, but there is equally no reason, political or economic, why identical products should not be exchanged across borders within the West. The question is whether 'the rest' can be, or need be, integrated into this process. The best answer to this can be seen in observing the attempts of third-world elites to attain equal status through the rhetoric of economic self-determination and a new international economic order in the 1960s and the 1970s. They inherited the structures of colonialism, and the question was whether they could break out of what had become neo-colonialism. Even their attempts to change the percentage of rent out of the extraction of natural resources, including cheap labour, was successful only in the one instance of oil production. Although third-world States were founded on a rhetoric of nationalism, it has been easy, by means of the rules favouring freedom of trade and investment and the reinforcement of Western intellectual property rights, to assure that third-world State nationalism, as an independent political element, is demonised as a source of corruption and economic irrationality. International economic law, as well as the more informal exercise of US-led Western hegemonic economic power, has virtually completely delegitimised the third-world State as an independent initiator of a locally coherent or cohesive economic development. All development must be 'outward', export-oriented towards the West.

Have developments since the 1980s done anything to render the classical colonial and neo-colonial divisions more fluid and less confrontational? Again it would appear that the 1990s have seen a more direct reassertion of Western rule over the South.[26] When the rhetoric of the new international economic order was in full swing it appeared that the world system accepted the permanence of new states that would attempt to develop some measure of social cohesion within their boundaries, on the basis of which they may develop complete economies along the lines of Western industrialisation

26. Ibid., 154–287.

since the nineteenth century. On this basis new states could gradually be added as full members of the international order. Economic self-determination may then run parallel to the right to political self-determination, found in the UN Human Rights covenants.

However, new trends in international management and technology diffusion meant that such autonomous industrial-technological development was improbable. It made more sense for Northern-based transnational corporations (TNCs) to farm out subsidiary activities in terms of a global strategy over which they could retain control. The primary reason for locating in the South would, as usual, be the cost of labour. The ultimate aim would be re-export to the North, which meant that there was no economic need to consider the expansion of consumer demand within local Southern markets. The reinforcement of intellectual property rights through the Uruguay Round would ensure the retention of overall direction. Indeed, even these relatively advanced industrial activities could be confined to a small number of newly industrialising countries, which the North may encourage for strategic reasons – the states on the rim of China, Taiwan, South Korea, and perhaps Indonesia. Beyond that it was necessary to ensure that possession of natural resources did not provide a basis for the development of indigenous industrial development through processing. Efforts by Ghana and Jamaica to develop bauxite production into aluminium, and so forth, could be crushed. Gulf oil dollars could be channelled into Western TNCs and rogue nationalist states, such as Iraq, Iran, Libya, China, and so forth, could be identified as not suitable to be partners in the international system and integrated into its international economic law regime.

None of this is to say that there is a complete, consciously worked out strategy of control. However, circumstances favoured an ever-tightening grip. The debt crisis of the early 1980s was brought on by a wide variety of factors, including the US arms build-up against the Soviet Union. However, the debt crisis favoured buying up potential independent industrial development in countries such as Mexico through debt–equity swaps. It enabled the IMF and World Bank structural adjustment programmes (SAPs) to stress the need to orient particularly agricultural developments to cash crop exports, which could pay off debts. Especially in Africa, public funds were directed away from education and training to cash crop exports of vegetables and fruit to Europe. In other words, the economic activity of the individual South countries could be both directed from outside and for the interests of the North. Throughout, there was a net transfer of wealth from the South to the North, so that Northern control could continue and the possibility of an expanded socio-economic base within Southern countries be foreclosed.

Hence has come the argument, introducing this chapter, that the period 1980–2000 has seen such a weakening of the State infrastructure in the South that the North is on the point of having to complement its IGO (WB/IMF/WTO)-led SAPs and its decentralised, subcontracting-led TNC management strategies, with a new, overtly military-political role for the North. Hence the aim now in both the EU and the US is to think of the development of rapid-reaction forces of a policing character and the evolution of doctrines of humanitarian intervention to assuage the acute crises and divisions in numerous Southern countries. Explicit doctrines of the export of the rule of law and democracy are on offer, with the threat of economic sanction and even military intervention albeit within a context in which the economic options at a global level have already been set by the TNCs and IGOs. Democracy, the rule of law, globalisation of human rights, and so forth, serve to prevent the Southern countries from deriving any legitimacy from the development of local State structures, which could serve to ensure the gradual evolution of local socio-economic solidarity or cohesion. This is reflected in the detail of WTO hostility to policies of subsidisation of local agriculture or industry, restrictions on foreign ownership, and, hugely inconsistently in terms of liberal ideology, in the maintenance of intellectual property rights. However, the rhetorical character of this ideology must be underlined. The disapproval of economic nationalism in Western-educated opinion is attributable to the economic imperialism of the pre-1914 years and to the aggressively protectionist nationalism of the 1930s. In both cases the culprit was taken to be Germany, which is the home of List-based theories of economic development through State cultivation of national industry based on the national market as a preliminary to participation as an equal in international commerce. It is believed that such a territorially and probably ethnically based view of economic development made inevitable German thinking in terms of the size of colonial empires, and encouraged Germany, in the 1930s, to set about constructing an identikit colonial empire in Eastern Europe, which would enable it to remain autarkic in relation to the global system dominated by Anglo-American economic power.[27]

27. See Hans-Erich Volkmann, 'Die NS-Wirtschaft in Vorbereitung des Krieges,' in Wilhelm Deist et al. (eds), *Ursachen und Voraussetzungen des Zweiten Weltkrieges* (1989) 211–435.

Hence, there is perhaps an unconscious Western tendency to see any serious, or apparently serious, opponent to its world economic strategies in terms of new Hitlers, especially in the Arab world. At the same time such a historically based ideology also serves the present political interests of Western countries.

It is well known that many services, such as the media, entertainment, computer software, and the food industry, directly embody cultural values and symbols, or so-called 'cultural baggage', although certain goods, such as clothing, cars, toys, and so on, do likewise.[28] In particular the media and audio-visual sectors swamp world markets. US films now account for 70 per cent of the market in Europe, more than 90 per cent in the UK and Ireland, and virtually 100 per cent of the Caribbean market. Supposedly American 'industrial cinema' now 'controls 80 per cent of the world's culture'. This is in spite of the fact that, under the Uruguay Round, there was no agreement for liberalizing the audio-visual sector. Indeed, the free trade argument that a deficit in one sector will be countered by a surplus in another 'is a furphy [i.e. rumor] . . . because the more US culture we are forced to watch on prime-time television the less of our own we see'. American films and TV programmes account for 40 per cent of the world market and audio-visuals are the second largest US export sector after aircraft, and yet imports account for barely 2 per cent of the domestic US market. It has been argued that language has always been about power first and culture and learning second. 'Blue jeans and Hollywood played their part in this, but it was Cruise missiles and Stealth bombers that became crucial to the process.'[29] Eighty per cent of home pages on the web are in English, compared to 4.5 per cent in German and 3.1 per cent in Japanese. While there are many studies to argue the cultural superficiality of globalised English, on the face of it the political passivity of most governments of the world towards Anglo-American hegemony appears to bear out the success of methodological individualism as a global role model. The positive rhetoric of the neoliberal international economic order is that it spreads to and implants in the non-Western world the legal values of democracy, the rule of law, and, above all, human rights.

28. Biel, *The New Imperialism*, 183 and what follows, 184–5.
29. R. McCrum, 'They are Talking our Language', *The Observer Review* (18 March 2001).

THE NATURE OF CONSENT, VALIDITY AND LEGAL OBLIGATION IN INTERNATIONAL ECONOMIC AND FINANCIAL LAW

Closer attention needs to be paid to the notion of imposed legal acquiescence. It is a concept essential to but not explicitly developed in analytical jurisprudence. Hart explains that for a legal system to exist, it is only necessary for the majority to accept, to acquiesce passively in the system. How the officials, who internalise the rules, and the others, who acquiesce, are distinguished or identified is left open.[30] The so-called consensus upon which international law rests includes the crucial legal legitimisation of economic coercion. This is clearly illustrated by the legislative history of the Vienna Convention on the Law of Treaties. Again, it was the Western countries that managed to repel the argument that economic coercion or pressure could constitute a violence that vitiated consent to an agreement. Only a threat or use of military force against a State was excluded. Overwhelming economic pressure would always be permissible.[31]

Economic hegemony, at the global level, means that the pressure of combined individual Western wishes and desires expresses itself in an overwhelming form on the rest of the world. The background to these wishes and desires is a methodological individualism that insists that each individual's claims and desires have automatic legitimacy and can compel fulfilment through whatever level of pressure is necessary. This value-subjective, morally anarchic philosophy is the essential anthropological basis for the free market economy. It supposes that human demands are not subject to external criticism and the success of these demands depends entirely on the strength with which they are pressed forward.

An elaboration of the idea of enforced legal acquiescence needs to situate it in the context of contractarian and voluntarist schools of liberalism. The word 'phagocyte' refers to a type of body or cell that engulfs bacteria, and so forth. In his polemic *The Hidden Face*

---

30. H. L. A. Hart, *The Concept of Law* (1961) 116–17.
31. Sir Ian Sinclair, *The Vienna Convention on the Law of Treaties*, 2nd edition (1984) gives an excellent account of the Western Third World confrontation on this issue in the drafting of the Convention. The West threatened to drop the whole idea of the convention if the Third World countries persisted with their proposal to regulate the use of economic pressure or force. The issue is not mentioned by Anthony Aust, *Modem Treaty Law and Practice* (2000), which may now be the standard current work on the subject, based very largely on the Vienna Convention.

of the United Nations (in French) (2000), Michel Schooyans borrows this word from Solzhenitsyn's famous Harvard Lecture (1978) to describe the tendency present in our society for law to appropriate morality. This may seem surprising in the face of the liberalisation of Western society from traditional, especially Christian values, in the 1960s and the 1970s. The State withdrew from wide areas of personal life no longer regarded as of public interest. However, Schooyans points sharply to a sting in the tail of this liberalisation, which he connects with the concept of an international legal order that takes coercion/sanction as its lynchpin.[32]

The Western (that is, European-North American) concept of the person, the subject of human rights, is radically voluntarist. It is based upon the unrestrained will of the individual in a radically subjectivist environment. There is no framework of rational discussion that can resolve differences and the tendency is increasingly towards a manipulation of assent through interest groups that reflect economic and military interests. The outcome is a forced consensus. Since human rights cannot be based upon objective understanding of either the value of the person or of reason, the consensus needed to reach decisions in democracies is increasingly the subject of coercive manipulation (popularly known as *spin*), causing alienation and withdrawal from the political process. The critique of voluntarism is that where each is free to choose his truth and act according to conscience, where all human beings are only individuals and have no common nature, or naturally grounded sociability, the meaning of words such as 'law', 'person', 'morality', 'family', and 'nation' depends upon consensual definitions that each one of us pleases to give.[33] Since there is no necessary element of reason in assent, it means simply adherence to a decision, without any necessary rapport with the truth of what is agreed. Consensus means acquiescence given to a project, a decision not to oppose it.[34]

Since we do not agree on any absolute values everything in the way of legitimacy, and presumably also the so-called rule of law, rests upon agreement about procedure, the process of consultation that precedes decision. The Habermasian theory of a free communicative space is explicitly based upon a post-metaphysical rejection of natural law, but fairness in communication is not enough to found

---

32. M. Schooyans, *La face cachée de l'ONU* (2000).
33. Ibid., 37.
34. Ibid., 39.

norms and values. It is politically agnostic about the actual context in which communication takes place.[35] In fact, it is essential to trace exactly the processes whereby individuals reach consensus in self-styled liberal democratic Western states. If there is no acceptance that there can be rationally objective ways of resolving differences of opinion about what is good or bad, it is inevitable that an anarchy of affirmations will, in fact, be resolved through the pressure, if necessary violent, of a preponderance of voices.

It is here that voluntarist individualism fits so well with the market economy. Exchange value dominates over nostalgia for use-value to mean that there are no values in common, but instead an individualist competitive struggle in the market as a place of exchange. The ultimate logic here is not a recognition of the absolute equality in dignity of all human beings, but the elimination of the inefficient, whether the individual or the nation. It is the frequency, density, and intensity of desire that is expressed in the multiplicity of choice that comes to dominate. Whatever holds out is legitimate.[36]

This is still a very elementary account of the relationship between liberalism, whether in its 'modernist' or 'post-modern' variety, the violence of the market, and the rhetoric of human rights as liberal democracy and the rule of law. Baudrillard also argues that the practice of politics and the practice of economics have increasingly converged to become the same type of discourse. The freedom to think is the freedom to consume. At the root of this transformation is the annihilation of all finality in the contents of production.[37] Work

---

35. Ibid., 41–2. This is in spite of Habermas's early work on the public space of rational debate since the Enlightenment, which I discuss in 'Changing Models of the International System', in *Perestroika and International Law*, W. Butler (ed.) (1990) 13–30. Schooyans is repeating a standard conservative critique of the procedural liberalism of Rawls, Habermas, and others, which may have first been made by Alistair MacIntyre in *AfterVirtue* (1987). In 'Critical International Law, Recent Trends in the Theory of International Law', *EJIL* 2 (1991) 66–96 I suggest that critical legal studies, as applied to international law, simply absorbs MacIntyre's critique of liberalism to produce the indeterminacy of legal concepts, without committing itself to explaining the existing structures of international law as hegemonic.
36. Ibid. This is a summary of the whole first section of Schooyan's book, *L'Empire du consensus*.
37. See further in Anthony Carty (ed.), *Post-modern Law* (1990) 'Postmodernism in the Theory and Sociology of Law,' at 82–5, in the section, 'Baudrillard and the End of the Social'.

reproduces itself and consumes itself like anything else. It exchanges itself with non-work in a complete equivalence of exchanges. There is no eschatology that may found itself on the social.

The roots of political passivity are here. Public opinion is itself a commodity. Opinion polls exist somewhere beyond any social production of opinion. They rebound incessantly in their own images: the representation of the masses is merely a simulation, as the response to a referendum (the father of opinion polls) is always induced by the question. It is not a matter of a single person *producing* an opinion; rather everyone has to *reproduce* public opinion, in the sense that all opinions are swallowed up in a general average, and then reappear at the level of individual choice. For opinion, as for material goods, production is dead, long live reproduction. Let spin be born.[38]

One may try to continue these reflections with some speculation upon the most well-known historical case of controversy about unequal or coerced economic treaties, the nineteenth-century treaties between Western powers and China. Here the analysis of *Treaties, Unequal*, which Anne Peters has done, is also very helpful, because she provides a broad overview of the history as well as placing it in the contemporary context of a 'realist' vision of modern international law as it is actually practiced.[39] She begins with the remarks that 'the pejorative term "unequal treaty" (or more polemical ones such as "coercive", "predatory" or "enslaving" treaties) refers . . . to the treaties between European powers, the United States of America . . . and . . . mainly Asian States'.[40] She comments that '[c]urrent international law as it stands does not accept a special legal category of unequal treaties with special legal effects'.[41] Peters' very thorough study shows the predominant experience of China in the debate. The modern notion of unequal treaties was developed by the Chinese in the 1920s and overwhelmingly scholarship has been concerned with the Chinese experience.[42]

Peters recognises that the issue of unequal treaties has actually become part of Chinese identity. The issue:

> became a focal point for nascent nationalism and was a driving force for institutional and legal reform. Notably in China, the unequal treaties also functioned as a scapegoat for interior problems and backwardness.

---

38. Ibid.
39. Anne Peters, *Treaties, Unequal* <http://opil. ouplaw.com/home/EPIL>.
40. Ibid., paragraph 1.
41. Ibid., paragraph 2.
42. Ibid., paragraphs 4 and 7.

> On the other hand their abrogation became one of the aims of the Chinese revolution of 1911 and was one of the three people's principles besides democracy and socialism. The treaty rhetoric has been integrated into the common heritage of Chineseness.[43]

Peters traces the changing Chinese consciousness through the nineteenth century. To begin with Asian countries were not concerned with extra-territoriality or customs regimes, merely wishing to retain control over certain cities and prevent foreign intrusion. This was because they lacked the conceptual understanding of legal identity necessary to object. '[O]nly later, the standard reproach of the non-Western parties emerged that the special privileges granted by the treaties significantly aggravated war-lordism and contributed to, if not caused, instability and governance problems in the host States.'[44] Nonetheless, Peters claims that these 'changes in attitudes and subjective assessments' did not warrant any changes in legal obligations, for instance as constituting a supposed element of changed circumstances.[45]

Her characterisation of the general system of international law of treaties is what is most important for the present argument about the nihilism underlying so-called international economic and financial law. Her argument is remarkable in its brutality and confirms very much the contempt that Dufour heaps on the whole of Western social culture attributable to the triad of Mandeville, Adam Smith and the Marquis de Sade.[46] She begins her analysis of contemporary unequal treaties, with question mark, with the words '[r]esort to economic and political pressure exploiting the extreme power disparities is a pervasive feature of inter-State relations. The result is treaties which are in procedural or substantive terms unbalanced'.[47] Peters gives a very comprehensive picture of unequal treaties usually connected with the United States, concerning its military bases and its opposition to the International Criminal Court, as well. Peters correctly identifies the legal situation as one going to the foundational structure of international law. So she says 'the freedom of the will of

43. Ibid., paragraph 66.
44. Ibid., paragraph 25.
45. Ibid., paragraph 57.
46. The word 'triad' signifies not simply triangularity but also the underground criminal gangs that operate in Chinese communities in Hong Kong and other parts of South East Asia.
47. Ibid., paragraph 60.

States is as yet no requirement of the validity of international treaties, mostly because an international institution which could effectively secure the genuine voluntariness of consent is lacking'.[48]

Peters appears to argue that this is an anomaly of international society that lacks the sense of community of national society, with its more developed domestic contract law.[49] However, her conceptual confusion really goes to the very absence of any conceptual logic or coherence in the post-Enlightenment concept of autonomous will. So Peters says:

> [t]he concept of a treaty is premised on the concept of contractual freedom (or in the inter-State context: sovereignty). By upholding unequal or otherwise unfair treaties, international law accepts the imbalances in social and political power that are reflected in international treaties.[50]

How can Peters continue to use the word 'treaties' at the end of the last sentence? The reason is that the whole idea of 'unequal' is itself unconvincing to her. So she continues:

> [T]he concept of unequal treaties is extremely vague. Both the prerequisites and the legal consequences of the inequality of a treaty are unclear. Which types of power or influence are relevant? How would they be measured? At what point would the inequalities in bargaining power and in the contents of the treaty be so intolerable as to flaw a treaty?[51]

One can imagine Mandeville, Smith, and de Sade laughing at the very idea of an international law of treaties. If one is to call for a global, compulsory system of adjudication, as Peters does – an impossible demand – one may as well simply accept, as Dufour insists, that we are now in a jungle that it is only obfuscating to characterise as legal.

However, an even broader perspective of international law based upon power and interest is provided by Jack Goldsmith and Eric Posner, in *The Limits of International Law*, a fairly comprehensive vision of the economic approach to international law, from Harvard and Chicago.[52] The lucidly expounded view of this work is that private,

48. Ibid., paragraph 71.
49. Ibid., paragraphs 71–3.
50. Ibid., paragraph 73.
51. Ibid., paragraph 75.
52. J. Goldsmith and E. Posner, *The Limits of International Law* (2005).

individual interest trumps any concept of the public good, and in line with Dufour's anti-history of Western political ethics, Goldsmith and Posner celebrate the dissolution of any moral or legal obligation in international relations. This is the very meaning and essence of the economic approach to law and brings international law into line with the general intellectual, cultural and political climate so far described in this chapter. What begins with a slight hesitation in the voice of Blaire Pascal – in Dufour's history – ends with the triumphalist cynicism of Goldsmith and Posner. No one has any obligation, least of all the powerful such as the USA, a frequently mentioned actor.

The fundamental structure of customary international law is grounded in a material practice of States, itself motivated and shaped by a legal conviction of States. Well, Goldsmith, and Posner tell us that such a legal conviction is an unnecessary hypothesis for the explanation of State conduct. Customary law changes with power constellations. States change their views frequently and always do what is in their best interests.[53] Using throughout their work the rhetoric of economic jargon, the authors say that equilibrium means that States will continue behaving in a particular way as long as the underlying payoffs do not change.[54]Coercion is a feature of the acquiescence of smaller States in rules. Where a coalition of stronger States with convergent interests forces others to engage in actions that serve the interests of the coalition this has the appearance of customary law, but is produced by force. Again economic jargon prevails:

> In equilibrium the large state makes the threat, the small state does not engage in X, and the large state does not punish the small state. . .
>
> Coincidence of interest exists when a state's incremental payoff from an action is independent of the action of the other state. Coercion exists when the strong state's payoff depends on the weak state's action and the strong state would punish the weak state if the weak state chose the action that does not maximize the strong state's payoff.[55]

In opposition to the 'traditionalists' who consider that 'a sense of legal obligation' puts some 'drag' on deviations from customary law as the cost of compliance increases, the authors' theory insists that payoffs from co-operation or deviation are the sole determinants of whether States engage in co-operative behaviour that is then labelled

53. (2005) 25–7.
54. Ibid., 28.
55. Ibid., 29.

customary law. So customary law is not an exogenous influence on State behaviour. There exists no sense of legal obligation.[56]

Factors such as reputation and retaliation do exercise an indeterminate compliance pull on States, although reputation in one field such as the environment may not extend to another such as trade or human rights.[57] However, Goldsmith and Posner make an important qualification, presumably with their own country in mind, following the neo-institutionalist American international relations specialist Keohane. They say:

> States can benefit from reputations for toughness or even for irrationality and unreliability. Powerful states may do better by violating international law when doing so shows that they will retaliate against threats to national security.[58]

The authors make a very risky comparison then with Nazi Germany concerning treaty obligations. Versailles was a poor treaty because Britain and France were too weak and the US too indifferent to enforce it against a resurgent Germany. They continue:

> It is hard to believe that Germany's (and Turkey's) reputation for compliance with treaties were weakened. Perhaps their reputations for compliance with poorly negotiated treaties were weakened, but that could add another element of noise to an already ambiguous variable.[59]

The authors oblige by providing an approach to ethical matters as whimsical as the world described by Baudrillard, Dufour, and, above all, Haaland, would lead one to expect. They characterize ethical rhetoric in foreign policy as a form of concealment from outsiders of the insider knowledge of whether they have 'high' or 'low' discount rates, that is, whether they are more or less unreliable.[60] This is a prelude to Goldsmith and Posner saying that ideals a State can invoke may be anything:

> A state may justify a violation of a border by saying the border reflects historic injustice, or that the other nation by persecuting minorities, forfeited its sovereign rights under international ethical norms. It could say that the border is the result of a treaty that is invalid because it violates

56. Ibid., 39.
57. Ibid., 102.
58. Ibid., 102–3.
59. Ibid., 103.
60. Ibid., 180–1.

> an international legal formality. It could say that it was commanded by God to strike down the infidels . . . We conjecture that the appeal to the basis of obligation will occur at the lowest level of abstraction consistent with characteristics of the intended audience.[61]

There follows a very confused discussion of the analogy of the State with a corporation, and at the same time, a less explicit analogy of a State with a liberal democracy, where public decisions have some measure of domestic accountability. The context is the reiteration of the theme that States have no moral obligation to follow international law, when what they call the instrumental calculus suggests a departure from international law. They add, for good measure, that international law imposes no moral obligation – how could it? – that requires contrary action.[62]

The main interest here in presenting these very critical reflections by Goldsmith and Posner is to bear out the argument that the so-called economic approach to international law reflects the methodological individualism of the Anglo-American culture that cannot conceive of a positive or constructive role for a national community (except implicitly their own – see later on the Iraq War) to take any measures to assure its own cohesion in a globalised world. The argument is largely inconclusive and leaves one no alternative but to quote it at length. Otherwise summaries will be treated with disbelief:

> On the one hand, if international law takes the state as the primary obligation-bearing agent, then it can have no direct moral force for the individuals or groups who control the state (???). . .On the other hand, if international law takes the individual or nonstate group as the primary moral agent, then it can claim the agent's loyalty but it must give up its claim to regulate the relationships between states.[63]

> (A) state, like a corporation, is not an agent whose well-being demands moral consideration. . .States are not individuals, and what is true for individuals is not necessarily true for states. . .When a state at time 1 promises that it will act in a certain way at time 2, the state at time 1 is committing a different entity, the state at time 2, which might be as different from the state at time 1 as. . . a liberal democracy. . ., . . .or a different population . . . or a population with different interests from a corrupt dictatorship.[64]

61. Ibid, 181–2.
62. Ibid., 185 et seq. to 197.
63. Ibid., 188.
64. Ibid., 190.

If one compares a State to a corporation, one may say that the shareholders are always bound by taking up voluntarily the obligations of the company. However, people born into a country do not consent in a similar way to take on the obligations of the country.[65] A State does not have a life plan and the promises that it makes cannot be said to be morally binding because they enhance the autonomy of individuals living in the State, the only conceivable moral basis by which states could be bound. Yet the State binding large numbers of people, binds people not yet born, who have not yet immigrated and so forth, and who have no power. [66] In any case, most States in history and even recently have not been liberal democracies concerned about increasing individual autonomy. Why would such non-liberal democratic States comply with international law against their interests? It would be hard to say that treaties that liberal democracies make with such States should create any moral obligations, since such States do not give any special weight to the autonomy of their citizens.[67]

It is impossible for Goldsmith and Posner to construct any theory of the relationship of the institution of State to its people or population. The State has no life plan, no autonomy, and no experience of welfare. These belong to individual people, for whom, nonetheless states are vehicles through which citizens pursue their goals. They accept that one can meaningfully talk of citizens of the State enjoying in the aggregate benefits, but the main source of doubt remains that States do not always act in the interests of their citizens. They may not have representative institutions or they may have what the authors call 'bad' institutions. 'In a world populated by bad states, it is doubtful that people are better off with international legal obligations.'[68] For the authors these are fatal arguments for the moral character of international law because it insists on the sovereignty equality of States, and 'that international obligations are not vulnerable to ambiguity about the quality of domestic political institutions, in which case many existing treaties and rules of customary international law would be thrown in doubt'.[69]

Goldsmith and Posner have demonstrated an unwillingness to accept any form of political organisation as credible and hence there cannot be any form of moral obligation attaching to political

65. Ibid., 191.
66. Ibid.
67. Ibid., 192.
68. Ibid., 194.
69. Ibid.

communities. That says as much about their ethos as public lawyers as it says about anything else. However, it is possible to read into their apparent nihilism two things. First, the existence of the public space is denied. However confused this position, it is symptomatic of the contemporary political culture described so well by Dufour and Halland. They conclude their book by saying:

> The international lawyer's task is like that of a lawyer called in to interpret a letter of intent or nonbinding employment manual: the lawyer can use his or her knowledge of business or employment norms . . . to shed light on the meaning of the documents, but the documents themselves do not create legal obligations even though they contain promissory or quasi-promissory language.[70]

Second, Goldsmith and Posner are part of a very wide segment of American political culture that simply does not accept that the United States is a part of any international legal community. Having a form of government infinitely superior to that of any other country and being endowed with innumerable gifts, talents, and a special destiny above all others, it should have regard, from beginning to end, to its own interests alone. The authors offer an illustration from recent discussion of the US invasion of Iraq in 2003. In order to discredit the admittedly absurd types of legal arguments that international lawyers use, they remark how some say the US invasion was illegal. They note that the vocabulary of international law allows them to say that they are contributing to the change of international law. This type of cynical argument the present author has also used to discredit the language of customary law.[71] The authors point out that when people criticise the US for intervening in Iraq, this is a claim that the status quo is good. International laws are good and should not be changed. Now to allow pre-emptive self-defence for the US in Iraq, it is to say that international law should be – or is already being – changed. They continue:

> As the debate between the two sides develops, international law, as an institution that exerts its own moral force independent of its content, falls away. The reason that it can exert no moral force comparable to the moral force of domestic law is that it has no democratic pedigree or epistemic authority; it reflects what states have been doing in the recent past and does not necessarily reflect the moral judgments or interests or

70. Ibid., 203.

71. A. Carty, 'The UK Invasion of Iraq as a Recent UK Contribution to International Law', *European Journal of International Law* 16 (2005) 143–51.

> needs of individuals. It can have no democratic pedigree because there are no international institutions that reliably convert the world's public's needs and interests into international law and that can change existing international law when the world public's needs and interests change.[72]

The economic approach to international law means that the United States need offer no more account to the world of its use of its economic power, than of its political or military power. As President Obama's lawyers counselling the use of drones see America as confronted by 'badlands', so Harvard and Chicago law professors Goldsmith and Posner see America as surrounded by 'bad states'. What is America to do?

AN ECONOMIC HISTORY OF INTERNATIONAL LAW FROM WESTPHALIA AND VATTEL'S EQUALITY OF STATES TO AN AMERICAN-LED COALITION OF THE DEMOCRACIES

In their classical study *Chaos and Governance in the Modern World System*, Arrighi and Silver set out the historical framework of modern capitalism in its development from industrial to finance capitalism. Just as the hegemony of the Dutch Republic, and after it the British Empire, exported capital to finance their eventual rivals, so also did the US from 1945 until the 1970s. The crisis of US hegemony has been marked by the abandonment of the dollar gold standard and the floating of currencies in the early 1970s. Just as with the former hegemonies, the US had built effective rivals out of Western Europe, Japan, and, increasingly, the Pacific Rim of China, Korea, and Taiwan.[73]

Arrighi and Silver consider most exhaustively the historical dimension of a series of capitalist hegemonies and identify the original structure of international law as attributable to the character of Dutch hegemony.

> When it was first established under Dutch hegemony, national sovereignty rested on a mutual recognition by European states of each other's juridical autonomy and territorial integrity (legal sovereignty), and on a balance of power among states that guaranteed their factual sovereignty against the attempts of any State to become so powerful as to dominate all the others.[74]

---

72. Ibid., 199.
73. G. Arrighi and B. J. Silver (eds), *Chaos and Governance in the Modern World System* (1999), generally, and especially chapter 1, 'Geopolitics and High Finance', 37–96.
74. Arrighi and Sliver, *Chaos* 92.

So the major distinction of the argument in Arrighi and Silver is to place in historical context the limitations of the Westphalian System of international law, based upon the sovereign equality of States. This was reflected in the original Dutch system of hegemony, which prevailed from 1648 until the Napoleonic Wars. When British hegemony replaced the Dutch in the nineteenth century other States enjoyed only nominal independence at a time when British industrial and naval supremacy guaranteed a global *Pax Britannica*. Britain called into independence the Latin American States, but they remained under British economic tutelage until 1914.

With the coming of American hegemony after 1945, even the semblance or fiction of the Westphalian system disappeared. After 1945, the British fiction of a balance of power that could still assure a factual sovereign equality of States was discarded even as a fiction. As Anthony Giddens is quoted, US influence on shaping the new global order both under Wilson and under Roosevelt, 'represented an attempted incorporation of US constitutional prescriptions globally rather than a continuation of the balance of power doctrine'.[75] In other words, while the symptoms of the present crisis in international law are clear to all, the nature of recent developments in US policy with respect to international law is seriously misunderstood. It is not now that the Westphalian model of international law is being challenged. This was buried, at the latest, with the onset of the Second World War, perhaps even with the Treaty of Versailles. The US has never in the twentieth century accepted that the constitution of a State was an internal matter. The export of its own constitutional model was the object of two world wars. The semi-sovereign German and Japanese protectorates were its models for the organisation of world society. There was no dissent from this in the West.

It is mistaken to claim that it is now the case, for instance, that the UN Charter is being ignored or the equality of States is being denied. There is not a present and unprecedented American overthrow of international norms. The American project of international society, at least since 1945 (and in terms of its war aims), was always quite different from classical international law. It was the export of its constitutional model of market democracy against the totalitarian socialism of the Soviet Union and China. By the early 1950s it had locked the whole planet into a coalition to this end.

However, since the 1970s there has been a radical bifurcation of military and financial global power. This has been most remarkable

75. Ibid., 93. See most extensively, P. Bobbitt, *The Shield of Achilles: War and Peace and the Course of History* (2002).

since the 1980s when the Reagan military build-up was financed through manipulation of interest rates on the dollar to siphon world liquidity into the United States.[76] The difference now is that the changing underlying economic structures of international society mean that the US does not have the material resources to be assured of its ability to enforce its project against possible new foes, nor can it rely any longer upon its economically resurgent erstwhile allies. This leads it to change from acting as a hegemonic power that continues to enjoy international legitimacy, to becoming a power that, clearly since its invasion of Iraq in the spring of 2003, tries to rely exclusively on its own political and military strength to force through its will.

The main preoccupation of the international law agenda of the US, here acting alone except for British support, has been to develop doctrines of pre-emptive attack, armed intervention, the spreading of military bases through agreement with host States, and the global strengthening of military policing against terrorism. This agenda now dominates the international scene. There are US military protectorates in Afghanistan and Iraq. Others may be in the offing for North Korea, Iran, and Syria. While there is less enthusiasm for intervention in Africa and Latin America, further protectorates, or very large measures of military assistance and co-operation, are in place or are likely at least, in Sierra Leone, Colombia, the Congo, and Liberia.

The underlying principle of both US and British policy is that such States are not sovereign and equal members of international society. Hence, the US undertakes international military actions, first without troubling to find the consent of the UN and, second, without even looking to have the support of the North Atlantic Treaty Organization (NATO). In Kosovo, Afghanistan, and Iraq the US has waged wars that are all in contravention of the basic international norms of sovereign equality of States and of the elementary need for community authority to legitimate the exercise of force against individual members of the society of States.

The Geo-Political Contradictions of this Contemporary International Order with the US as its Sole Centre-Point – The US as the Focal Point for the Concentration of Finance Capital and its Future Strategic Options

Now it will be asked whether international law can offer any autonomous prescriptions in response by delving also among the first

---

76. Arrighi and Silver, *Chaos* 88–96, 284.

Marxist theories of imperialism and the nation,[77] while considering specifically the quality and possibilities of US relations with other powers.

There are several apparent contradictions in capitalism. Industrial or productive capitalism tends to become, gradually, financial capitalism. That is, such productive capitalism accumulates greater and greater profit, which it then has increasing difficulty placing, as it is not necessary or perhaps even possible to reinvest the capital in productive processes to serve an ever-shrinking market. This is because of the exploitative conditions inherent in the ownership of the means of production under capitalism. Profit comes from the transfer of the surplus value of labour, necessitating a reduction in the scope and extent of consumer demand.[78] It then drifts into increasingly scare – because demanded – assets, such as derivatives and real estate, which acquire speculative values.

The surplus capital is exported into production abroad that then becomes significantly competitive with the home producers, while still competing for the same limited consumer markets. Because of the capitalism-induced concentration of markets, almost the only effective outlet for the increased productive capacity of these rivals is the US itself. Equally, the consumer boom in the West, and particularly in the US, is credit-led, marked by the capacity of US oligarchies and its 'coalition' to corner surplus liquidity.[79]

So international economic relations are increasingly marked by a dependency of the greatest consumer of world manufactures and natural resources, the United States, on the producers, China, Korea,

---

77. V. Kubalkova and A. Cruickshank, *Marxism and International Relations* (1989). One could give weight to Soviet or Chinese doctrines of international law, or also the whole range of other post-1945 Marxist theories of international relations, but the turn of the millennium, remarkably, allows focus on issues in a manner similar to the immediate pre-1914 period, that is, where there is a crisis of hegemony, this time of the United States, while earlier, of Great Britain.
78. E. Todd, *Weltmacht, USA Ein Nachruf* (2003) 95, referring to the taboo character surrounding discussion of shrinking demand among economists considering globalisation. The only exception he can find is Chalmers Johnson, *Ein Imperium verfaellt, Wann endet das Amerikanische Jahrhundert?* (2000) 252.
79. Todd, in *Weltmacht USA* 32–6, identifies this feature of advanced capitalism as affecting equally all the so-called Western democracies. In particular, France and Great Britain are governed by remote oligarchies that preside over increasingly polarised societies.

Western Europe, Japan, and the Pacific Rim, through the medium of increasing American debt. An advantage that the US has had from the time after 1945, when it dominated world production and trade, is the dollar. By fixing the value of its own currency as the world currency, it can pay its debts by printing money.[80]

However, the full context of the usefulness of this power can only be understood if another aspect of the concentration of wealth and avoidance of income redistribution is stressed. The way out of surplus production for the US, since the 1930s, has been the war economy, military production financed by the State, first through domestic income, but eventually through the control of world liquidity.[81] That is, the US found its way out of the Great Depression by adopting the 'warfare–welfare' economy of armaments, which retained its impetus, after the defeat of Germany and Japan, through the Czech Crisis (the Prague communist coup of February–March 1948) and the Korean War.

Since then the US has remained primarily a war economy driven by the need to confront external danger at a global level. This feeds effectively on the paranoid style that is fundamental to US foreign policy. Harvey explains that the internal configurations of power that were able to resist Roosevelt's modest attempts during the New Deal to rescue the economy from its contradictions through redistribution of wealth, meant instead the paranoid style of politics. The difficulty of achieving internal cohesion in an ethnically mixed society characterised by intense individualism and class division made for the construction of US politics around the fear of some 'other' (such as bolshevism, socialism, or anarchists).[82] This aggressive policy extends to an unequal military alliance system that ensures transfers of profit back to the US through compulsory purchases of American armaments, an effective export of the 'warfare–welfare' economy.[83]

It is widely recognised that these economic contradictions accentuate further political contradictions. First, there is the changing character of American military dominance at the global level. This dates from 1945 and the US reconstruction of Germany and Japan as semi-sovereign states, as US protectorates. Under a US military umbrella, they were free to redevelop their own industrial potential.

80. The least disputable aspect of this argument: see Arrighi and Silver, *Chaos* 284; Harvey, *New Imperialism* 128–9; Todd, *Weltmacht USA* 117–19.
81. Arrighi and Silver, *Chaos* 137, 147.
82. Harvey, *New Imperialism* 48–9.
83. Todd, *Weltmacht USA* 115–16.

By the time of the Korean War the US had ringed the Soviets and Chinese with an unprecedented number of military bases, which meant that not merely were there only two superpowers, there were, in fact, in the classical (Westphalian) international law sense only two (maybe three) sovereign States in the world, that is, States with the power to declare and wage war. Turkey, Israel, Japan, Germany, the UK, Italy, and many others were no longer autonomous, even legally.

The difficulty with overwhelming US global military dominance at present rests in the transformation of its capital base. As long as the military production was financed from within the US the latter saw no security threat to itself. Once the finance to support these military structures has started to come from outside, the picture becomes more uncertain. American military power is accompanied by increased indebtedness of the American State to foreign capital seeking profit within the US, either on the private stock exchange or in government securities. This began in the 1970s, but it has become acute in the course of the 1990s. These concrete developments are central to the whole 'global financial expansion that in the 1980s and 1990s reflated the power of the U.S. State and capital and correspondingly deflated the power of the movements that had precipitated the crisis of US hegemony'.[84]

The US has become financially dependent upon its industrial protectorates, Germany and Japan, as well as upon Arab oil states and Chinese interests (Singapore, Hong Kong, and Taiwan, but also Mainland China). These entities may not be hostile to America, but they are not necessarily committed to US political-military policies. At the same time, they do have the economic power to limit American action, even if self-destructively. Besides, even now, the US does not have the military and political resources to constrain positively the direction of these States and city-States. This creates uncertainty in the US about how to behave towards its erstwhile protectorate-allies.[85] Todd sees here a fundamental weakness of the global order. The US lays sole claim to military dominance at a global level, but it is, in fact, neither financially nor militarily capable of ensuring the monopoly of the use of force that has to be, since Weber, the characteristic of legality in modernity.[86]

84. Ibid., 284.
85. An identical argument by Todd, *Weltmacht USA* 110–11, who points to the particular role of Germany and Japan as subordinate powers, suffering huge military bases that they finance indirectly.
86. Ibid., 119.

Another political contradiction of late capitalism concerns the relations between the US, its 'coalition', and the so-called developing world. Again, Arrighi and Silvers' challenging insights into a true history of international law are completed by Harvey, with his theory of accumulation through dispossession. Capitalism has always been global, and always involved a huge transfer of value from the developing to the developed world. Dutch wealth was based upon the plunder of Spanish Indies gold and silver bullion. The exploitation of India from the eighteenth century was utterly crucial to Great Britain's world hegemony. British power was further enhanced through the humiliation of China in the nineteenth-century Opium Wars that allowed the full realisation of India's potential.[87]

The central thesis has to be that the so-called global order has always been and has never ceased to be based upon plunder. As Harvey puts it, the market-State will never produce a harmonious State in which everyone is better off. It will produce ever greater levels of social inequality. He argues that Marxism must not

> regulate accumulation based upon predation, fraud and violence to an 'original stage' that is no longer considered relevant . . . A general re-evaluation of the continuous role and persistence of the predatory practices of 'primitive' or 'original' accumulation within the long historical geography of capital accumulation is, therefore, very much in order.[88]

Harvey insists that the fundamental drive to accumulation by dispossession is as old as capitalist imperialism itself. The crisis would not be happening 'if there had not emerged chronic problems of over accumulation of capital through expanded reproduction *coupled with a political refusal to attempt any solution to these problems by internal reform*' (author's emphasis).[89] He describes the opportunities open to those who can manipulate a monopoly of credit mechanisms in traditional Marxist terms. Monopoly control of credit systems allows unlimited possibilities to operate a credit squeeze, to drive a drying up of liquidity, and to drive enterprises into bankruptcy.[90] Accumulation by dispossession allows the release of a set of assets (including labour power) at very low (and in some instances zero) cost. Over-accumulated capital can seize hold of such assets and immediately turn them to profitable use.[91]

---

87. Arrighi and Silver, *Chaos* 219–46.
88. Harvey, *The New Imperialism* 144.
89. Ibid., 181.
90. Ibid., 155.
91. Ibid., 149.

> Some of the mechanisms of primitive accumulation that Marx emphasised have been fine-tuned to play an even stronger role now than in the past. The credit system and finance capital became, as Lenin, Hilferding, and Luxemburg all remarked at the beginning of the twentieth century, major levers of predation, fraud, and thievery. The strong wave of financialisation that set in after 1973 has been every bit as spectacular for its speculative and predatory style. Stock promotions, ponzi schemes, structured asset destruction through inflation, asset-stripping through mergers and acquisitions, and the promotion of levels of debt incumbency that reduce whole populations, even in the advanced capitalist countries, to debt peonage, to say nothing of corporate fraud and dispossession of assets (the raiding of pension funds and their decimation by stock and corporate collapses) by credit and stock manipulations – all of these are central features of what contemporary capitalism is about. The collapse of Enron dispossessed many workers of their livelihoods and their pension rights. But above all we have to look at the speculative raiding carried out by hedge funds and other major institutions of finance capital as the cutting edge of accumulation by dispossession in recent times.[92]

The question is how to explain this, and also whether any constructive response is possible. Writing in 1999 Arrighi and Silver did not consider that serious conflict between the US, its erstwhile Western allies, and the significant Pacific Rim States was inevitable, despite the bifurcation of military and financial global power, provided there is not '*US resistance to the loss of power, and prestige (though not necessarily of wealth and welfare) that the recentering of the global economy on East Asia entails*' (author's emphasis).[93] Capitalism is a global phenomenon. Even China has long embarked upon a process of primitive accumulation, which Harvey characterises as an internally imposed accumulation by dispossession, comparable to the Tudor enclosures.[94] Todd also acknowledges that advanced capitalism affects social structures, democracy, and the rule of law in all major Western societies, including France.[95]

An early Marxist theory of 'ultra-imperialism' at the beginning of the twentieth century proposed that a peaceful adjustment of the relations of production (including international relations) to the

92. Ibid., 147.
93. Arrighi and Silver, *Chaos* 270. They see a balance of power in East Asia as possible.
94. Harvey, *The New Imperialism* 153–4.
95. Todd, *Weltmacht USA* 32–6.

worldwide forces of production was possible. Karl Kautsky thought that this adjustment could be brought about by capitalism itself. Capitalism would go through an additional State, which would see an aggrandisement of the policy of cartels into a foreign policy. 'This phase of ultra- or super-imperialism involving the union of imperialists across the globe would bring to an end their struggles with one another. The notion, in other words, of a co-operative effort in the Grotian tradition enabling a joint exploitation of the world by internationally merged finance capital.'[96]

However, writing at the end of 2002 and in the late spring of 2003 respectively, Todd and Harvey consider that present US foreign and consequently international law policy do indicate a very firm intention to resist any loss of power and prestige. The US is evidently willing to accept open conflict with other powers. For both authors, American actions are necessitated by the internal contradictions of its political-military and economic-social relations, also with its trading partners, particularly China. Aggressive political and military policies abroad have their roots in economic and social contradictions at home. This is something that Marxists like Harvey, 'postmodernists' like Campbell and Christian moral theologians like O'Donovan can all see very well from their different perspectives. Economic structures shape the agenda of contemporary international law in the following respects. Most importantly, the US realises that its economic pre-eminence in the global system is seriously threatened in the medium term. Its economic dependence on its Western allies, particularly Japan and the European Union, means that it feels compelled to choose issues on which to exercise its political power in a primarily coercive military dimension in order to force an acknowledgement of its supremacy.[97] Obvious examples at the moment are the consolidation of NATO forces under US leadership in eastern Europe on the Russian border and the focus on a confrontation with China in the South China Sea, under the umbrella of ASEAN.

This is where the exact nature of the evidence Todd and Harvey adduce to arraign the US is interesting. Todd's argument is based on an analysis of the material situation of the US and the material

---

96. Kubalkova and Cruickshank, *Marxism and International Relations* 52. This assumption underlies my contribution to A. Qureshi, *Perspectives in International Economic Law* (2002), 'The National as a Meta-Concept of International Economic Law' 65.
97. This is the clear overall argument of both of the books of Todd and Harvey.

consequences of its actions. The US is no longer necessary for the maintenance of 'freedom', democracy, and the rule of law in the world, given the disappearance of the 'socialist world'. The country has, since the 1970s and especially since 1995–2000, seen its economic situation radically altered to its disadvantage – the world's largest debtor, and significantly less productive than its main trade rivals. The same US embarks upon apparently ludicrous military adventures against extremely weak developing countries and penetrates into the Central Asian landmass under the pretext of pursuing a terrorism that it equates with the Arab-Muslim region, despite the limited pull of militant Islam outside Pakistan and Saudi Arabia. It acquires bases in several former Soviet Central Asian republics, Afghanistan, and, eventually Iraq (Todd is writing in December 2002), all through unilateral action, without consulting NATO or the United Nations. A centrepiece of this policy is to block any settlement of the Palestinian–Israeli conflict and to keep the European Union marginal to a mediation of the conflict.

Europe, Japan, China, and Russia have no immediate interest to quarrel with one another and especially no economic interest to confront the Arab and Muslim world. They have every assurance that energy will be supplied because the Arabs and Iran need that for their own development. At the same time Israel's quarrel with the Palestinians is a serious source of conflict of interest for all of America's traditional allies. It could weaken or complicate their relations with the source of an essential energy supply. So the assertion of unqualified US solidarity with Israel fits together with a plan to maintain a literally physical control of the oil resources of the Middle East. It enables the US to view with equanimity the possible destabilisation of the source of its allies' oil supplies through a generalised Arab-Muslim hostility towards 'the West'.[98]

The kernel of Todd's structural argument is that the US is behaving irrationally because both its internal and international situation have become unstable. It is fixated on the unilateral use of force to ensure control of territory and oil in the Middle East and Central Asia as a way of maintaining dominance over its erstwhile allies. In this context Westphalian and UN Charter rules of international law do not apply to the US's relations with the Middle East and Central Asia. Doctrines of pre-emptive strike against terrorist states, or humanitarian intervention against brutal dictatorships,

98. Todd, *Weltmacht USA* 36–8, 56–8, 146–54, 164–82.

can be variously used and are being used to underpin a volatile Western–Middle Eastern relationship. The balancing of Israeli and Palestinian rights to self-determination is not important compared to keeping the European Union marginal to the political relations of the Middle East.

Writing in the spring of 2003, Harvey possesses the fact that the war with Iraq is in full swing. He agrees with Todd that the starting point of US action is its increasingly serious economic weakness. His argument has a classical Marxist framework, considering the options between a Kautsky style 'ultra-imperialism' of the Western powers and Lenin's scenario of a violent competition among the imperialist powers – meaning, effectively, all powers, including China.[99] He is also influenced by the tradition of geopolitics of the 1900s of Halford Mackinder, which treats control of the Eurasian landmass as central to world domination. However, beyond that Harvey relies primarily on an 'intentionalist' explanation of US policy. He refers to planning documents of US leaders, which are openly available, and also the writings of influential opinion leaders within the US. These are not the equivalent of open access to the minutes of meetings of key decision-makers, but they suppose that access to US elite intentions is possible. At the same time, these elites are, for the moment, able to direct the course of US power.[100]

Harvey consider that both intentions and actions (for example, the defence strategy documents of 1991–2 and the language justifying the invasion of Iraq) show a clear opinion for a military solution to the weakness of the US. Alliances and traditional international law are to be discarded in favour of unilateral and military action, in US interests. These actions are to demonstrate the absolute military and political supremacy of the country globally. Territorial and physical control of Middle East oil is sufficient for the US to maintain its dominance for the near future.[101] As Harvey puts it,

> if it (United States) can move on (as seems possible) from Iraq to Iran and consolidate its position in Turkey and Uzbekistan as a strategic presence in relation to Caspian basin oil reserves (which the Chinese are

---

99. Harvey, *The New Imperialism* 75, 209; see also, more generally Kubalkova and Cruickshank, *Marxism and International Relations* 52–3, that the development of capitalism is so uneven that conflict is inevitable.
100. Ibid., 18–25, 74–86, 183–212.
101. Ibid., 19.

> desperately trying to butt into), then the US, through firm control of the global oil spigot, might hope to keep effective control over the global economy and secure its own dominance for the next fifty years.[102,103]

All of this dramatic confrontational strategy is understandable given the immense danger that the present international economic situation poses for the US. The constructive alternative would be for the US to turn away from imperialism and engage in both a massive redistribution of wealth within its borders and a redistribution of capital flows into the production and renewal of physical and social infrastructures. This would mean an internal reorganisation of class power relations and transformation of social relations that the US has refused to consider since the Civil War. More deficit financing, much higher taxation, and strong State direction are what dominant class forces within the US will not even consider.[104] At the same time, the economic, particularly financial threat from East Asia is huge. Arrighi and Silver think that the immediate major task for the US is to accommodate itself to this constructively. Harvey thinks that, on balance, the US is unlikely to take this course. The ferocity of the primitive capital accumulation that is taking place in China may well spark a rate of economic growth there capable of absorbing much of the world's capital surplus. There may be revolution and political breakdown in China caused by the stress of present social change. However, if there is not,

> the drawing off of surplus capital into China will be calamitous for the US economy which feeds off capital inflows to support its own unproductive consumption, both in the military and in the private sector . . . In such a situation, the US would be sorely tempted to use its power over oil to hold back China, sparking a geopolitical conflict at the very minimum in Central Asia and perhaps spreading into a more global conflict.[105]

---

102. Ibid., 78.
103. These arguments are at present, as already said, bolstered by the US-NATO-led build-up in Eastern Europe and mobilisation of military forces against Russia, as well as the military and naval build-up in the South China Sea, where the US is providing military equipment and training to Vietnam and Philippines, as well as encouraging its protectorate, Japan, to do the same. See further John Pilger, 'Why Hilary Clinton is more dangerous than Donald Trump', *New Matilda* <www.newmatilda.com>, accessed 23 March 2016.
104. Ibid., 75–6.
105. Ibid., 208–9.

The Leninist scenario of violent competition among capitalist blocs is most likely. The more explicit the US project becomes, the more it will almost certainly force an alliance between France, Germany, Russia, and China, which more reflective American figures such as Kissinger believe will not necessarily lose in a struggle with the US.[106] Arguing from within social democratic parameters, Hutton and Todd hope that the European Union can balance the economic power of the US more peacefully. The key instrument is the aggressive use of the Euro as a political weapon, to enforce European social policies both within the European economic area and in international development aid policy.[107]

Now the question presents itself of whether there could have been anything careless or even pre-meditated in the US private capital markets corrupting the European markets with toxic derivatives, which have contributed into turning the Euro into a paper tiger. Undoubtedly, Dufour and Halland would prefer to designate Europe and America as one cultural area – the West, and scoff at the Euro idealism of Hutton and Todd.

In any case, Harvey insists that their project cannot hope to be realistic unless it involves an explicit rejection of neoliberal economic policy, which indeed both Todd and Hutton would also advocate. There must be a strong revival of sustained accumulation through expanded reproduction (read: curbing the speculative powers of finance capital, decentralising and controlling monopolies, and significant redistribution of wealth). Otherwise, this Kautsky-style benevolent 'New Deal' imperialism can only sink deeper into the quagmire of a politics of accumulation by dispossession throughout the world in order to keep the motor of accumulation from stalling.[108]

Contemporary US policy, which for the moment enjoys British support, appears nihilistic in relation to the existing Westphalian international legal order, making it a pure fiction. It appears at the same time, consciously, but completely unrealistically, to be a project to restore political control of large parts of the non-Western world that was temporarily relinquished in the 1950s and the 1960s. There is much argument that the granting of independence was premature and that it has to be undone because there are simply not

106. Ibid., 200.

107. Todd, *Weltmacht USA* 211–38; Hutton, *The World We Are In* esp. 400–11.

108. Harvey, *The New Imperialism* 211–12.

adequate political institutions, viz. State structures in large parts of the globe.[109]

Again, as with the present US treatment of its erstwhile allies, this apparently radical suspension of traditional Westphalian and UN Charter law in relation to large parts of the South has to be seen in its longer historical context. It is, in terms of time-scale, merely a phase in the development of international law since the sixteenth century. Arrighi and Silver have most brilliantly captured this phase as one of a crisis of US capitalist hegemony. They give full place to changing developments in the history of international law since Dutch hegemony ushered in the Westphalian system. The League of Nations and the United Nations mark the transition from British to American hegemony.

The latter's hegemony is now fundamentally in question. The US attempt to reverse the course of history, to reintroduce colonial-type international protectorates, is another aspect of the nihilism that will simply not face the responsibilities of global management in terms of necessary economic and social change. Optimistic European voices argue that a reassertion of an economic balance of power, among Europe, Russia, Japan, China, and so on and the US (possibly eventually India and Brazil) make inevitable a return to the dialectics of dialogue in the resolution of international conflict. This supposes that the Americans can adjust to a reduced but still significant role in the international economy. In relation to the South, this optimistic Europeanism argues that European, Japanese, and Chinese capitalism is more socially oriented than the predatory Anglo-American neoliberal market economy States. Unlike the US and the UK, they can negotiate compromise relations with different cultures, premised upon a slow process of gradualist reform and integration.

Concretely, this means Europe absorbing Russia and the Middle East into its economic-social zone, in which a postmodern, agnostic absence of the military dimension to politics will prevail. Arguably, Japan and China can take the same lead in East Asia. In this picture the US goes off into the wilderness from which it emerged at the beginning of the twentieth century. It is left with the North American Free Trade Agreement (NAFTA). Todd and Hutton, from

109. This is argued most forcefully by such British figures as R. Cooper ('The New Imperialism', *The Observer*, 7 April 2002), a Blair advisor, and Niall Ferguson, a historian of the British empire and international economic and financial history.

England and France, place much of hope in developments in such directions. They can point to the failure of neoliberalism to make decisive breakthroughs in France and Germany, not to mention reversals of economic strategy in Putin's Russia and, finally, the great enigma of China.

None of this optimism can be grounded in the rather more Leninist imperialist scenario outlined by Harvey. The concrete flaw in European optimism is that the US is aware of its strategic precariousness and has already moved to anticipate it. It enjoys a political military precedence if not dominance, which can impede any alternative global project. Japanese, other East Asian and European capital markets are locked into the radically skewed American capital market as part of capital's natural search for maximum profit. European and East Asian industrial production are equally locked in the embrace of this market. The latter is not only skewed but also twisted, since an integral part of the consuming power of this market is the surplus capital of the exporters to America.

On the outside stands the economically marginal, disenfranchised world proletariat, threatening, or being seen to threaten, illegal immigration, international crime (especially people and drug trafficking), and, of course, terrorism. Marxism would surely require that this proletariat must become more radical as it becomes more economically marginal. The latter must happen because of the continuing transfer of capital resources from the South to the North, an uninterrupted process since the sixteenth century. The will and the means do not really exist in the West (Europe and Japan will not go along with the US) to restore political control over the South. So the disorder it represents will gradually engulf the West.

That is, unless a social-democratic alternative – whether or not dubbed Kautsky-style 'ultra-imperialism' – can support a true development of the same social-democratic model, a substantive economic self-determination of peoples in the developing world.[110] However, Marxist analyses of the impact of international political economy upon the general structure of international law remain the most convincing for the present.

---

110. As the author has already suggested, particularly in 'The National as a Meta-Concept of International Economic Law', in *Perspectives in International Economic Law*, Qureshi (ed.); and in A. Carty, 'Liberal Rhetoric and the Democratisation of the World Economy', in *Ethics* (1988) 65.

DOMESTIC SOCIO-ECONOMIC REFORM AS THE STARTING POINT FOR THE STABILISATION OF THE GLOBAL ECONOMIC ORDER – WITH THE REFORM OF ANGLO-AMERICAN FINANCIAL MARKETS TOP OF THE LIST

Law may refer to the command enforced by a sovereign State, the positivist's equation of law with the State. The word 'law' in 'international law' may refer more generally to the legal relations among equal and independent States according to the Westphalian system. *Marxism can easily identify the first sense of 'law' as an instrument of 'the capitalists' who control the State. This is a very useful shorthand for the assumption of a rule-of-thumb political sociology that a State bureaucratic apparatus is effectively controlled by a clique or oligarchy in its own interests.* The difficulty is understanding the relations between a dominant capitalist State and a whole range of other States in the international system. Concretely, this means asking how the US relates to the other major Western powers, including Japan, and, then, to what are loosely called the developing, or simply significantly poorer countries, including China, India, Brazil, and innumerable other smaller countries.

However, before coming, in conclusion, to the question of whether the US really does enjoy an uncontested actual control of a whole range of other States in the present international system, it is necessary to return to the domestic scene within national States, and, in particular, the USA itself. Given that the starting point of contemporary international law is the system of Vattel, it has to be remembered that the entire first volume of his work was taken up with describing the role of the Nation (his capital N) in ensuring the development of its own welfare. If this could be assured, in Vattel's scheme most other issues would take care of themselves, except for the occasional problem of the rogue State. So it is entirely within the compass of a systemic philosophy of international law to address directly, as of concern to the entire international community, whether a particular State – especially a key State such as the US – is actually able to focus effectively on the development of the welfare of its own people. As has been seen, the central argument of Harvey is that the failure of socio-economic reform in 1930s America is the root cause of the immense violence that this State compulsively inflicts on the whole planet. In other words, democratic reform within the US is essential for the development of world peace.

We have seen in the extended analysis of the so-called economic approach to international law of Goldsmith and Possner that they have huge difficulty in constructing any concept of a political collectivity. Earlier, in our reflections on international legal personality, we have also observed O'Donovan's severe critique of liberal contractarianism's compulsive resolution of its absence of a theory of collective political identity, by resort to an essentially racist – Rawls style – enforcement of democratic political ideology on other members of the international community. An essential historical aspect of this anti-nationalism, which he deplores, is the reaction in Europe to fascism and Nazi racism. However, it remains a crucial aspect of the work of a philosophy of international law to address directly – even if it cannot answer in a day – how to achieve social cohesion along with economic well-being in the advanced states of the world, particularly in the West.

This is the context in which to revisit Michael Hardt and Antonio Negri's *Empire*, a poststructuralist and, at the same time, post-Marxist critique of globalisation.[111] The rhetorical, virtually magical style of this work makes it difficult to engage with its arguments. However, it is extremely important to understand not only its anti-nationalist tone, excluding explicitly any concept of economic self-determination of peoples or indeed any form of collective political action, while also offering a bemusing glorification of the gridlocked American constitution, without any reference to the polarised nature of present American political society (written just before the advent of the G. W. Bush Presidency).

Its mystical adulation of speculative currency flows and MNEs is irrepressible. For instance, the following is typical of the authors' utterly apolitical and ahistorical fetishisation of late 1990s (that is, pre 2007–8 Financial Crisis) economic life: 'The huge transnational corporations construct the fundamental connective fabric of the bio-political world in certain important respects.' Now they (that is, the MNEs), 'directly structure and articulate territories and populations' and so forth.[112] In the same nonsensical style they pronounce that the supposedly complex apparatus that selects investments and directs financial and monetary manoeuvres determines 'the new bio-political structuring of the world'. They tell us 'There is nothing, no "naked life", no external standpoint, that can be posed outside this field permeated by money; nothing escapes money.'

The authors stand in hopeless awe of what they call the great industrial and financial powers that produce not just commodities, but

111. M. Hardt and A. Negri, *Empire* (2000).
112. Ibid., 31.

subjectivities, that is – wait for it – 'agentic subjectivities within the bio-political context: they produce needs, social relations, bodies, and minds – which is to say, they produce producers'.[113] In metaphysical terms, what Hardt and Negri are doing is simply to deny any dialectic between structure and agency. Structure is everything. This makes it metaphysically impossible for them to conceive of anyone or any particular grouping having actions ascribed to them. So they tell us:

> The machine is self-validating, auto-poetic – that is systemic. It constructs social fabrics that evacuate or render ineffective any contradiction; it creates situations in which, before coercively neutralizing difference, seem to absorb it in an insignificant play of self-generating and self-regulating equilibria.[114]

There are 400 pages of this convoluted rhetoric.

Hardt and Negri object that the concepts of nation and nation State faithfully reproduce the patrimonial State's totalising identity of both the territory and the population. Relying on sovereignty in the most rigid way, nation and nation State make the relation of sovereignty into a thing, often by naturalising it, 'and thus weed out every residue of social antagonism. The nation is a kind of ideological shortcut that attempts to free the concepts of sovereignty and modernity from the antagonism and crisis which define them.'[115] Apparently, Hardt and Negri know that Luxemburg's most powerful argument was 'that nation means dictatorship and is thus profoundly incompatible with any attempt at democratic organization'.[116]

The nation or the people it produces is contrasted with the multitude. Hardt and Negri make a caricature of the nation as a frenzied totalitarian beast that compels obedience of all its compatriots to a single imperious command. The multitude is:

> a multiplicity, a plane of singularities, an open set of relations, which is not homogenous or identical with itself and bears an indistinct, inclusive relation to those outside of it . . . the construction of an absolute racial difference is the essential ground for the conception of a homogenous national identity.[117]

113. Ibid., 32.
114. Ibid., 34.
115. Ibid., 95.
116. Ibid., 97.
117. Ibid., 103.

Even the nation as the dominated power will, in turn, play an inverse role in relation to the interior they protect and repress internal differences and so on.[118]

In contrast, the US has a constitution that favours the productive synergies of the multitude rather than trying to regulate them from above. This encourages the expansiveness of capitalism that, supposedly, does not know an outside and an inside (that is, it is all-absorbing). The US Constitution provides the opportunity for the de-centred expansion of capital.[119] This apparently makes the US especially suited as an instrument of the global events since the early 1970s. Hardt and Negri's account is rather neutral: 'Little by little, after the Vietnam War the new world market was organized: a world market that destroyed the fixed boundaries and hierarchical procedures of European imperialisms.' After US power had destroyed European colonialisms, 'the army of command wielded its power less through military hardware and more through the dollar . . . an enormous step forward towards the construction of Empire'.[120]

The second mechanism for its construction was a process of decentring the sites and the flows of production. The transnationals transferred the technology necessary for constructing the new productive axis of the subordinate countries and mobilised the labour force and local productive capacities in these countries. Rather strangely, the authors conclude this part of their argument as follows:

> These multiple flows began to converge essentially towards the United States, which guaranteed and co-ordinated, when it did not directly command, the movement and operations of the transnationals. This was a decisive phase of Empire. Through the activities of the transnational corporations, the mediation and equalisation of the rates of profit were unhinged from the power of the dominant nation-states.[121]

So, one may ask, why did Nixon have the wit to decouple the dollar from the gold standard and put a surcharge of 10 per cent on all imports from Europe to the United States, a transfer of the entire American debt to Europe? It 'thus reminded the Europeans of the initial terms of the agreement, of its (the US) hegemony as the highest point of exploitation and capitalist command'.[122]

118. Ibid., 106.
119. Ibid., 161–7.
120. Ibid., 246.
121. Ibid., 247.
122. Ibid., 266.

Yet nation-State resistance must always be rejected as an option, being a metaphysical impossibility. If it is argued that through the imposition of imperialist domination the underdevelopment of subordinated economies was created and then sustained by their continued integration into dominant capitalist economies, it is still an invalid conclusion that disarticulated developing economies should aim for relative isolation to achieve their own full articulation. Instead, the tendential realisation of the world market should destroy any notion that today a country or region could isolate itself or delink itself from the global networks of power. The interactions of the world market have resulted in a generalised disarticulation of all economies.[123]

The fetishisation of the US economic policy decisions of the 1970s follows. In italics the authors announce that the State has been defeated and that corporations rule the Earth. Politics has disappeared and consensus is determined by economic factors such as the equilibria of trade balances and speculation on the value of currencies. The mechanisms of political mediation function through the categories of bureaucratic mediation and managerial sociology. This means that single government has been disarticulated and invested in a series of separate bodies, banks, international organisms of planning and so on.[124] Notwithstanding these categorical statements the authors still insist that at the top of the pyramid of world power is the US with a group of nation States that 'control the primary global monetary instruments and thus have the ability to regulate international exchanges. Only the United States itself has the global use of force.' On a second tier, under this umbrella come the transnationals that organise what the authors call the networks, already many times described.[125] Never tired of contradicting themselves, the authors tell us once again that it is foolish to harbour nostalgia for the nation State, either as a cultural or economic-juridical structure. Its decline can be traced through the evolution of a whole series of bodies such as the GATT, the WTO, the World Bank, and the IMF. Even if the nation were to try to resist, it could only be worse, since 'the nation carries with it a whole series of repressive structures and ideologies'.[126]

The resistance to a dichotomised focus on third-world nation State and US imperialism is in favour of the postcolonial hero, 'who continually transgresses territorial and racial boundaries, who destroys

123. Ibid., 283–4.
124. Ibid., 308.
125. Ibid., 309–10.
126. Ibid., 336.

particularisms . . . liberation means the destruction of boundaries and patterns of forced migrations'. For the most wretched of Earth, 'its new nomad singularity is the most creative force . . . The power to circulate is a primary determination of the virtuality of the multitude, and circulating is the first ethical act of a counter-imperial ontology.'[127]

So the authors are not denying the focused power of the US and its imperial allies. Rather, they claim that this power is irrelevant to the future liberation of their postmodern hero. The means to get beyond the crisis of empire 'is the ontological displacement of the subject'.[128] They offer a kind of millennial spirituality. Calling on St Francis of Assisi, they say that once again we find ourselves in Francis's situation,

> posing against the misery of power the joy of being . . . bio-power, communism, cooperation and revolution remain together, in love, simplicity and also innocence . . . This is the irrepressible lightness and joy of being communist.[129]

The authors could mean that the world economic and political chaos they celebrate will unleash (it had not done so in 1999 but may be doing so at present) tens of millions of illegal immigrants defying the boundaries of States. However, there is little evidence that the Western powers, especially the Anglo-Americans, feel that they have to give up the national institutional power to resist these flows. Populist politics in the UK and the US at the time of writing (summer 2016) indicate otherwise.

Presumably the poststructuralist view of the global penetration of 'capital discourse' means that it is impossible to speak of independent agency in international relations. In this sense, the US does not exist as an entity, and, ipso facto, can hardly have a plan of world domination. The US is deconstructed as having no essence prior to international society. Intentionality is a mere effect of discourse and not a cause in its own right. Following Saussure's linguistic structuralism, meaning stems from relations of difference between words rather than reference to the world, in this case the consciousness of individuals.[130] Todd's French discourse of critique of the US is, perhaps, embedded in relations of French hostility to the US that

127. Ibid., 363.
128. Ibid., 384.
129. Ibid., 413.
130. A. Wendt, *Social Theory of International Politics* (1999) 178.

may be traced back to Roosevelt's treatment of de Gaulle in North Africa in the winter of 1942/3. That opposition itself may be traced back into the mists of time. Wittgenstein has called 'mentalism' the belief that subjective mental states cause actions. Instead, we merely ascribe motives in terms of public criteria that make behaviour intelligible. Therefore, it is better for social scientists to eschew intentions as causes of actions and focus on the structures of shared knowledge that give them content.[131] This would place Todd firmly within a huge literary industry of French anti-Americanism.

Capitalism is a discourse that produces resistances, because it has to strive to absorb and exclude its 'other', whatever is not capitalist. Harvey has no difficulty with using postmodern political theory to describe the workings of capitalism.[132] Capitalism can be said necessarily to create its own 'other'. It can make use of some non-capitalist formation or it can actively manufacture its 'other'. There is an organic relation between expanded reproduction and the often violent processes of dispossession that have shaped the historical geography of capitalism. This forms the heart of his central argument about accumulation by dispossession.[133] However, Harvey objects to placing all struggles against dispossession 'under some homogenising banner like that of Hardt and Negri's "multitude" that will magically rise up to inherit the earth'.[134] Wendt makes a similar objection to poststructuralism, or what he calls wholism, in social theory. He argues that no matter how much the meaning of an individual's thought is socially constituted, all that matters for explaining his behaviour is how matters seem to him. In any case, what is the mechanism by which culture moves a person's body, if not through the mind or the self. 'A purely constitutive analysis of intentionality is inherently static, giving us no sense of how agents and structures interact through time'.[135] Individuals have minds in virtue of independent brains and exist partially in virtue of their own thoughts. These give the self an 'auto-genetic'

131. Ibid., 179.
132. See, for instance, D. Harvey, *The Condition of Postmodernity* (1989), which explains the break from fixed to floating currencies as marking the end of the balance between organised labour, large corporate capital and the nation state, and that Bennett highlights as a watershed in the spread of modern cultural pessimism, *Cultural Pessimism*, 146.
133. Harvey, *The New Imperialism* 141–2.
134. Ibid., 169.
135. Wendt, *Social Theory of International Politics* 180–1.

quality, and are the basis for what Mead calls the 'I', an agent's sense of itself as a distinct locus of thought, choice, and activity 'Without this self-constituting substrate, culture would have no raw material to exert its constitutive effects upon, nor could agents resist those effects'.[136]

So the vital distinction that the legal, political, or other historian *has to struggle to make* is between the following two styles of argument. Wittgensteinians say that, in the hypothetical court case, the jury can only judge the guilt of the defendant – having no direct access to his mind – through social rules of thumb to infer his motives from the situation (a history of conflict with the victim, something linking him to the crime scene, and so on). They go further and argue that the defendant's motives cannot be known apart from these rules of thumb and so there is no reason to treat the former as springs of action in the first place.[137] At the same time, many now distinguish between two kinds of mental content. 'Narrow' content refers to the meanings of actions in a person's head that motivate his actions, while 'broad' content refers to the shared meanings that make the actions intelligible to others.[138] While Wendt draws these distinctions from the philosophy of agency and structure, they are always perfectly familiar to historians.

It is very much the argument of this book that there are evolving structures of the world economy and world politics that circumscribe the actions of individuals, within States and across State boundaries, whether at a conscious or unconscious level. Indeed, it is also argued that there is a single world political economic ideology – Anglo-American – that dominates world debates about market economy and liberal democracy. Even more so, it is argued that these ideologies of late capitalism take on marks of postmodern hedonism, irrationalism, and materialism that are extremely difficult to clarify in particular situations. However, the argument of the 'new' natural law of the Introductory Chapter, combined with the radical social theory of agency of Wendt, just outlined, indicate that it is perfectly possible, and, ethically, absolutely essential, for a philosophy of international law to focus upon and clarify what are the responsibilities of individuals in situations of economic and financial challenge, just as much as in political and military contexts.

136. Ibid., 181–2.
137. Ibid., 179.
138. Ibid., 181.

Possibilities of National and International Financial Reform

What follows now are two final stages of analysis of 2007–8. These follow out of the structural picture of international economic and financial relations provided by Todd and Harvey, but the context of crisis provides the possibility to illustrate the distinction just drawn by Wendt between 'broad content' and 'narrow content'. The first stage is to explain the particular role of derivatives and the trading culture surrounding them in the build up to the financial crisis and the second stage is to outline the evolving economic and financial structures that explain and make possible the exercise of overwhelming financial power by private banks in relation not only to individuals but also to states. This section develops the arguments of Todd and Harvey, giving more specific focus to events that have occurred from 2007 to the present.

THE 2008 FINANCIAL CRISIS FROM THE VANTAGE POINT OF THE PRIVATE BANKERS, ESPECIALLY IN NEW YORK[139]

> In the murky and curious period from early February to June 2007, the subprime mortgage market resembled a giant helium balloon, bound to earth by a dozen or so big Wall Street firms. Each firm held its rope; one by one, they realized that no matter how strongly they pulled, the balloon would eventually lift them off their feet. In June, one by one, they silently released their grip.[140]

What Happened to the Top Financial Institutions of the US?

In September 2008, Fannie and Freddie were insolvent. Lehman Brothers filed for bankruptcy. Merrill Lynch was taken over by the Bank of America. AIG, the largest and most reputable issuance company in the world, survived the turbulence only with federal funding.[141] Goldman Sachs is probably the only one, among other big shots on Wall Street, which sensed the upcoming storm and turned it around, shorting the collaterialised debt obligations (CDOs), timely making tons of money in the Financial Crisis. Warren Buffet injected

---

139. This Part I is written by Han Yu, a lawyer formerly with Linklaters Hong Kong, is a postgraduate student in the Columbia Law School, NYC.
140. Michael Lewis, *The Big Short* (2010) 209.
141. *The Federal Reserve and the Financial Crisis*, 2013, Princeton, Lectures by Ben S. Bernanke, pp. 72–3.

Goldman with approximately $5 billion in the form of preferred shares.[142] JPMorgan Chase did not default on their large amount of CDO products and their other business, including retail business and commercial banking business, saved them from going bust. Bear Stearns was even sold to JPMorgan Chase at a fire-sale price. Credit Suisse was not deeply involved into the subprime business and the asset management and private banking business were steady enough to steer clear of the crisis.

How Does the Financial Crisis Develop?

As we all know, the US dollar was set free as the Bretton Woods system dissolved in the 1970s. The innovation of various financial instruments began to spring up. The 1973 oil shock led into a massive influx of capital running back home to New York. Reagan's Imperial Circle (see above Todd and Harvey) further promoted the prosperity and size of the financial industry in the 1980s in both London and New York. After entering the 1990s, the end of Cold War and advancement of technology enormously encouraged cross-border investments and speculations, as the economy reached its peak. This was followed by the burst of the doc-com bubble. Disappointed by the sovereign debt crisis, and the stock market crisis of traditional industry (see below Streeck, *Buying Time*) and the dangers of the new technology, people shifted their attention to the seemingly sound and solid real-estate industry.

Picturing the whole financial system as a big football court the game time, unfortunately, was during a stormy season. The major players are investment banks, insurance companies, credit-rating agencies and numerous investors. What they were going after were 'fancy' derivatives products. It was so tempting that every player was needed to co-operate and to compete. Sadly, not everyone knew exactly what was inside of the 'fancy' ball. But it did not matter as everyone was fighting for it. It must be good for scores.

Creating fancy products takes time. They evolved from Mortgage Backed Securities (MBS) to Collateralised Mortgage Obligations (CMO), eventually, to Credit Default Swaps (CDS) and a big bomb.

MBS was a result of the huge demand for housing loans. The initiators of MBS were various investment banks and trust companies aiming to provide guarantee for individuals. The initial struc-

142. Greg Smith, *Why I Left Goldman Sachs* (2012) 187.

ture designed was a Special Purpose Vehicle (SPV), issuing bonds. The purpose of setting up a SPV is to segregate the risks from the original company and to benefit from favourable tax rules. Bondholders, namely the investors, bought the bonds and received the housing Principal and Interest. In other words, the investment banks acted as the agents, with all risks being assumed by those investors. The potential of bond defaults got the credit-rating agencies involved and those bonds were grouped and sold on the basis of investors' risk preferences. But good quality assets were not everywhere. To dilute the risks of an asset, the smartest banks came up with the idea of repackaging. From their perspectives, the concurrent defaults of bonds was unlikely to happen, something that they purported to prove by 'accurate' mathematics models.

The newly bundled securities were named as CMO. The name speaks for itself. Normally, the collateral provided by big insurance companies or investment banks served as the insurance for the low-rating bonds. As for the rating, at that moment, it never occurred to anyone that the most reliable turned to be the least reliable. Highly reputable as Fitch, Moody's, and S&P were as Credit Rating Agencies, they let investors down and tarnished their reputations by colluding with investment banks. 'It was as if they had bought cheap fire insurance on a house engulfed in flames.'[143] What was in their eyes was solely the high return rather than the corresponding high risks. Investment banks successfully shifted part of the risks by the means of sharing a certain portion of their profits with the insurance companies, but the number of such insurance companies is limited. These 'genius' banks created CDS to trade the defaulting risks. The buyers to such contracts compensated the seller's losses upon the default of specified assets. Although a CDS looks like insurance, it has more destructive power. It is not necessary for the sellers to have interests in the assets. A CDS is open to various financial entities and individuals. More importantly, the CDSs backfired and gave rise to an endless loop. Investors borrowed money from banks; banks sold the loans to insurance companies; and insurance companies repackaged these liabilities to be appealing investment products that were bought by investors. In summary, investors make investment with the borrowed money. The overestimated housing price resulted in the decline of demand, hence the decline of housing prices. The subsequent default of repayments was the last thing the banks wanted to

143. Lewis, *The Big Short* (2010) 164.

see as the house, as the collateral, was worthless. Yet the insurance companies could just announce a bankruptcy and had no need to pay back the investor who buys their fund products. The insurance companies could just walk away and leave the public to suffer the losses after declaring bankruptcy.

Evil Derivatives or Evil Bankers?

Bankers love money, but as we all know, love is blind. The invention of derivatives by no means makes the financial crash inevitable. It is just a tool.

PROS: Hedge Risks and Reduce Uncertainty about Future Prices

Under the microscope of the media, derivatives are too evil to be accepted. However, the truth is that a derivative is just a contract that links its value with the performance of its underlying assets, such as equity, bond, interest rate and and so on. The basic derivatives include forwards, options, futures, and swaps. One feature of derivatives instruments is to enter into a contract specifying conditions to be met at present and to fulfil the agreed obligations in the future – or you could say they are contractual agreements between two willing market participants that allow one party to sell exposure to specific risks and the other to gain exposure to the same risks, all in a relatively low-cost manner. Derivatives contracts are everywhere. When you step into a bookstore and request to reserve a book and the saleswoman tells you that the books are sold out, you enter into a derivate style contract. Actually, this is a forward contract (a form of derivatives contract). Derivatives are frequently used to protect financial institutions from subjection to undesired price movements. Without derivatives products, banks may have no choice but to expose themselves to great potential losses resulting from other transactions and the risk-adjusted costs will be higher, but entering into a derivative contract whose value moves in the opposite direction to their existing contracts enables parties to hedge the original risks. An option is also an appropriate example here. It is designed to attain disproportionately large returns if they become profitable. Put simply, it is a derivative granting a right to the buyer in terms of handling the underlying assets at the agreed strike price. What the buyer needs to pay is the relatively lower amount of premium. Should it be used correctly with cautions, it would add great value to companies and the whole financial market.

There is one point to be noted, that the nature of hedging is to distribute risks rather than eliminate risks. A lot of people have misunderstandings of risks and hedging. Risk is not an enemy. Hedging risks does not mean destroying enemies of financial stability. In fact, profits are proportional to risks and we are supposed to embrace an appropriate amount of risks. Even some measure of speculation, therefore, encourages higher levels of liquidity and thereby accelerates market efficiency. Such guessing at future prices can be helpful in building up a fair market. However, the same purely economic logic does not necessarily apply to political governance (the contraction of sovereign debt) because it is driven by non-economic social and political goals (of which more later).

CONS: *Lack Oversight and Make Financial Market Complicated*

The derivatives create a market encouraging proper risks for the investors, making a balance between risk and return. This should make the cost of capital go down and provide more investment options for market participants. However, the benefits are overstated to some extent. In practice, derivatives are often used to take advantage of legal loopholes and to skirt around regulatory blind spots. A Market Access Product is one of such applications. According to the Hong Kong Exchange (HKEX), 'structured products on non-Hong Kong underlying assets listed under Chapter 15A of the Listing Rules are called Market Access Products (MAPs). MAPs can take the form of Derivative Warrants (DWs), Callable Bull/Bear Contracts (CBBC) or equity Linked Instruments (ELIs).'[144] The MAP allows investors to get exposure to various underlying assets, which one may be not allowed to trade directly in one jurisdiction or that are not open to foreign investors. There are a lot of regulatory concerns involved, such as foreign exchange controls aiming to maintain financial stability or various other higher procedural requirements imposed on the foreign market participants. You could compare this term MAP to the 'market access' used in the international trading. When we think of the WTO, the related terms that pop up must include tariff or non-tariff measures. They are all referred to as the barriers set by countries. So the key of its operation is to issue products open to foreign investors, say Participatory Notes, and all capital gains or dividends of

144. 'Structured Products on Non-Hong Kong Underlying Assets-HKEx' <www.hkex.com.hk/eng/prod/secprod/dwrc/structured_products_on_nhkua.htm>.

the underlying instruments belong to the investors. There is no need to register with domestic regulators, to disclose their information, to comply with the domestic tax policy and and so on. You could imagine how ideal a way the MAP is to launder money.

People Matter

In retrospect, the 2008 financial crisis, like a magnifying lens, reflects how greedy people are. Ironically, the mainstream media made sharp criticisms about the CDO pricing model, the Gaussian copula models that was invented by David X. Li, a quantitative analyst. Some headlines even exaggerated it as 'a formula that killed Wall Street'[145]. However, the first default was triggered by the poor people who were unable to afford the houses they bought but insisted on getting a loan. At the same time, Ivry puts the blame squarely on racist bankers selling loans they knew to be bad to black people who were in fact entitled to more advantageous loans. The banks were under pressure to make the loans by the Bush Presidency.[146] In any case, the first gatekeepers of such high-risk derivatives should have been sophisticated investment banks who ended up only bragging about their rising revenues and joking about their primary and most important responsibilities. As at the time of writing another glaring example of this is a court case in London where the Libyan Investment Authority is suing Goldman Sachs for a loss of about 1.2 billion US$ in transactions where Goldman still allegedly took in the region of 200 million US$. It is presenting evidence that Goldman regarded them with a racial contempt and hired prostitutes as part of their business style.[147]

The US is not alone. The sovereign debt crisis in Europe and the A share crisis in China also have their roots in the greediness of people. European people also want to earn more but work less, borrow more but repay less. Without derivatives, the meltdown of European's economy in 2010 was still inevitable (see the next section on Steeck). In 2014, the Chinese government treated stock investors to a feast by artificially lifting up the stock price to an unbelievable level. Investors want more and invest more and lose more in the end.

145. Felix Salmon, 'Recipe for Disaster: The Formula That Killed Wall Street', 23 February 2009 <www.wired.com/2009/02/wp-quant>.
146. Bob Ivry, *The Seven Sins of Wall Street* (2014).
147. Jill Treanor, 'Goldman Sachs Hired Prostitutes to Win Libyan Business – Court Told', *The Guardian*, 13 June 2016 <www.theguardian.com/business/2016/jun/13/goldman-sachs-hired-prostitutes-to-win-libyan-business-court-told>.

We all believe we are able to survive good times and bad times never come. History repeats itself.[148]

The Financial Crisis is Inevitable but is Predictable

People just choose what they want to believe: the housing price will never fall down, the credit-rating agencies have credit and investment banks have morality or moral standards. The Federal Reserve once analysed an advertisement posted during the financial crisis. The advertisement says: '1% Low Start Rate, Stated Income, No Documentation Loans, 100% Finance Available, Interest Only Loans, Debt Consolidation'. '1% Low Start Rate' means the rate in the first year is 1 per cent, but you have no idea of the rest of the years of the loan. 'Stated Income' means 'you tell the company what your income is, and they write it down; that is all the checking you do'. '100% Finance Available' means 'no down payment is required'. Debt consolidation allows one to borrow money and add in all credit card debt and everything else that the buyer owns, to put all that into one big mortgage payment, for which the buyer only pays with the 1 per cent start rate.[149] Without doubt, the conditions are stimulating recklessness and such practices are questionable. All conditions sound tempting and allure you into an illusion that there exist free cakes. A reasonable person may sniff out the hidden cost from sentences unwritten and jump out of the trap. But 'a reasonable person' is only an assumption in economics textbooks.

As described in the *Big Short*, 'The data from the mortgage services was worse every month – the loans underlying the bonds were going bad at faster rates – and yet the price of insuring those loans was rising. "Logic had failed me," Bury said, "I could not explain the outcome I was seeing."'[150] Not everyone was blind, at least those from short siders. They were using reasons and facts against the whole market. And they were right.

There are and were numerous public sources to track the credibility of the CDS for sophisticated investors. For the adjustable-rate mortgage (ARMs) whose interest rates keep going up, the interest

148. At the time of writing, the IMF is visiting China and warning it that its corporate debt market is extremely seriously bloated – including shadow banking – and that a government rescue with sovereign funds will be necessary; see *Financial Times* week ending 11 June 2016.

149. *The Federal Reserve and The Financial Crisis* 68.

150. Lewis, *The Big Short* 184.

rate could be an indicator of the pressure on the borrowers. For the house itself, there is a direct data, loan-to-value ratio, showing bank's tolerance to the housing risks. For the ultimate user of houses, the FICO Score provided by FICO could be used as 'the standard measure of consumer credit risk in the United States'.[151]

The Greedy and Corrupt Investment Banks

As discussed at the beginning, almost all banks on Wall Street were struck down by the financial crisis. They are as miserable as sin. Just as the US Securities and Exchange Commission (SEC) lists on its action letter, these banks are also punished by the SEC for their misconducts 'that led to or arose from the financial crisis'.[152] They took advantage of and exploited investors, their competitors, and committed self-harm.

Exploit the Competitors

The derivatives transactions were also entered into between the top investment banks:

> Taking losses is never much fun for a Wall Street firm, but the pain can be mitigated by offsetting profits, which Goldman had in abundance in 2007, thanks to the mortgage-trading group that they set up as a 'the big short' against their own investors. What's more, the profits Goldman made from 'the big short' allowed the firm to put the squeeze on its competitors, including Bear Stearns, Merrill Lynch, and Lehman Brothers, and at least one counterparty, AIG, exacerbating their problems – and fomenting the eventual crisis – because Goldman alone could take the write-down with impunity. The rest of Wall Street squirmed, knowing that big losses had to be taken on mortgage-related securities and that they did not have nearly enough profits to offset them.[153]

The money robbed outside goes to top executives inside. Look at the payroll list in 2008: Thomas Montag in Merril Lynch received in the region of $39.4 million; the salary of CEO Richard Fuld in Lehman

151. 'Experian R Credit Report' <www.fico.com/en/about-us#at_glance>
152. 'Security and Exchange Commission Enforcement Actions Addressing Misconduct That Led to or Arose from the Financial Crisis' <www.sec.gov/spotlight/enf-actions-fc.shtml>
153. W. D. Cohan, *Money and Power – How Goldman Sachs Came to Rule the World* (2012) 4–5.

Brothers was about $184 million; and CEO James Cayne in Bear Sterns enjoyed in the region of $163 million.[154]

It was explained at the beginning how the collusion between investment banks, rating agencies and insurance companies deceives and exploits investors. Wall Street gets a way around by 'playing on client's fear and greed'. The typical sales pitch documents normally advocate that their bespoke derivatives are ready to help you outperform peers and survive through the difficult financial time.[155] Derivatives products are complicated but ratings attached to derivatives products are straightforward. Investment banks were busy with flickering investors and risk education was not on their agenda. Knowing nothing about the products did not prevent investors from believing that the more complicated, the better. Investment banks are cruel.

They not only prey on investors, but they also prey on one another. As Milton Friedman put it, '[I]f an exchange between two parties is voluntary, it will not take place unless both believe they will benefit from it.' A typical example is Goldman Sachs's mortgage-trading group that set up 'the big short', as explained above.[156]

Money Talks – Goldman Sachs

As already noted, the top five executives at Goldman split approximately $322 million between them during the 2008 Crisis.[157] Speaking of Goldman Sachs, people respect them, hate them and are afraid of them.

> The firm has been described as everything form 'a cunning cat that always lands on its feet' to, now famously, 'a great vampire squid wrapped around the face of humanity, relentlessly jamming its blood funnel into anything that smells like money' by Rolling Stone writer Matt Taibbi.[158]

---

154. 'Michael Corbery Executive Pay and the Financial Crisis: A Refresher Course', *Wall Street Journal*, 18 September 2009, <http://blogs.wsj.com/deals/2009/09/18/executive-pay-and-the-financial-crisis-a-refresher-course/> Top five executives at Goldman split $322 million; see Cohan, *Money and Power – How Goldman Sachs Came to Rule The World* 4–5.
155. Smith, *Why I Left Goldman Sachs* 171.
156. See footnote 153 above.
157. Ibid.
158. Cohan, *Money and Power* 1.

Goldman is the only bank making profits facing the turmoil of the financial crisis. But its short strategies also worsened the sliding market and cornered all market players. Money or reputation, Goldman chose the first. Simply put, 'Goldman Sachs was merely the first to dash through the exit – and then it closed the door behind it.'[159] In 2010, the US Senate organised hearings about Goldman's short. Senator Levin said, '[H]e remains mystified by CEO Blankfein's denials when the documentary evidence – including e-mails and board presentations – points overwhelmingly to Goldman having profited handsomely from the bet'.[160] In *SEC v. Goldman Sachs*, Goldman, in the end, agreed to pay in the region of $550 million to set the SEC's charges, but without admitting or denying any guilt.[161]

Goldman's reputation was tarnished again when it was discovered to have helped Greece and Italy mask their debt and sugar up their budgets through complex derivatives in the 2000s. Without Goldman's being the accomplice, it may have taken longer for Greece to be accepted as the member of the Euro, but the debt crisis may then have been avoidable. The derivatives product that Goldman tailored for Greece was the CDS. In this case, the default of Greece's payment would be a big blow to sovereign debt and a strike to the EU's ambitions. To reduce the negative effects to the minimum, Greece proposed a voluntary debt-restructuring agreement and had the International Swap Derivatives Association (ISDA) on board agreeing not to consider such agreements as a credit event so that buyers of CDS cannot bring legal proceedings asking for compensations.

> On 27th of February 2012, the ISDA received a query about whether the voluntary acceptance by some private banks of a haircut on their holdings of Greek debt could be defined as a credit event. On the 1st of March, ISDA issued a note clarifying that, according to the facts recorded until that date, this event could not be considered as a default event.[162]

---

159. Lewis, *The Big Short* 209.
160. Cohan, *Money and Power* 7.
161. Securities and Exchange Commission Press release 2010-123 <https://www.sec.gov/news/press/2010/2010-123.htm>.
162. The credit Default Swap Market Report, The Board of the International Organization of Securities Commission FR 05/12 June 2012 <https://www.iosco.org/library/pubdocs/pdf/IOSCOPD385.pdf>.

Under the agreement, investors holding Greek bonds had nothing but to accept the 53.5 per cent losses of the notional value of their bonds.

Besides, Goldman was turning a blind eye to the Chinese Wall. On the one hand, Goldman advised hedge funds on how to benefit from Greece's chaos by questioning its repayment ability and selling Euro to drive up the price of CDS. As long as the European Central Bank extended a lifeline to Greece, Goldman could benefit with tons of money again. On the other hand, Goldman also tried to win contracts from the European governments to help them walk away from the chaos by providing loans and arranging financing.[163]

What Goldman did brings into question what the world looks like if every bank is betting on the failures of others, instead of on success and no one tries to build up a healthier market for economies.

Where Does the Insanity Come From?

We have analysed above the advertisement offering the adjustable interest rates. Most people were aware of the fact that the interest rates were beyond their ability. But, as the opportunities were there, they firmly believed that their houses could be sold at a higher price before the adjustment of interest rates as long as the housing price kept going up.

Here are two obvious questions. First, what makes everyone believe that the housing price keeps going up? Second, even if the rating agency takes partial blame for faking the ratings, what if widespread default occurs? Or do people just not believe that they can become victims by any chance?

On the first question, one needs to touch upon the psychological side. As a member of society, everyone wants to feel needed and to succeed at least in the eyes of other people. The fear of being losers pushes us to go after higher goals. Why was the demand of housing so high? The mixture of desperation and hope of the poor people make them have zero resistance to good houses that they were dreaming about. Owning represents power. It is crucial to self-cognition. Once they have made the decision of buying the house, they will adjust expectations to be in line with their behaviour. Accordingly, it is not hard to understand why they held expectations of the housing price going up. The analysis also applies to rating agencies. 'The rating

163. Smith, *Why I Left Goldman Sachs* 313.

agencies were morally bankrupt and living in fear of becoming actually bankrupt. They are scared to death about doing nothing because they'll look like fools if they do nothing.'[164]

On the second question, one of the functions of Morgan Stanley's quants was to teach the rating agencies about how to evaluate CDOs[165] and rating agencies were under pressure to give good ratings to clients due to competition from other rating agencies.[166] It is not uncommon to see the stress tests performed in investment banks. But the outcome also depends on people's expectation on potential losses. In Morgan Stanley, Howie Hubler's

> bet had been 'stress tested' for scenarios in which subprime pools experienced losses of 6 percent, the highest losses from recent history. Now traders were asked to imagine what would become of their bet if losses reached 10 percent.[167] As a senior Morgan Stanley executive outside Hubler's group put it, 'They did not want to show you the results. They kept saying, *That State of the world can't happen*.'[168]

But black swan theory teaches us that nothing is impossible.

Regulator's Role

Financial sector regulators have been constantly criticised due to the financial crisis. They were accused of encouraging the real-estate industry and mortgage development without corresponding strong policies and regulations. The accusations are not entirely groundless. 'The exclusion of derivatives from the ambit of US regulation in 1999 is now almost universally recognized to have been a mistake.'[169]

But did the regulators respond to the financial crisis quickly and effectively? During the 2008 financial crisis, the Secretary of Treasury was Henry Paulson, a former CEO of Goldman Sachs. His initial measures were not helpful in terms of comforting the public, not to

---

164. Lewis, *The Big Short* 176.
165. Ibid., 201.
166. 'S&P was worried that if they demanded the data from Wall Street, Wall Street would just go to Moody's for their ratings.' Lewis, *The Big Short* 171.
167. Ibid., 211–12.
168. Ibid.
169. John Kay, *Other People's Money, The Real Business of Finance* (2015) 234.

mention that there was not too much transparency and he was not tough enough on the investment banks on Wall Street. In 2014, he was asked to testify for the 2008 federal bailout package extended to AIG in a lawsuit 'alleging the AIG rescue cheated shareholders of $40 billion'.[170]

As discussed at the beginning of this section, banks on the Wall Street were hit badly, but this did not justify their misconduct. Neither did it exempt them from being punished. During and after the financial crisis, regulators made efforts to discipline the financial market. For example, the US Securities and Exchange Commission (SEC) took actions against these banks for their misconduct 'that led to or arose from the financial crisis'.[171] Banks paid hundreds of millions to settle the charges and pledged to reform their business practices.

One summary conclusion comes to mind in the face of this whole story:

> Surely, there is no law, ethical guideline or moral injunction against profit. But Goldman Sachs – it did not just make money, it profited by taking advantage of its client's reasonable expectations that it would not sell products that it did not want to succeed and that there was no conflict of economic interest between the firm and the customers that it had pledged to serve.[172]

THE EVOLVING STRUCTURE OF THE GLOBAL ECONOMY AND THE FUTURE SHAPE OF A GLOBAL PUBLIC ECONOMIC AND FINANCIAL LAW

There are many interpretations of the long-term nature of the growing fiscal and credit crisis of the West, but there are three that are here going to be highlighted. What one really needs to understand is how the nature of present global liquidity is being managed almost exclusively by the banks just described and how their practices have

170. 'Damian Paletta and Leslie Scism Former Treasury Secretary Paulson Testifies in AIG Bailout Suit', *Wall Street Journal*, 6 October 2014 <http://www.wsj.com/articles/former-treasury-secretary-paulson-testifies-in-aig-bailout-suit-1412614061>.
171. US Securities and Exchange Commission, 'SWEC Enforcement Actions Addressing Misconduct That Led to or Arose from the Financial Crisis' <http://www.sec.gov/spotlight/enf-actions-fc.shtml>.
172. Cohan, *Money and Power* 19.

become so politically crucial and potentially lethal. The interpretation offered by Wolfgang Streeck in his *Buying Time, The Delayed Crisis of Democratic Capitalism* (2013/14), in combination with Giles Chance, *China and the Credit Crisis: The Emergence of a New World Order* (2010) and Joseph Stiglitz, with his *Globalization and its Discontents* (2002) is that there has occurred since the 1970s at the latest a massive change in the international division of labour, which has combined with a massive re-orientation of political power, based on changing economic wealth, within Western political societies. The consensus social-democratic welfare State of the period 1945–70+ was based upon a Fordist style of second-stage mass industrial production for domestic and external markets in the fields of finished hard consumer goods, such as cars, aircraft, electronics and shipping pharmaceuticals. This style of production ensured high employment with relatively high income distribution across the middle classes, blue-colour workers and so on in the West. It also provided a very wide tax base in the population – with staggered income tax and property/inheritance tax – to make affordable very high standards of social welfare, especially in health, education, social security and pensions. During this time, the Western State could function fiscally, without much debt-covered public spending. Indeed, the mid-1960s marked a high point of social-democratic politics in the US and the UK.[173]

However, from the 1970s onwards, with competition from Japan, and the Asian tigers in particular in the same standardised production of what is known as consumer durables, the heart was hollowed out of the Fordist style of mass production in the West, as the latter was driven more and more into high-technology, relatively low-labour-intensive production for niche markets. This led to an increasingly highly skilled but much smaller European professional class, unwilling to accept a compensatory increase in tax to make up for the declining income of wider sectors of society. Right across Europe and North America more conservative governments came to power that were low-tax oriented, anxious to free up the investment possibilities of wealth already accumulated during the boom periods by deregulating financial markets and indeed encouraging competition among such markets, especially London and New York and, after that, Tokyo, Hong Kong and Frankfurt.[174]

---

173. Streeck, *Buying Time* 1–46.
174. Ibid., 47–96.

This change in the international division of labour was accentuated with the collapse of Eastern European communism and the opening-up policy of China, which has from the 1990s to the financial crisis of 2007–8 and onwards, come to overwhelm remaining traces of Fordist production in the West.[175] Increasingly, it has become clear that not merely is the distribution of capital, or total wealth within Western societies, changing, in the direction of an ever-decreasing minority, but also there is a radical redistribution of capital across continents. It began sharply with the Organization of the Petroleum Exporting Countries (OPEC) Revolution of 1971–3, when the oil price hike led to a huge transfer of wealth to the mainly Middle East oil producers. Through the 1970s onwards, wealth has transferred to Japan and the Asian tigers, with the final radical push coming with China's rise from the 1990s onwards. This has very largely worked to swamp Western financial centres, especially London and New York (in competition with each other), with, first, Middle East petrol dollars, and then Russian petrol and energy dollars and, finally, vast Japanese and especially Chinese surpluses from long years of increasing trade surpluses. This increase in the quantity of Western financial management is accentuated by the non-convertibility of the Chinese Yuan.[176] There were attempts by Western states to retain control of this process. For instance, the Johnston Democratic Presidency attempted to control dollar outflow in the 1960s and failed. France tried under the Mitterrand Socialist Presidency after 1981 to resist the trend, but they were both easily overwhelmed by the mobility of capital.

These developments have created the global paradox that while the wealth production of the world has significantly moved east and even south out of the North Atlantic area, the finance capital, liquidity, has moved back into the same area to be managed. The credit threat, the danger of financial crisis on a global, systemic scale lies only partially in defective management of derivatives in non-transparent and internationally linked securitised instruments. The problem lies more fundamentally at the political level within the West.

---

175. Chance, *China and the Credit Crisis* 1–48.

176. <http://en.wikipedia.org/wiki/Stock_exchange>. Figures for January 2015 Monthly Reports World Federation of Exchanges show that for 32 trillion dollars of issued shares of companies alone were in New York, with 6.2 trillion for London and 4.4 trillion for Tokyo and 4 trillion Shanghai and 3.3 trillion for Hong Kong.

Western political elites, constrained by a shrinking fiscal base and by the weakening of the economic base of the social-democratic political constituency, have responded by encouraging their populations to make up stagnant and decreasing incomes through the pursuit of lifestyle through credit. The housing boom played a central part as the focus on housing as an investment asset in the West encouraged re-mortgaging, the foundation of the eventually toxic securitised derivatives. At the same time a new financial elite evolved in the West, especially New York and London, which actually managed not merely UK or US money, but global flows, themselves seeking not merely further outlets of profit outside their own regional productive reinvestment, but also, quite simply, stability in a world financial system in which the only denominations for wealth were in notoriously unstable currencies such as the dollar and the Euro. More than 75 per cent of derivatives are taken up with trying to provide security against currency and interest-rate fluctuations. Of course the non-European (Chinese, Russian, oil, primarily Arab Middle East and Japanese) capital also goes into prime market properties in Western capitals, pushing up London, New York, Paris and so forth properties as assets. This phenomenon is also a reflection of the instability of the main and secondary international currencies.

What has happened with the financial crisis of 2007–8 is that the private banking encouragement of private debt, itself encouraged by the State, but without direct State financial participation, reached beyond breaking point. The derivatives market played a part in this, especially the US subprime market. The Western banking sector failed to restrain the now socially disrupted Western consumer market in the face of footloose global credit awash in Western financial centres. The responsibility of this rests partially with Western banks and governments, but also partially with the decisions of non-Western capital to house itself in the West, whether for safety or for profit.

The final stage in this scenario is that after the Financial Crisis of 2007–8, Western governments have bought their way out of the spectre of recession, the collapse of private banking and consumer purchasing power, through colossal accumulations of sovereign debt, the first debtor not being Greece but the US and the UK. This debt is contracted without any attempt to address the underlying structural weaknesses in the Western place within the world economy. In the emergency circumstances of 2007–8 this was hardly surprising. Massive infusions of credit into the banking system and into the capacity for consumer spending in the West were essential to avoid an immediate and total collapse of financial confidence and with it the whole system of world trade. However, the continuing looming threat is that without structural change of the international financial order, with each month that passes the Western States are accumulating an ever larger share of sovereign debt.[177] In terms of external debt, this is, clearly, overwhelmingly in Western hands. External debt is the

> total public and private debt owed to nonresidents repayable in internationally accepted currencies, goods, or services, where the public debt is the money or credit owed by any level of government, from central to local, and the private debt the money or credit owed by private households or private corporations based in the country under consideration'.

Here the figures are staggering. US external debt is 19.2 trillion with a percentage of GDP 114; for the others, respectively, UK 9.6 and percentage 569; China 1.2 and percentage 16.2; and Japan 2.8 and percentage 60.[178] And this is in currencies – particularly the dollar and the Euro – that are being constantly destabilised by their sovereign masters the Federal Reserve and the European Central Bank, through quantitative easing. Here is the heart of the continuing ticking bomb of another and indeed definitive financial collapse and economic collapse, at least in so far as the real world economy requires both liquidity and stable trading partners, East and West, at the global level.[179]

There is a solution for which the whole world trading and financial community is responsible. It is the reform of the world financial system. Giles Chance focuses on this. He refers to the UN Commission of Experts (headed by Stiglitz) 2009 and the Chinese Central Bank (Zhou Xioachuan) calling for the dollar's role to be taken over by an expanded IMF Special Drawing Rights System that would consist of a basket of currencies, reflecting their importance in international trade and finance. This change would also have to be reflected in the governing structure of the IMF, which would become, overnight, an all-powerful

177. Public debt not necessarily larger than those of Asian countries but it is not matched by production and trade balances able to finance it. For example, the US has 15.9 trillion $US public debt, percentage of GDP at 93.6; UK 2.8 trillion and percentage at 103.7; and China 1.95 trillion and percentage GDP at 17.7. The Economist: The Economist Intelligence Unit: The Global Debt Clock <http://www.economist.com/content/global_debt_clock>.
178. List of Countries by Extent of External Debt as Percentage of GDP <http://en.wikipedia.org/wiki/List_of_countries_by_external_debt>.
179. Streeck, *Buying Time* 97–164.

World Central Bank, to the extent that the capital-surplus countries were prepared to transfer their capital into the SDRs.[180] At one fell-blow, London and New York would be seriously reduced as financial centres and the power of Western States to manage the increasing social disruption caused by their declining economic importance, would be abolished to the extent that capital-surplus countries sought increased security in SDRs. In other words, it is virtually inconceivable that the West would take the initiative for regulatory reform in this vital field. The initiative and build-up of pressure would have to come from the 'Eastern' States, but they could only hope to make the transition through an elaborately evolving consensus. Otherwise, confidence in the dollar and the Euro would immediately collapse. At present, the greatest risk of collapse comes from a serious hike in US dollar interest rates.

It is Stiglitz who brings us back to Vattel and the idea of economic self-determination. It is also a primary function of the State itself to restore its own financial sovereignty. It may seem a wild idea, but a small number of countries such as China are in a position to do so, with their present capital and currency controls. In any case, one needs at least, as a lawyer, simply to set out what reforms are required and then explain how they are being blocked. Then, it is hoped, the mist of Hardt and Negri's *Empire* will evaporate. Joseph Stiglitz, a former chief economist to the WB, and chief economic advisor to President Clinton, considers that it is possible to adopt a non-mystical approach to international monetary problems, particularly as they affect developing countries. He sets out two starting principles for his argument in favour of government intervention in the market. It should happen where there is imperfect information and where social cohesion is threatened. In this event an economy will not function rationally. Starting from these principles Stiglitz argues quite simply that no case has been made for capital market liberalisation.[181]

In summary, for Stiglitz monopoly concentration of capital, in the interest of a small number of creditor States, particularly the US, operating through a secretive, undemocratic IMF, serves acutely dysfunctionally the interests of most developing, that is, poor countries. The creditor States resist change simply because it is in their financial interest to do so. Immediate prospects for the necessary political reform at the global level are not good.[182] The IMF rhetoric that liberalisation would enhance world economic stability by diversifying sources of funding is

180. Chance, *China and the Financial Crisis* 71–90.
181. J. Stiglitz, *Globalization and its Discontents* (2002).
182. Ibid., 223–8.

nonsense. Banks prefer to lend to those who do not need the money. The limited competition in financial markets means that lower interest rates do not follow. The so-called freedom of capital flow is very bad for developing countries, because there is no control of the flow of hot money in and out of countries – short-term loans and contracts that are usually only bets on exchange-rate movements. It consists of money that cannot be used to build factories and so forth because companies do not make long-term investments with it. Such a financial climate can only destabilise long-term investments. There are bound to be adverse effects on growth in this environment because countries have to set aside in their reserves amounts equal to their short-term foreign-denominated loans; for example, if country A borrows $100 million at 18 per cent it should deposit the same in US Treasury bills at 4 per cent, thereby losing 14 per cent.[183]

Where benefits are not paid for, or compensated, global collective action is necessary, that is, externalities to achieve global economic stability. The mind-set of the IMF is that it will vote to suit creditors and a change in weighted voting cannot come with the US using its effective veto. Yet the contributions are actually coming from the developing countries as the IMF is always repaid. Stiglitz is not also sanguine that the necessary reforms in this institution will come. Indeed, if there was even open debate in the IMF it is not clear that the interest of creditors would always come before those of workers and small businesses. Secrecy always allows special interests full sway and engenders suspicion.[184]

The institutional solutions are clear. Banking and tax restrictions must be imposed to ensure effective restrictions on short-term capital flows. A bankruptcy provision is needed that expedites restructuring and gives greater presumption for a continuation of existing management, thereby inducing more diligence in creditors. The IMF role in debt restructuring is fundamentally wrong. The IMF is a major creditor, representing major creditors, and a bankruptcy system can never allow creditors to make bankruptcy judgements.[185]

The rest of the institutional changes necessary are perfectly clear. They have nothing to do with bureaucracy and efficiency and everything to do with the equity that political choice must realise. The risk-based capital adequacy standards imposed on developing country

183. Ibid., 65–7.
184. Ibid., again 223–8.
185. Ibid., 237.

banks are inappropriate. The IMF must be required to expand substantially its Special Drawing Rights to finance global public goods to sustain the world economy. The risks of currency fluctuation must be absorbed by the creditors and the concerns of workers and small businesses have to be balanced against those of creditors. There must be global taxation to finance development. It is quite simply because alternative policies affect different groups differently that it is the role of the political process – not international bureaucrats – to sort out the choices.[186] So, why does Stiglitz have cause not to be sanguine about these obvious reforms to the world financial system?

FURTHER READING

Arrighi, Giovanni and Beverly J. Silver, *Chaos and Governance in the Modern World System* (1999).

Bernanke, Ben, *The Federal Reserve and the Financial Crisis* (2013).

Chance, Giles, *China and the Credit Crisis: The Emergence of a New World Order* (2010).

William D. Cohan, *Money and Power: How Goldman Sachs Came to Rule the World* (2011).

de Graaf, John, David Wann and Thomas H. Naylor, *Affluenza: How Overconsumption is Killing US – and How We Can Fight Back*, 3rd edition (2014).

Firth, Simon, *Derivatives Law and Practice* (2003).

Goldsmith, Jack and Eric Posner, *The Limits of International Law* (2005).

Ivry, Bob, *The Seven Deadly Sins of Wall Street, Big Banks, Their Washington Lackeys and the Financial Crisis* (2014).

Kay, John, *Other People's Money: Masters of the Universe or Servants of the People* (2015).

Kennedy, David, *A World of Struggle: How Power, Law and Expertise Shape Global Political Economy* (2016).

Lewis, Michael, *The Big Short: Inside the Doomsday Machine*, movie tie-in edition (2015).

Senate Subcommittee on Investigations, *Wall Street and the Financial Collapse* (2011) Cosimo Report.

Smith, Greg, *Why I Left Goldman Sachs: A Wall Street Story* (2012).

Stiglitz, Joseph, *Globalization and its Discontents* (2002).

Streeck, Wolfgang, *Buying Time: The Delayed Crisis of Democratic Capitalism* (2014).

186. Ibid., 238–48.

Index

EU Authorised Representative:
Easy Access System Europe Mustamäe tee 50, 10621 Tallinn, Estonia
gpsr.requests@easproject.com

Printed and bound by CPI Group (UK) Ltd, Croydon, CR0 4YY
14/09/2026
02216781-0011